Redesigning Innovative Healthcare Operation and the Role of Knowledge Management

M. Saito, Waseda University, Japan

N. Wickramasinghe, Illinois Institute of Technology, USA

M. Fujii, Nonprofit Organization TBI Rehabilitation Center, Japan

E. Geisler, Illinois Institute of Technology, USA

Medical Information Science

REFERENCE

MEDICAL INFORMATION SCIENCE REFERENCE

Hershey · New York

Director of Editorial Content:	Kristin Klinger
Senior Managing Editor:	Jamie Snavely
Assistant Managing Editor:	Michael Brehm
Publishing Assistant:	Sean Woznicki
Typesetter:	Sean Woznicki
Cover Design:	Lisa Tosheff
Printed at:	Yurchak Printing Inc.

Published in the United States of America by
Medical Information Science Reference (an imprint of IGI Global)
701 E. Chocolate Avenue
Hershey PA 17033
Tel: 717-533-8845
Fax: 717-533-8661
E-mail: cust@igi-global.com
Web site: http://www.igi-global.com/reference

Library of Congress Cataloging-in-Publication Data

Saito, Murako.
  Redesigning innovative healthcare operation and the role of knowledge management / by Murako Saito and Nilmini Wickramasinghe ; with Masako Fujii and Eliezer Geisler.

      p. cm.

  Summary: "This book offers a compilation of chapters on how knowledge impacts the layout and design of the medical industry"--Provided by publisher.
  Includes bibliographical references and index.
  ISBN 978-1-60566-284-8 (hardcover) -- ISBN 978-1-60566-285-5 (ebook) 1. Health services administration. 2. Knowledge management. 3. Health care reform. 4. Medical informatics. I. Wickramasinghe, Nilmini. II. Title.

 RA971.2.S25 2010
 362.1068--dc22
                                   2009007893

British Cataloguing in Publication Data
A Cataloguing in Publication record for this book is available from the British Library.

All work contributed to this book is new, previously-unpublished material. The views expressed in this book are those of the authors, but not necessarily of the publisher.

Table of Contents

Section 1:
Fundamental Aspects of Knowledge and Knowledge Management

Chapter 1
   Nilmini Wickramasinghe, Illinois Institute of Technology, USA

Section 2:
Approaches to Healthcare Operations Management

Section 4:
Case Studies Illustrating Key Issues and Investigations at the Community Level

Chapter 18
**Further Directions in Cognitive Rehabilitation in Community- and
Home-based Daily Trainings in Clients with Severe Traumatic
Brain Injury** **266**
    Masako Fujii, Nonprofit Organization TBI Rehabilitation Center, Japan

Foreword

Over my years in healthcare management, research and education as a CEO, professor and public policy participant, it has become clear to me that information and insights from multiple sources are the key to success–if they can be effectively captured, integrated, and managed. However we have often isolated aspects of this to individual functional areas–information technology, transaction systems, archival/retrieval systems, market research and intelligence, research and development, and the like. The Epilogue to this book describes a family tree of related approaches. Yet it is the sum total, integrated in some way, that creates competitive advantage and intellectual property for the organization and produces community benefit to society as a whole. Knowledge management is our best attempt yet to provide that level of integration and, thus, to realize the latent value in our organizations and systems.

This book builds an extensive conceptual framework for integration across all of the contributing fields. The scope of topics is large but appropriate ranging from the philosophical nature of science (Chapter 4) to consideration of information processing and interpretation models (Chapter 6) to conceptual and empirical studies of applications in health (Sections 3 and 4). Here the reader can gain the base necessary to appreciate and develop a meaningful approach to knowledge management in healthcare operations.

Yet the value of the book for me lies in the foundation it provides for much broader applications. My current professional concerns regarding quality as a board member of the Joint Commission mesh with my ongoing focus on payment, insurance, and economic value in health services. From this perspective, it is obvious to me that quality must become a core management objective and its metrics, a central measure of organizational success on a par with financial viability indicators. Likewise payment systems that recognize patient outcomes and satisfaction as well as processes and protocols force organizations to think across traditional functional boarders. Yet we tend to measure and manage quality, finance, and market attractiveness in separate silos. We often have great stores of knowledge in fragmented form but fail to manage it effectively towards broader objectives.

In this world, knowledge management, as presented here, offers a way to cross the boundaries of function and organization. It provides a core management tool for survival and prosperity, not only for organizations but also for whole health systems. This book is not a detailed handbook to achieve this but a precursor that points the way for its audience in organizing and understanding the elements of emerging knowledge management in healthcare operations. It provides a solid foundation for those wishing to realize the promise.

J. B. Silvers, PhD
William and Elizabeth Treuhaft Professor of Health Systems Management
Weatherhead School of Management
Case Western Reserve University
Cleveland, Ohio
November 25, 2008

JB Silvers *is the Treuhaft Professor of Health Systems Management at the Weatherhead School of Management with a joint appointment in the school of Medicine at Case Western Reserve University. He has published in the journal of Finance, Journal of the American Medical Association, Medical Care, Health Services Research and many others. From 1997 to 2000, while on leave, he was President and CEO of a health insurance company. Currently he serves on the board of The Joint Commission, and for seven years was a Commissioner on the Prospective Payment Assessment Commission Advising Congress on Medicare Payment.*

Preface

In 2005, two of the authors of this book attended to the 4th International Conference on the Hospital of the Future at Aalborg, Denmark. We took this opportunity to discuss the idea of a collaborative work concerning the application of knowledge management (KM) to various aspects of healthcare sector. We believed then and today are convinced that it is essential for healthcare globally to embrace the tools, techniques, technologies and tactics of KM to effect superior healthcare operations and we trust that this book helps to convey to our readers not only the importance of KM, buy why it is so integral in redesigning innovative healthcare operations.

In coping with the current complex and dynamic situation in the healthcare field, it is imperative for the creation of new ideas and values to foster an innovative workplace that enables an organization's most critical resource, its knowledge workers to collaborate across and within disciplines. This can only be possible by embracing a socio-technical systems methodology (Emery and Trist, 1965, Miller, 1999), new pluralism and a multi-paradigm intervention (Habermas, 1978, Drucker, 1992, Jackson,2000), which combine psycho-social, cognitive-psychological perspectives with physical/mechanical and information technology perspectives. In such an integrated approach, enterprise visions and the responsibility necessary to propel organizational strategy are shared and strengthened, and individual value consciousness is aligned with a collective one. In contrast, cognitive misfits between the internal and external world in individuals and collectives, and also among any stakeholders, frequently happen in the current society which in turn leads collaborative work to be misdirected, and thereby the collaboration becomes difficult and problematic. Organizational performance can be improved by cognitive reliability and validity, and can be developed by the viability of the participants. Timely and appropriate application of knowledge management methodology is essential to change the healthcare fields by sharing and spreading new value of knowledge beyond the barriers among academic disciplines, or beyond a particular interest limited to a specific field. In the organization embraced by socio-technical methodology, knowledge management plays a crucial role in enhancing organizational resilience/adaptability and in improving organizational performance especially during turbulence in uncertain and complex society. Given the state of healthcare operations globally – contending with exponentially increasing costs, myriads of technology options and in most instances aging population problems – the tools and techniques of KM offer a welcome oasis after an extensive trek through the Sahara desert, indeed, one might be tempted to state that KM might be the panacea for healthcare in this 21 century.

In an attempt to navigate through the relatively unchartered waters of knowledge management for innovative organizations and more especially the role of knowledge management in redesigning innovative organizations, this book presents essential theories, concepts, methodologies and evidence-based applications. In particular, the reader will find the key tools and techniques necessary for the designing of an innovative healthcare operations presented in the following chapters. Knowledge management provides two thinking modes, normal scientific and post normal scientific modes. In normal science, the problems are solved by nomothetic approaches to causality, while in the post normal scientific thinking mode, the problems are appreciated by hermeneutic approaches to an a causal phase of social event service. Knowledge management plays an essential role in continuously transforming the organization into a dynamic and resilient organization by facilitating the interpretation of current issues in the field. Hence, knowledge management provides efficient and effective methodologies for creating a reliable organizational climate/culture which will emerge synergetic power of amplifying together (Haken, 1978, Shimuzu,1992), not simply fusing and living together, and for creating an innovative work atmosphere where collaboration and alignment among different disciplines can ensue. Given the universal need to embrace the key tools and techniques of knowledge management and yet the challenge to apply these tools and techniques appropriately in the manufacturing and service sectors as well as the community at large, this book focuses on underscoring both the universal need for knowledge management and the importance of contextual applicability and understanding the different nuances on the events, as in management by the participants' value which leads to an innovative operations.

This book is recommended for university students, researchers, practitioners or service-providers primarily in the healthcare field as well as in those who are interested in knowledge management and are eager to develop their current understanding of organizational environments in order to transform them into innovative ones, such as managers and leaders in team work/projects, management staff in industry, professional healthcare workers, nurses, physicians, hospital administration managers.

This book is written with four explicit sections and has two implicit parts. Section I and II combined make up the first implicit part of the book which focuses on the essential concepts and critical aspects of KM Specifically Section I provides an introduction to the fundamental aspects of knowledge and knowledge management, while Section II provides exposure to important methodologies and emphasizes the importance of socio-technical perspective for effective KM. Thus Section I and II provide the reader with the essential tools and technologies for harnessing good KM practices. Section III and IV make up the second half of the book. In these two sections the attentions turns to evidence of examples in various areas of the healthcare sector(Section III) and then to evidence in local communities and family lives in Section IV. Given that healthcare operations have significant impact not only to healthcare-providers and patients but also the community, it is important to illustrate the impact of redesigned healthcare operations and/or the importance of redesigning existing healthcare operations to/for these various stakeholders.

Section 1: Fundamental Aspect of Knowledge and Knowledge Management

This first section consists of four chapters: "Knowledge Economy for the Innovative Organization" by Wickramasinghe, "Managing Knowledge for Enhancing the Participants through Organizational Learning and Leadership" by Saito, "Permitting the True Potential of Knowledge Assets to be Utilized with KMI" by Wickramasinghe, and "Normal Science and Post-Normal Sciences" by Geisler.

Together these four chapters outline fundamental considerations regarding critical aspects of the knowledge construct (i.e., the dualities found within the knowledge construct as discussed in Chapter 1 and the connection between knowledge management, organizational learning, and leadership as discussed in Chapter 2). Chapter 3 discusses the fundamental components necessary to develop an appropriate and robust knowledge management infrastructure (KMI) and finally Chapter 4 presents important implications and considerations for methodologies for knowledge management that can only be fully appreciated through the understanding of significant aspects of normal and post-normal sciences.

Knowledge management is a nascent evolving field. Our goal in this section is to provide readers with the essential core elements of the KM discipline so that they have a solid foundation, exposure, and understanding of the key concepts. Given that the primary focus of this book is the use of KM for redesigning healthcare operations, we naturally focus our attention on those key aspects of KM that we believe are most beneficial when applied to any/all healthcare scenarios. Specifically, it is necessary to understand the roles for people and technology as well as how to develop appropriate and solid KM infrastructures so that the true potential of all knowledge assets can be maximized. This in turn requires appropriate leadership, good metrics, and a need to break away from rigid and outdated structures and/or archaic approaches to viewing problems and scenarios.

On the completion of this section, the reader should have a solid grounding in the fundamental core principles that are necessary in order to understand the role for knowledge management in redesigning innovative healthcare processes.

Chapter 1 (Wickramasinghe) describes the knowledge economy for innovating organization by providing definitions of basic concepts, knowledge, knowledge economy, knowledge management, and explains the knowledge spiral in information processing in society as well as knowledge creation from two major perspectives, i.e. the people-oriented perspective and technology-oriented perspective.

Chapter 2 (Saito) explains that managing knowledge facilitates the process of organizational learning and enhances organizational climate/culture in which the participants feel confident and are inspired in contributing to the organization in order to harness competitive advantages. Organizational learning capabilities and organizational learning process models are described in relevance of knowledge management to organizational learning and technology

Chapter 3 (Wickramasinghe) discusses the importance of establishing and sustaining an appropriateknowledge management infrastructure (KMI) in order to provide the organization with the best possible foundation from which to leverage its intellectual assets.

Chapter 4 (Geisler) provides the key attributes of normal science and the recently heralded post-normal science and argues the subjugation of post-normal science to social, economic urgencies and exigencies is only a matter of degree. This chapter brings researchers in the area of social sciences an inquiry into theory-in-use as well as espoused and established theories.

Section 2: Approaches to Healthcare Operations Management

This section presents six chapters as follows: Chapter 5, "Whole Systems/Holistic Approaches to the Continuation of Organizational Transformation," by Saito. Chapter 6, "Knowledge Information Processing Levels and Knowledge Information Interpretation," by Saito. Chapter 7, "The Intelligence Continuum and Emergency and Disaster Scenarios," by Wickramasinghe. Chapter 8 "Evaluation of Human Action: Foucault's Power/Knowledge Corollary," by Wickramasinghe. Chapter 9, "Key Considerations for the Adoption and Implementation of Knowledge Management in Healthcare Operations," by Wickramasinghe and Geisler, and finally Chapter 10, "Realizing the Healthcare Value Proposition: The Need for KM and Technology," by Wickramasinghe.

As already discussed in the preface, integral to the presentation of knowledge management issues in this book is the embracing of the sociotechnical perspective; a perspective that takes into consideration both human and technology issues that must complement and coordinate if superior operations are to be effected. In order to develop a full appreciation of the importance of such a sociotechnical perspective to facilitate ones understanding of the role of knowledge management in redesigning innovative healthcare organizations, it is vital to first investigate key concepts, including whole systems and holistic approaches, as discussed in Chapter 5, the knowledge-information processing dynamic presented in Chapter 6, as well as the dynamics of intelligence both human and machine (or artificial) as presented in Chapter 7, and finally and often one of the most daunting aspects in the application of knowledge management initiatives, namely that of the power dynamic, which is presented in Chapter 8. Chapters 9 and 10 then begin to focus explicitly on healthcare contexts and present key issues concerning the adoption and implementation of KM, as well as the role of KM for realizing the healthcare value proposition. Taken together, Sections 1 and 2 provide the fundamental principles of KM and human action. In Sections 3 and 4, instances of these key aspects are highlighted in various healthcare contexts.

On the completion of this section, the reader should be well equipped to understand most, if not all, the key aspects of sociotechnical dynamics.

Chapter 5 (Saito) describes conceptual framework of whole systems, holistic or integral social systems, and the classification/categorization of human cognition-action at the individual level as well as the organizational culture in the collective level. Typology of methodologies for intervening complex social systems and for changing organizational culture is also explained.

Chapter 6 (Saito) provides knowledge information processing loops and explains the multiplicity of knowledge information processing. The three throughputs of knowledge information and organizational learning, the feed back and feed forward processes of knowledge information, holistic management and knowledge information interpretation are described for the argument of future study in aligning of misfit between operation management and human action

Chapter 7 (Wickramasinghe) presents the model of the intelligence continuum. This model outlines a structured approach that is particularly useful in emergency and disaster scenarios in order to make effective and decisive decisions which draw upon the power of the extant knowledge base.

Chapter 8 (Wickramasinghe) discusses the need to incorporate post modern philosophies such as that the work of Foucault with classical theories such as agency theory, to develop a rich lens for understanding the dynamics of knowledge and its management in innovating organizations.

Chapter 9 (Wickramasinghe) describes key considerations for the adoption and implementation of knowledge management in healthcare operation,

Chapter 10 (Wickramasinghe) describes that it is only possible to realize the healthcare value proposition by embracing the tools, techniques, strategies and protocols of KM.

Section 3: Case Studies Illustrating Key Workplace Issues

This section presents four chapters all by Saito as follows: "Perceived Organizational Environment and Perceived Reliability in the Case of Hospital Nurses," Chapter 11, "Roles of Interpersonal Relationship in Improving Organizational Performance in the Case of Hospital Nurses," Chapter 12, "Interference of Mood States at Work with Perceived Performance, Perceived Efficacy, and Perceived Health," Chapter 13, and finally, "Causal Relationship Among Perceived Organizational Environment, Leadership, and Organizational Learning in Industrial Workers," Chapter 14.

The chapters in this section focus on critical current workplace issues in hospitals (in Chapter 11 and 12) and also in industry (Chapters 13 and 14). Effective application of knowledge management tools are made when the participants can understand the current situations of their workplace and share the reality. The participants need appreciation process for sharing the reality. Case studies or field studies are very important for the purpose of identifying the realty in workplace. Without the evidence obtained by case studies or investigations, redesigning innovative workplace operations is unlikely to result in successful outcomes.

The relationship between job cognition and incident behaviors of hospital nurses is presented in Chapter 11. In Chapter 12 nurses' behaviors at a subsystem level without any strategies is described. Significant interference of mood state at work with perceived self-efficacy, perceived performance, and perceived health forms the focus of Chapter 13. Finally, in Chapter 14 crucial roles of organizational learning and leadership as a leverage for the development of organizational performance in industry provides a good example of how to identify the reality and then start appreciative steps by means of knowledge management tools. The results of these four chapters suggests that understanding and sharing the current workplace information is critical in order to make workplace operations superior through the appropriate application of knowledge management methodologies.

On the completion of this section, readers will be equipped to identify key current workplace issues and to adopt appropriate methodologies of knowledge management in order to effect appropriate organizational redesign to enable effective and superior operations whether in the healthcare sector or manufacturing.

Chapter 11 (Saito) presents evidence on the relationship of perceived organizational condition and the performance reliability which are observed in hospitals in Japan. Occurrence of erroneous actions relates to organizational control and also relates to specific working time during 24 hours. Cognitive reliability on work conditions and work environment played critical roles in improving work performance and reducing human errors during the course of providing high quality of care.

Chapter 12 (Saito) provides evidence on the relationship between interpersonal relationship and organizational performances in the case of hospital nurses. Team reciprocity, communication accuracy and performance reliability representing organizational performance are provided and compared by emotional regulation, communication type and appreciation level of professional nursing work.

Chapter 13 (Saito) presents evidence on the interference of mood states at work with perceived performance, perceived efficacy and perceived health by using industrial workers. Mood states at work are influential moderators in affecting workers' perceptions. The perceptions of performance, self-efficacy, and health status significantly differed among mood states at work, and a vigorous mood at work had positive effects on workers' perceptions which leads to the enhancement of work ability and interpersonal management competency. It is important to note that while this chapter does not discuss healthcare operations, but the lessons from it are most pertinent to the healthcare sector.

Chapter 14 (Saito) provides some evidence on organizational learning observed in industries in Japan, and discusses organizational learning as a leverage in developing organizational performance. Mediating roles of organizational learning and leadership by type are crucial in improving organizational performances and in changing organizational climate coping with complex social environment. As with the previous chapter, we note that whiloe this chapter not specifically discuss healthcare operations, but the lessons from it are most pertinent to the healthcare sector.

Section 4: Case Studies Illustrating Key Issues and Investigations at the Community Level

The final section presents four chapters as follows: Chapter 15, "Eye-Movement and Performance during Reading of Cerebral Palsy Patients," by Karashima, Chapter 16, "Roles of Home Care and Rehabilitation Equipment for the Aged who Need Care in Improving Performance," by Nishiguchi, Chapter 17, "The First Attempt of Intensive Approaches in Cognitive Rehabilitation in Clients with Severe Traumatic Brain Injury (TBI)," by Fujii, Chapter 18, "Further Directions in Cognitive Rehabilitation in Community- and Home-based Daily Trainings in Clients with Severe Traumatic Brain Injury (TBI)," by Fujii.

The objective of these chapters is to provide readers with empirical studies and investigations dealing with the CP patients, the aged, and the TBI clients in community life, which illustrate current problems in their lives without the benefits of the appropriate adoption of the tools and technologies of knowledge management. The idea of this book is to highlight all areas in innovative healthcare operations where the tools, techniques, and technologies of KM can be utilized. The empirical studies which make up Section 4 emphasizes an area within healthcare; namely, that of home-based and community-based care, one that is less well understood and more often than receives less attention, and shows that the need for KM is just as important and relevant in this context to facilitate the designing of innovative operations.

Supporting tools and technologies for the TBI patients, CP patients, or the aged peoples who have a social handicap have been developed in each disciplinary section. However, a particular disciplinary knowledge is not adequate for active people who want to develop their own future life styles. People require foresight in their future lives in society as well as deep insight into the current circumstances. Knowledge on sociotechnical systems in addition to the specific disciplinary knowledge is needed for the people who search future perspective/scenario of their lives. Redesigning appropriate mechanisms of sociotechnical systems makes socially handicapped people become empowered to see their desired reality. Appropriate application of knowledge management methodologies are hardly expected without the prudent inquiries to future scenario as well as to current problems for the socially handicapped people.

On the completion of this section, the reader will be equipped with some key points to understand how socially handicapped people perform their own cognition-behavioral coupling processes. Their reactions in cognition and behavior levels are so characteristic that you can not understand without adequate analytical data and study results, and also their future perspectives vary depending up their living environments whether or not they have family support and satisfactory living surroundings. Moreover, this section highlights that KM plays as an important role in the community, as well as other contexts of healthcare.

Chapter 15 (Karashima) provides experimental evidence of eye-movement and performance in reading still documents of Japanese characters (Experiment 1) and scrolling documents (Experiment 2) by comparing between cerebral palsy (CP)patients and students. Characteristic eye-movement and performance of CP patients were clarified by comparing reading time, eye fixation duration, frequency of fixation, and the intervals between eye fixation in Experiment 1, and the most comfortable scrolling speed in Experiment 2. Appropriate daily care supported by the tools of knowledge management as well as by specific disciplinary technology is required for redesigning the social lives of the CP patients with characteristic eye-movements.

Chapter 16 (Nishiguchi) presents a barrier-free design for the aged who need home care and rehabilitation equipment. Home care and rehabilitation equipment are described as the method to remove barriers in daily activities, such as transferring the individual from bed or chair, mobility, eating, dressing, taking bath, verbal and auditory communication. The effectiveness of homecare and rehabilitation equipment is also described in emphasizing the importance of environmental adjustment for the aged, and the difference between male and female users in the feelings of satisfaction and well-being.

Chapter 17 (Fujii) describes the roles of home-based daily cognitive rehabilitation in two severe traumatic brain injury (TBI) clients, Client A and Client B. This chapter provides evidence on how the regular practice of work book training is effective and how ho0me-based practice is efficient for the clients. The step-by-step processes in their home and the community where the TBI clients were engaged and the reliable relationship among stakeholders, care-givers, supervisors and the clients, provided the clues and tips for clients to get suitable to their new job and to successful social reentry.

Chapter 18 (Fujii) provides the outcomes of the cognitive rehabilitation tests carried out by using young clients with severe traumatic brain injury (TBI). This Chapter suggests that the cognitive deficits of the TBI clients are improved first in attention, reading abilities, memory and executive function. After long-term training for social re-entry, memory in TBI clients are further improved.

Evidence-based practice leverages in developing knowledge management and in creating new values which change organizational environment. The organizational environment continues to be transformed and enhanced by preparing a set of scenario for the future by means of multi-modal methodological approaches, and juxtaposing hermeneutic approaches as well as nomothetic approaches. The authors, belonging to different disciplines, present some evidence of current circumstances and the need for organizational change in various healthcare scenarios. Viewpoints range from Management Systems Engineering, Human Factors Engineering, Brain Research, Management Sciences, Information Sciences, to Social and Health Sciences, Cognitive Psychology, Industrial Organizational Psychology, and Rehabilitation Psychology. The chapters we have prepared in this book are designed to help all the readers to gain deeper insights and a broader understanding of knowledge management and how it impact a multiplicity of interwoven disciplines, fields and events, and moreover that application of knowledge management to any organizational context will indeed facilitate superior outcomes. The studies and investigations presented in this book are only some examples intended to illustrate key points rather than be representative of all scenarios that require knowledge management. Most of our studies were to determine the reason why these kinds of events happened and to suggest how to take an action in operations, while a few of the studies describe the application of knowledge management methodology suitable to each event. What we present then in the following pages is a sample of the role of knowledge management in redesigning innovative operations and we underscore the need for on going research in this key area. We hope that all our readers will enjoy this book and find some hints and tips in the chapters introduced in this book as they try to grapple with the role of knowledge management in their own areas of interest and specialization.

REFERENCES

Drucker, P.F. (1992) *The age of discontinuity: Guidelines to our changing society.* Transaction Publishers, New Brunswick and London

Emery, F.E. & Trist, E.L. (1965) The causal texture of organizational environment. *Human Relations, 18*(1), 21-32.

Harbarmas, J.(1978). *Knowledge and Human Interests.* Heinemann.

Harken, H. (1978) *Synergies: An introduction.* The 2nd edition. Springer-Verlag.

Jackson, M.C. (2000). *Systems Approaches to Management.* Kluwer Academic/ Plenum Publishers.

Miller, E. (1999). *The Tavistock Institute Contribution Job and Organizational Design,* Vols. I and II. Ashgate Dartmouth.

Shimizu, H (1992) *Life and Place: Science creating meanings and values* (in Japanese). NTT publishers, Tokyo

Murako Saito and Nilmini Wickramasinghe
September 2008

Acknowledgment

This book would not have been possible without the cooperation and assistance of many people: the contributors, reviewers, our colleagues, and the staff at IGI Global. The authors would especially like to thank Mehdi Khosrow-Pour for inviting us to produce this book, Jan Travers for managing this project, as well as Rebecca Beistline and Christine Bufton for assisting us through the process and keeping us on schedule. We also acknowledge our respective universities for affording us the time to work on this project and are indebted to our colleagues and students for many stimulating discussions.

Section 1
Fundamental Aspects of Knowledge and Knowledge Management

This first section consists of four chapters: "Knowledge Economy for the Innovative Organization" by Wickramasinghe, "Managing Knowledge for Enhancing the Participants through Organizational Learning and Leadership" by Saito, "Permitting the True Potential of Knowledge Assets to be Utilized with KMI" by Wickramasinghe, and "Normal Science and Post-Normal Sciences" by Geisler.

Together these four chapters outline fundamental considerations regarding critical aspects of the knowledge construct (i.e., the dualities found within the knowledge construct as discussed in Chapter 1 and the connection between knowledge management, organizational learning, and leadership as discussed in Chapter 2). Chapter 3 discusses the fundamental components necessary to develop an appropriate and robust knowledge management infrastructure (KMI) and finally Chapter 4 presents important implications and considerations for methodologies for knowledge management that can only be fully appreciated through the understanding of significant aspects of normal and post-normal sciences.

Knowledge management is a nascent evolving field. Our goal in this section is to provide readers with the essential core elements of the KM discipline so that they have a solid foundation, exposure, and understanding of the key concepts. Given that the primary focus of this book is the use of KM for redesigning healthcare operations, we naturally focus our attention on those key aspects of KM that we believe are most beneficial when applied to any/all healthcare scenarios. Specifically, it is necessary to understand the roles for people and technology as well as how to develop appropriate and solid KM infrastructures so that the true potential of all knowledge assets can be maximized. This in turn requires appropriate leadership, good metrics, and a need to break away from rigid and outdated structures and/or archaic approaches to viewing problems and scenarios.

On the completion of this section, the reader should have a solid grounding in the fundamental core principles that are necessary in order to understand the role for knowledge management in redesigning innovative healthcare processes.

Chapter 1
Knowledge Economy for Innovating Organizations[1]

Nilmini Wickramasinghe
Illinois Institute of Technology, USA

ABSTRACT

Today's knowledge economy is dynamic, complex, and global. Every organization faces numerous challenges in trying to survive let alone thrive in such an environment. It is essential for innovating organizations to understand the key drivers of the knowledge economy so that they can better position themselves and thereby reap the rewards of a sustainable competitive advantage. The following addresses this by discussing knowledge and the key drives of the knowledge economy.

INTRODUCTION

In today's knowledge-based economy sustainable strategic advantages are gained more from an organization's knowledge assets than from its more traditional types of assets; namely land, labor and capital. Knowledge however, is a compound construct, exhibiting many manifestations of the phenomenon of duality such as subjectivity and objectivity as well as having tacit and explicit forms. Overlooking this phenomenon of duality in the knowledge construct however, will serve only to detract from the ability to realize the true potential of any organization's intangible

DOI: 10.4018/978-1-60566-284-8.ch001

assets. This is particularly problematic for an innovating organization, since it has such a high reliance on leveraging the cumulative expertise that resides within it to continually improve and innovate. Hence without a good understanding of the knowledge economy and how to effectively manage knowledge in such an environment, the innovating organization will find itself in an inferior position relative to this environment rather than enjoying a sustainable competitive advantage afforded by maximizing the benefits of its distinctive competencies.

This chapter contends that by understanding the phenomenon of duality and how it relates to the knowledge construct not only will innovating organizations firstly be able to better understand the compound knowledge construct and its management but also this will facilitate their superior functioning in the knowledge economy.

In this chapter, many specific manifestations of the duality phenomenon as it relates to knowledge and its management are highlighted such as the subjective and objective perspectives, the consensus versus disensus perspective, the Lokean / Leibnitzian aspects of knowledge versus the Hegelian / Kantian aspects, and the people versus technology dimensions. Throughout the chapter no one perspective is singled out as correct or incorrect rather the emphasis is on the fact that these respective duals not only underscore the duality phenomenon at different levels but are all useful, necessary and important for an innovating organization to fully appreciate the compound quality exhibited by the knowledge construct and thereby embrace superior knowledge management strategies, techniques, tools and processes. In addition, a sound understanding of the duality phenomenon as it relates to knowledge will not only facilitate a better understanding of how to embrace knowledge management (an important strategy in today's knowledge economy (Drucker, 1993)), but also address key needs such as identified by Nonaka that " … few managers grasp the true nature of knowledge creating companies – let alone how to manage it" (Holsapple and Joshi, 2002, p.47) and Ann Stuart that "[m]any managers would be hard pressed to explain precisely and concisely, what this evolving business trend (knowledge management) means" (ibid, p.47).

THE KNOWLEDGE ECONOMY

In general, economists are agreed that the world has experienced three distinct ages – the Agrarian Age, the Industrial Age, and now the Information Age (Persaud, 2001; Woodall, 2000). The hallmark of the Information Age, is the rapid adoption and diffusion of ICT (information communication technologies) which has had a dramatic effect on the way business is conducted as well as on the life styles of people. An important consequence of globalization and rapid technological change has been the generation of vast amounts of raw data and information, and the concomitant

Table 1. Critical components of the knowledge economy

Economy	Critical Components
Traditional	• Land (natural resources) • Labor • Capital
Knowledge	• Creativity • Information & data • Intellectual Capital • Innovation

growth of the capabilities to process them into pertinent information and knowledge applicable to the solutions of business problems. Knowledge then has become a major organizational tool in gaining and sustaining competitive advantage.

Traditionally, economists have emphasized land and the associated natural resources, labor, and capital as the essential primary ingredients for the economic enterprise. However, in the Information Age, knowledge is now being considered to be as important as the three original prerequisites. Hence, the new term Knowledge Economy has emerged and managing knowledge has became one of the primary skills organizations need to acquire in order to survive and prosper. Table 1 contrasts the critical components of the knowledge economy with the traditional economy

Knowledge

There exist many plausible definitions of knowledge. For the purposes of this chapter the definition of knowledge given by Davenport and Prusak (1998, p.5) will be used because it is not only broad and thus serves to capture the breadth of the construct but also and perhaps more importantly for this discussion, it serves to underscore that especially in an organizational context, knowledge is not a simple homogeneous construct, rather a compound construct:

Knowledge is a fluid mix of framed experiences, values, contextual information, and expert insights that provides a framework for evaluating and incorporating new experiences and information. It originates and is applied in the minds of knowers. In organizations, it is often embedded not only in documents or repositories but also in organizational routines, processes, practices and norms. Davenport and Prusak (1998, p.5)

KNOWLEDGE AND ITS MANAGEMENT FOR INNOVATING ORGANIZATIONS

In trying to understand knowledge, knowledge management and related concepts such as organizational learning and organizational memory, numerous researchers have employed the structure of an inquiring organization (Churchman, 1971; Malhotra, 1997, Courtney et al., 1998; Courtney, 2001 and Hall et al. 2003a). By doing so, they are able to view knowledge creation and thereby examine knowledge, its management as well as organizational learning and organizational memory through a systems lens. Since inquiring organizations employ inquiring systems consisting of interrelated processes, procedures and other measures for producing knowledge on a problem or issues of significance (Courtney et al, 2000; Mitroff and Linstone, 1993), knowledge and its management then become integral to all major activities of inquiring organizations. To be successful today, the modern organization must be a learning organization (Senge, 1990). By viewing such a learning organization as an inquiring system and thus an inquiring organization, it is not only possible but useful to do so in order to identify knowledge creation, in particular "valid" knowledge produced (Malhotra, 1997, Courtney et al., 1998; Courtney, 2001 and Hall et al. 2003b).

These inquiring organizations have typically been discussed as different types, corresponding to the different types of inquiring systems first identified by Churchman (Courtney et al, 2000). Specifically, Churchman's Leibnitzian inquirer, Lockean inquirer, Hegelain inquirer, Kantian inquirer and Singerian inquirer which in turn have led to the Leibnitzian inquiring organization, the Lockean inquiring organization, the Hegelian inquiring organization, the Kantian inquiring organization and the Singerian inquiring organization. Such a singular perspective however, appears limiting given the compound nature of knowledge itself. Innovating organizations are indeed inquiring organizations at both the micro and macro level. More particularly without the embracing of one or more of these different types of inquiry it becomes difficult for the innovating organization to continuously innovate in a knowledge economy. Essential to all of these types of inquiry in the context of knowledge management (KM) however, is an understanding of the types of knowledge since different methods of inquiry will provide greater or lesser knowledge of one or another type and depending on the nature of the innovating organization a particular type of knowledge would be more or less useful and relevant.

TYPES OF KNOWLEDGE

In trying to understand the knowledge construct it is necessary first to recognize the binary nature of knowledge; namely its objective and subjective components (Wickramasinghe and Mills, 2001). Knowledge can exist as an object, in essentially two forms; explicit or factual knowledge and tacit or "know how"(Polyani, 1958, 1966; Haynes, 1999, 2000). It is well established that while both types of knowledge are important, tacit knowledge is more difficult to identify and thus manage (Nonaka, 1994, 2001). Of equal importance, though perhaps less well defined, knowledge also has a subjective component and can be viewed as an ongoing phenomenon, being shaped by social practices of communities (Boland and Tenkasi, 1995). The objective elements of knowledge can be thought of as primarily having an impact on process while the subjective elements typically impact innovation. Both effective and efficient processes as well as the functions of supporting and fostering innovation are key concerns of knowledge management. Thus, we have an interesting duality in knowledge management that some have called a contradiction (Schultze, 1998) and others describe as the *loose-tight* nature of knowledge management (Malhotra, 2000).

The *loose-tight* nature of knowledge management comes into being because of the need to recognize and draw upon some distinct philosophical perspectives; namely, the Lockean / Leibnitzian stream and the Hegelian /Kantian stream. Models of convergence and compliance representing the *tight* side are grounded in a Lockean / Leibnitzian tradition. These models are essential to provide the information processing aspects of knowledge management, most notably by enabling efficiencies of scale and scope and thus supporting the objective view of knowledge management. In contrast, the *loose* side provides agility and flexibility in the tradition of a Hegelian / Kantian perspective. Such models recognize the importance of divergence of meaning which is essential to support the "sense-making", subjective view of knowledge management. Figure 1 depicts the Yin-Yang model of knowledge management (Wickramasinghe and Mills, 2001). The principle of Yin-Yang is at the very roots of Chinese thinking and is centered around the notion of polarity or duality not to be confused with the ideas of opposition or conflict (Watts, 1992). By incorporating this Yin-Yang concept of duality and the need to have or recognize the existence of both components present yet not necessarily in equal amounts is appropriate for describing knowledge management from a holistic perspective. Further, by recognizing the manifestations of duality that exist with the knowledge construct as identified in Figure 1 and thereby taking such a holistic perspective, not only are both sides of these duals recognized (i.e. the loose and tight perspectives, subjective/objective, consensus/disensus, Lokean/Lebnitzian vs Hegelian/Kantian) but also, and more importantly, both are required (at least to some extent) in order

Figure 1. **Yin Yang model of knowledge management** *(adapted from Wickramas-inghe and Mills, 2001)*

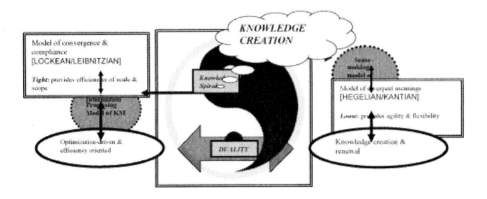

for knowledge management to truly flourish.

Such a holistic perspective then strongly suggests that focusing on only one component or having a singular perspective of an inquiring system without any regard for the other side of any given dual is limiting and likely to lead to a less complete picture of knowledge creation; hence the need to recognize the duality phenomenon for innovating organizations. The importance for innovating organizations then, becomes two fold; a) to recognize and understand this underlying principle of duality and b) to utilize it by in essence finding the "right mix" of the duality, or harmonious balance between these duals for the specific context; given the context dependent nature of wisdom. Thus, the Lockean inquiring organization grounded in a Lockean inquiring system should not totally ignore aspects of a Hegelian or Kantian inquiry system in order to create a fuller picture of "valid" knowledge. It is important to note here however, that unlike with data this "right mix" is neither programmable nor algorithmic and thus requires a deep understanding of the duality principle as well as the organization's specific context and what is key in that specific context, in this way "valid" knowledge should be resultant; and hence a state of wisdom achieved.

THE KNOWLEDGE SPIRAL

Knowledge is not static; rather it changes and evolves during the life of an organization. What is more, it is possible to change the form of knowledge; i.e., turn tacit knowledge into explicit and explicit knowledge into tacit or to turn the subjective form of knowledge into the objective form of knowledge (Wickramasinghe and Mills,

2001). This process of changing the form of knowledge is known as the knowledge spiral (Nonaka, 1994, 2001). Integral to this changing of knowledge through the knowledge spiral is that new knowledge is created (Nonaka, 1994) and this can bring many benefits to organizations. In the case of transferring tacit knowledge to explicit knowledge for example, an organization is able to capture the expertise of particular individuals; hence, this adds not only to the organizational memory but also enables single loop and double loop organizational learning to take place (Huber, 1984). Implicit in this is the underlying dualities and a dynamic equilibrium or "right mix" between dualities that is determined by context. In the process of creating "valid" knowledge, innovating organizations are in fact enacting these transformations and thus "experiencing" these dualities; however it is unconscious and to a great extent much of the knowledge that potentially could be acquired is never captured by ignoring the underlying dualities and taking a singular focus such as only a Lockean inquiring system as the lens to view knowledge creation.

KNOWLEDGE CREATION

The processes of creating and capturing knowledge, irrespective of the specific philosophical orientation (i.e. Lockean/Leibnitzian versus Hegelian/Kantian), has been approached from two major perspectives; namely a people-oriented perspective and a technology-oriented perspective; another duality.

THE PEOPLE-ORIENTED PERSPECTIVE TO KNOWLEDGE CREATION

This section briefly describes three well known people-oriented knowledge creation frameworks: namely, Nonaka's Knowledge Spiral, Spender's and Blackler's respective frameworks.

According to Nonaka (1994): 1) Tacit to tacit knowledge transformation usually occurs through apprenticeship type relations where the teacher or master passes on the skill to the apprentice. 2) Explicit to explicit knowledge transformation usually occurs via formal learning of facts. 3) Tacit to explicit knowledge transformation usually occurs when there is an articulation of nuances; for example, as in healthcare if a renowned surgeon is questioned as to why he does a particular procedure in a certain manner, by his articulation of the steps the tacit knowledge becomes explicit and 4) Explicit to tacit knowledge transformation usually occurs as new explicit knowledge is internalized it can then be used to broaden, reframe and extend one's tacit knowledge. These transformations are often referred to as the modes of socialization, combination, externalization and internalization respectively (Nonaka, 2001).

Spender draws a distinction between individual knowledge and social knowledge (yet another duality), each of which he claims can be implicit or explicit (Newell et al., 2002). From this framework we can see that Spender's definition of implicit knowledge corresponds to Nonaka's tacit knowledge. However, unlike Spender, Nonaka doesn't differentiate between individual and social dimensions of knowledge; rather he merely focuses on the nature and types of the knowledge itself. In contrast, Blackler (ibid) views knowledge creation from an organizational perspective, noting that knowledge can exist as encoded, embedded, embodied, encultured and/or embrained. In addition, Blackler emphasized that for different organizational types, different types of knowledge predominate, and highlights the connection between knowledge and organizational processes (ibid). Blackler's types of knowledge can be thought of in terms of spanning a continuum of tacit (implicit) through to explicit with embrained being predominantly tacit (implicit) and encoded being predominantly explicit while embedded, embodied and encultured types of knowledge exhibit varying degrees of a tacit (implicit) /explicit combination.

In trying to integrate these various perspectives, what we see is that Spender's and Blackler's perspectives complement Nonaka's conceptualization of knowledge creation and more importantly do not contradict his thesis of the knowledge spiral wherein the extant knowledge base is continually being expanded to a new knowledge base, be it tacit /explicit (in Nonaka's terminology), implicit / explicit (in Spender's terminology), or embrained / encultured / embodied / embedded / encoded (in Blackler's terminology). What is important to underscore here is that these three frameworks take a primarily people-oriented perspective of knowledge creation. In particular, Nonaka's framework, the most general of the three frameworks, describes knowledge creation in terms of knowledge transformations as discussed above that are all initiated by human cognitive activities. Needless to say that both Spender and Blackler's respective frameworks also view knowledge creation through a primarily people oriented perspective. Typically, Hegelian and Kantian inquiring systems would incorporate knowledge creation that is consistent with these people-oriented perspectives (Malhotra, 1997).

THE TECHNOLOGY-ORIENTED PERSPECTIVE TO KNOWLEDGE CREATION

In contrast to the above primarily people-oriented perspectives pertaining to knowledge creation, knowledge discovery in databases (KDD) (and more specifically data mining), approaches knowledge creation from a primarily technology-oriented

Figure 2. Technology perspective of knowledge creation (adapted from Wickramasinghe and von Lubitz (2007))

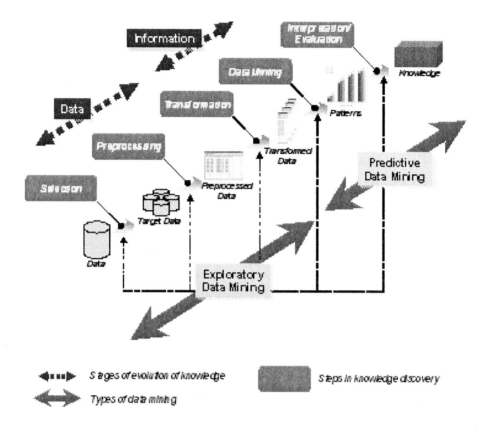

perspective. In particular, the KDD process focuses on how data is transformed into knowledge by identifying valid, novel, potentially useful, and ultimately understandable patterns in data (Fayyad et al., 1996). KDD is primarily used on data sets for creating knowledge through model building, or by finding patterns and relationships in data. How to manage such newly discovered knowledge and other organizational knowledge is at the core of knowledge management. Figure 2 summarizes the key steps within the KDD process; while it is beyond the scope of this chapter to describe in detail all the steps which constitute the KDD process, an important duality to highlight here is that between exploratory and predictive data mining. Typically, Lockean and Leibnizian inquiring systems would subscribe to a technology-oriented perspective for knowledge creation (Malhotra, 1997).

The preceding discussions then have highlighted some key aspects of knowledge creation from both a people-oriented perspective as well as a technology-oriented perspective. Irrespective of which knowledge creation perspective, the concept of duality is reflected in the knowledge creation process both between the people-oriented and technology-oriented perspectives as well as within each respective perspective; for example within the people-oriented perspective, we have the dualities of social versus individual and tacit versus explicit; while in the technology-oriented perspective, we have the duality of exploratory versus predictive data mining. Unlike the dualities identified in the Yin-Yang model of knowledge management though, these dualities represent instantiations of the duality principle at the micro-level. So it is possible then to have the manifestations of dualities with respect to the knowledge construct at both the macro and micro levels; yet another reason why the knowledge construct is compound in nature. The following section elaborates on these dualities at both the macro and micro levels with respect to the knowledge construct and the impact they have on knowledge management.

DUALITIES IN THE KNOWLEDGE CONSTRUCT

The previous section highlighted several dualities with respect to the knowledge construct and knowledge creation at both a macro and micro level. In so doing, we can see that in fact many dualities manifest themselves when we begin to understand the knowledge construct and its management. It would make sense then that our inquiring systems, which are creating knowledge through their activities, should also be viewed in such a light and embrace such a perspective. Before, discussing the benefits of embracing such a perspective, it is first useful to summarize the key dualities discussed and their benefits to knowledge management. Table 2 highlights these key dualities and why each side of the duality has importance with respect to knowledge management.

As noted in the introduction, any duality represents the existence of two irreducible aspects or perspectives. By recognizing both sides of a specific dual then, be it tacit/explicit, individual/social, Lockean/Leibnitzian vs Hegelian/Kantian, subjective/objective, consensus/disensus, loose/tight or people/technology, a more complete and richer picture of knowledge is created and hence the impact to knowledge management be it in terms of sharing knowledge, creating knowledge or enhancing the knowledge context, in turn is superior. On the other hand, taking a one-dimensional view, which is more often than not what too many organizations tend to do with respect to their own knowledge management initiatives, for example only recognizing the technology side of knowledge creation (and not being cognizant of the people side of knowledge creation; i.e. the Lockean and/or Leibnitzian innovating organization), or disregarding the existence of explicit knowledge (and only recognizing the existence of tacit knowledge; i.e. the Hegelian and/or Kantian

Table 2. Key knowledge management dualities

Duality	Importance of the Duality to KM
Tacit/Explicit	From Nonaka's knowledge spiral both tacit and explicit knowledge as well as the transformations of tacit to explicit and vice versa are important to KM. Only focusing on tacit (or only focusing on explicit) provides an incomplete picture with respect to knowledge creation.
Individual/Social	Spender and Blacker, in particular, highlight the significance of both sides of this duality. Only focusing on individually constructed knowledge limits us to a much narrower domain of knowledge creation. Especially given the gregarious nature of humans socially constructed knowledge should also form an important part of the total knowledge created.
Lokean/Leibnitzian vs. Hegelian / Kantian	These fundamental philosophical perspectives all highlight important facets of the knowledge context (a key dimension of wisdom) and thus when taken together facilitate the understanding of the full spectrum for knowledge management.
Subjective/Objective	The sides of this duality highlight both the complexities of knowledge capture relative to the knowledge type being captured as well as the importance of capturing all types of knowledge.
Consensus/Disensus	While the consensus side of this duality emphasizes convergence of thought the disensus side emphasizes the need for divergence; however both are reflections of group dynamics that are important for knowledge sharing/dissemination.
Loose/Tight	This duality also highlights the need for considering both internal and external organizational context in the framing of KM issues for supporting activities that lead to optimization as well as activities that lead to knowledge creation and renewal
People/Technology	This duality underscores the need for a socio-technical approach to knowledge creation because it highlights that knowledge can be created by technologies and people as well as it also being embedded in processes.

innovating organization) in knowledge creation will lead to a much narrower and limited resultant body of knowledge as well as an inferior and most likely less useful or appropriate knowledge management initiative which in turn detracts from the ability of innovating organizations to build on their distinctive competencies. Hence, we should not be surprised by the many discussions prevalent in the literature regarding the "nonsense of knowledge management" (Wilson, 2002).

Two key characteristics of innovating organizations are i) accuracy of the system basis and ii) continual review of the stored knowledge for accuracy in changing environments (Hall et al. 2003b). Surely a partial picture of knowledge would never be able to provide a similar level of accuracy as a fuller, richer picture; hence the benefit to innovating organizations of understanding the duality principle and incorporating the many manifestations of these, duals both macro and micro, with respect to the compound knowledge construct.

Understanding the duality principle necessitates an understanding of the "right mix" or dynamic equilibrium for the given context. Given this connection with the context and the non-programmable nature of the knowledge construct, such an understanding becomes a necessary albeit not sufficient step for innovating organizations to successfully leverage the full potential of their intangible and primarily people assets and thereby prosper in a dynamic and complex knowledge economy.

CONCLUSION

In the knowledge economy, technology plays an integral part in expanding economic potential (Persaud, 2001). Such economic potential is primarily reliant on maximizing the firm's intangible assets and requires the fostering of innovation and creation. To support such initiatives information is required. However, this information serves a dual purpose; it reduces operating costs and also facilitates idea generation and creativity. For example, the use of enterprise-wide systems permits organizations to decrease their transaction costs which allows them to decrease agency costs. This is because integrated information pertaining to specific tasks and activities can now be acquired in a timely fashion (Wickramasinghe, 2000). Furthermore, information accessed through various shared service modules supports the generation of new and innovative initiatives (Probst et al., 2000; Shapiro and Verian, 1999). Moreover, the continuous collection and analysis of this data and information generated from a variety of transactions throughout the supply chain facilitates idea generation and the rapid design and development of new products, processes or even new ways to meet requirements.

In order to maximize and leverage the potential advantage afforded to organizations it is imperative that an understanding of the dualities of the knowledge construct is gained. This is particularly vital for innovating organizations since their raison d'etre is to continually come up with new ideas, services and/or products. Integral to such activities is a thorough and complete understanding of the role and application of knowledge as well as key people and technology dimensions for the creation of germane knowledge.

This chapter has served to highlight several instances of the duality principle as it relates to knowledge and its management. These instances represented dualities at both the macro and micro levels. By so doing, the pervasive nature of the duality principle to knowledge as well as to knowledge management was emphasized. In presenting the duality principle as it relates to knowledge and its management it is important to recognize its macro and micro aspects, because these aspects are characteristics of any organizational setting. Furthermore, an appropriate mix of these dualities is determined by the specific organizational /environmental/technological /situational context, and is necessary but not sufficient in the formulation of an appropriate knowledge management strategy; while the understanding of the underlying principles is important for the achievement of wisdom. Given the importance of knowledge and its management to innovating organizations such an understanding then becomes essential if innovating organizations are to survive and thrive in the knowledge economy.

REFERENCES

Acs, Z. J., Carlsson, B., & Karlsson, C. (1999). *The linkages among entrepreneurship, SMEs, and the macroeconomy*. Cambridge: Cambridge University Press.

Boland, R., & Tenkasi, R. (1995). Perspective making perspective taking. *Organization Science, 6*, 350–372. doi:10.1287/orsc.6.4.350

Churchman, C. (1971). *The design of inquiring systems: Basic concepts of systems and organizations*. New York: Basic Books Inc.

Courtney, J. (2001). Decision making and knowledge management in inquiring organizations: Toward a new decision-making paradigm for DSS. *Decision Support Systems Special Issue on Knowledge Management, 31*, 17–38.

Courtney, J., Chae, B., & Hall, D. (2000). Developing inquiring organizations. *Journal of Knowledge Management and Innovation, 1*(1).

Courtney, J., Croasdell, D., & Paradice, D. (1998). Inquiring organizations. *Australian Journal of Information Systems, 6*(1).

Davenport, T., & Grover, V. (2001). Knowledge management. *Journal of Management Information Systems, 18*(1), 3–4.

Davenport, T., & Prusak, L. (1998). *Working knowledge*. Boston: Harvard Business School Press.

Drucker, P. (1993). *Post-capitalist society*. New York: Harper Collins.

Drucker, P. (1999). Beyond the information revolution. *Atlantic Monthly, 284*(4), 47–57.

Fayyad, Piatetsky-Shapiro, & Smyth (1996). From data mining to knowledge discovery: An overview. In Fayyad, Piatetsky-Shapiro, Smyth & Uthurusamy (Eds.), *Advances in knowledge discovery and data mining*. Menlo Park, CA: AAAI Press/ The MIT Press.

Hall, D., Guo, Y., & Davis, R. (2003a). Developing a value-based decision-making model for inquiring organizations. In *Proceedings of the 36ᵗʰ Hawaii International Conference on System Sciences.*

Hall, D., Paradice, D., & Courtney, J. (2003b). Building a theoretical foundation for a learning-oriented knowledge management system. *Journal of Information Technology Theory and Application, 5*(2), 63–89.

Haynes, J. D. (1999). Practical thinking and tacit knowing as a foundation for information systems. *Australian Journal of Information Systems, 6*(2), 57–64.

Haynes, J. D. (2000, August 9-12). Inquiring organizations and tacit knowing. *AMCIS*, California, *Association for Information Systems* (pp, 1544–1547).

Holsapple, C., & Joshi, K. (2002). Knowledge management: A threefold framework. *The Information Society, 18*, 47–64. doi:10.1080/01972240252818225

Huber, G. (1984). The nature and design of postindustrial organizations. *Management Science, 30*(8), 928–951. doi:10.1287/mnsc.30.8.928

Huber, G. (1990). A theory of the effects of advanced information technologies on organisational design, intelligence, and decision making. *Academy of Management Review, 15*(1), 47–71. doi:10.2307/258105

Malhotra, Y. (1997). Knowledge management for inquiring organizations. In *Proceedings of 3ⁿᵈ Americas Conference on Information Systems* (pp. 293-295).

Malhotra, Y. (2000). Knowledge management and new organizational form. In Malhotra (Ed.), *Knowledge management and virtual organizations.* Hershey, PA: Idea Group Publishing.

Newell, S., Robertson, M., Scarbrough, H., & Swan, J. (2002). *Managing knowledge work.* New York: Palgrave.

Nonaka, I. (1994). A dynamic theory of organizational knowledge creation. *Organization Science, 5*, 14–37. doi:10.1287/orsc.5.1.14

Nonaka, I., & Nishiguchi, T. (2001). *Knowledge emergence.* Oxford: Oxford University Press.

Persaud, A. (2001). The knowledge gap. *Foreign Affairs (Council on Foreign Relations), 80*(2), 107–117.

Polyani, M. (1958). *Personal knowledge: Towards a post-critical philosophy.* Chicago: University Press Chicago.

Polyani, M. (1966). *The tacit dimension London.* Routledge & Kegan Paul.

Porter, M. (1990). *The competitive advantage of nations.* Boston: Free Press.

Probst, G., Raub, S., & Romhardt, K. (2000). *Managing knowledge: Building blocks for success.* Chichester: Willey.

Schultze, U. (1998). Investigating the contradictions in knowledge management. Presentation at IFIP Dec.

Shapiro, C., & Varian, H. (1999). *Information rules.* Boston: Harvard Business School Press.

Watts, A. (1992). *Tao the watercourse way.* London: Arkanan.

Wickramasinghe, N. (2000). IS/IT as a tool to achieve goal alignment: A theoretical framework. *International J. HealthCare Technology Management, 2*(1/2/3/4), 163-180.

Wickramasinghe, N. (2003). Do we practise what we preach: Are knowledge management systems in practice truly reflective of knowledge management systems in theory? *Business Process Management Journal, 9*(3), 295–316. doi:10.1108/14637150310477902

Wickramasinghe, N. (2005). The phenomenon of duality: The key to facilitating the transition form knowledge management to wisdom for inquiring organizations (pp. 272-291). In Courtney, et al. (Eds.), *Inquiring organizations: Moving form knowledge management to wisdom.* Hershey, PA: Idea Group.

Wickramasinghe, N., & von Lubitz. (2007). *Knowledge-based organizations: Theories and fundamentals.* Hershey, PA: IGI Global.

Wickramasinghe, N., & Lamb, R. (2002). Enterprise-wide systems enabling physicians to manage care. *International Journal of Healthcare Technology and Management, 4*(3/4), 288–302. doi:10.1504/IJHTM.2002.001144

Wickramasinghe, N., & Mills, G. (2001). MARS: The electronic medical record system the core of the Kaiser galaxy. *International Journal of Healthcare Technology and Management, 3*(5/6), 406–423. doi:10.1504/IJHTM.2001.001119

Wilson, T. (2002). The nonsense of knowledge management. *Information Systems Research, 8*(1), 1–41.

Woodall, P. (2000). Survey: The new economy: Knowledge is power. *The Economist, 356*(8189), 27–32.

ENDNOTE

[1] This chapter includes a distillation of material from previous IGI publications by the author namely: Wickramasinghe, N. 2007 "Knowledge-Based Enterprise: Theories and Fundamentals" with D. von Lubitz Idea Group and Wickramasinghe, N. 2005 "The Phenomenon of Duality: A Key to Facilitate the Transition From Knowledge Management to Wisdom for Inquiring Organisations" pp. 272-291 in Eds Courtney, J., J. Haynes and D. Paradice "Inquiring Organisations: Moving from Knowledge Management to Wisdom" Idea Group.

Chapter 2

Managing Knowledge for Enhancing the Participants through Organizational Learning and Leadership

Murako Saito
Waseda University, Japan

ABSTRACT

Managing knowledge is essential to facilitate the process of organizational learning and to foster organizational culture in which the participants are inspired and feel confident to contribute to the organization and to enhance competitive advantages. The participants develop their capabilities driven by the process of cognition-action coupling at individual and collective levels. The role of knowledge management is inevitably to redesign the organization into an innovative one by inspiring the participants to create new values. The first topic in this chapter is on the conceptual models of business performance, such as our basic model of organizational adaptability and organizational learning capability model explaining organizational learning process (i.e., cognition-action coupling process in organizational environment). In the second topic, continuity of reflexive organizational learning for creating new values and the process models of organizational learning are discussed for harnessing organizational learning development (OLD). The final important topic is on the relevance of knowledge management to organizational learning and to technology. Innovation (i.e., knowledge generation and knowledge generalization) emerges in the recursive information processing harnessed by technology, which in turn leads

DOI: 10.4018/978-1-60566-284-8.ch002

to flexibility, adaptability of organization and inspires people to achieve shared goals. The focus of this chapter is placed on the participants of the organization who are most important business assets and a fundamental aspect in knowledge management in redesigning innovative organizations.

INTRODUCTION

It is by the strategic application of knowledge management underpinned by advanced technology that redesigning of an organization enables the development of the organization into being more effective and competitive and to cope with the changes in society. To become innovative means that the participants are inspired to develop through the course of organizational learning by sharing organizational visions and missions. Knowledge management facilitates the process of inquiry by creating new values to develop the future direction and for restructuring workplaces where the participants can achieve business goals for competitive advantage. Human assets for any businesses, such as in manufacturing, services, and in R&D, are enhanced by being activated and inspired through the process of cognition-action coupling at both levels of individuals and collectives. In the activated and inspired organizational climate, new values emerge through the cognition-action coupling processes, namely, the process of organizational learning. People feel confident helping each other to develop in the recursive or reflexive learning process and in the favorite climate of organizational environment provided with advanced information technology. Organizational learning development (OLD) plays a crucial role in sharing information, amplifying outcomes and innovating organizations for business prosperity.

The focus in this Chapter is on organizational learning and leadership which play important mediating and moderating roles in improving business performance. Business performance in an information society is harnessed by managing knowledge for fostering all the stakeholders of business. Fostering and empowering the participants are made in the process of organizational learning. In the recursive process of organizational learning, people understand why and how the organization functions and how to attain organizational goals. The participants as service-providers are able to acquire necessary information to develop their skills and careers. The participants as service-recipients are able to learn how to inquire and request the necessary information in the recursive process. The OLD is enhanced by a strategic reciprocal relationship on both sides of the participants. Leadership also plays another important role in improving organizational performance by aligning different cognitions and values among multi-disciplinary staff and teams, and by making strategic action for encouraging the participants to spread the information acquired.

The topics dealt with in the following sections are organizational learning and leadership as mediating or moderating roles in developing an innovative organization and appropriate processes for overcoming turbulence in a dynamic society. The roles of organizational learning and leadership are critical in making knowledge management initiatives successfully embraced in the workplace.

ORGANIZATIONAL LEARNING AND LEADERSHIP FOR IMPROVING ORGANIZATIONAL PERFORMANCE

Basic Model of Organizational Adaptability

Business resources, such as human resources, physical resources and information systems and technology are subsumed into a total system or a whole system of the enterprise. Organizational adaptability which is the main engine of the enterprise is to be empowered by human resources supported by advanced technologies and fostered by organizational learning and leadership. The basic model of organizational performance introduced by our studies (Saito et al, 1998, 2000, 2002) consists of three components, business constraints as the antecedents, organizational environment as a central part of the enterprise and business performance as the consequences as shown in Figure 1. The levers, at least two levers, i.e. organizational learning and leadership, are necessary to improve business performance and to cope with a dy-

Figure 1. Basic model of organizational adaptability

namic social environment Mediating or moderating roles of organizational learning and leadership are crucial to encourage the participants to follow a course of action with confidence in order to improve organizational performance. Leaders inspire their follower's organizational learning and lead them to attain successful outcomes appropriately aligned to the organization. Leadership fosters employee development. Networking among multiple disciplinary staff with multiple paradigms is fostered by the moderating roles of organizational learning and leadership, which leads to the change in the current organizational culture.

Learning capability in the organization is very important to enhance interpersonal coherence and team reciprocity which in turn may lead to organizational flexibility or resilience. Creation of ideas and their spread into the related organizations are brought about by the learning capability of the participants and their leadership. Through the organizational learning processes under appropriate leadership, the participants are inspired, and new ideas and values for all the stakeholders emerge. New ideas and knowledge are stored in a systematic data-base, and are used to generate explicit knowledge which is then shared among different disciplinary areas in order to improve business performance.

Empirical evidence on the causation of the relationship among business constraints, leadership, organizational learning and organizational performance in a healthcare context is described in Chapter 14.

Leadership in European Foundation for Quality Management (EFQM) as an Excellent Model

In excellent enterprises, leadership plays a critical role in motivating employees. In most European countries, the EFQM model shown in Figure 2, or Baldrige model which is known as a revision of the EFQM, is frequently adopted in the US healthcare sector. The antecedent in both models is leadership which drives organizational resources, such as people, policy and strategy, partnership resources, and activates the learning process which brings people results, customer results and society results to improve organizational performances, as shown in Figure 2.

Leaders, employees as followers, customers, shareholders and all the stakeholders are positively related to the development of organizational learning. Leadership development drives business prosperity by means of a causal value chain as shown in Figure 3. Employee satisfaction leads to customer satisfaction, customer satisfaction drives shareholder value which finally enhances business prosperity. Leadership development drives its members to create values for all the stakeholders related to the organization. Leadership plays a decisive role in enhancing business prosperity through internal and external organizational learning on multiple levels of organizational learning as descried in Chapter 14.

In our model shown in Figure 1, business visions and business culture as enterprise constraints are placed as the antecedents, but in the EFQM and Baldrige models, leadership was placed as the antecedent. Leadership works as a moderator or mediator instead of the antecedent variable in our model shown in Figure 1. There may be something different in the DNA of each culture in Western and Eastern. Leaders in the context of Japanese culture do not drive their followers to work as managers command to follow, but rather help and cooperate as a guardian to encourage their followers to work. In doing so, a higher contribution and better result has been obtained as a result of the workers having confidence in achieving

Figure 2. The European Foundation for quality management excellent model

Figure 3. Value chain to emerge business prosperity through organizational learning

their tasks and in improving self-efficacy. Our surveys suggested that, the workers having confidence and self-efficacy, do not want to be forced or led, but want to act as being professional in a discretionary or autopoietic manner (Saito and Seki, 1998, Saito,1998, Saito, Ikeda, Seki,2000, Saito,2006).

Organizational Learning Capabilities

Organizational transformation for adapting in a dynamic society is enabled by organizational learning capabilities of acquiring and generating new information and knowledge, and then of generalizing this knowledge with other members of the organization (Yeung, Urlich, Nason and von Glinow, 1999, Cameron and Quinn, 1999, Tsai, 2001, Todorora and Durisin, 2007). Knowledge management plays its roles in all the steps of information processing, such as acquiring, generating, sharing and implementing. Acquiring is for understanding the information and knowledge presented or given, generating is for creating new additional information and knowledge among the members with a similar mindset; while sharing is for understanding with all members having different mental models, or for generalizing the information and knowledge with different disciplinary fields. Implementing is for understanding the information and knowledge, and for taking action to achieve its goals, rendering services in the field with team members of different disciplinary mindsets.

Organizational learning capabilities include all the processes of acquiring, generating, sharing and implementing information so as to create and generalize knowledge. Social accidental issues reported remind us of the importance of knowledge management in all the steps of knowledge information processing, especially in the implementation of these steps. Team members for implementing final decisions are made by the persons with various mental models in accordance with field circumstances, so that interpretation of the issue or the way of implementation is not similar among team members. Team performance may not be predicted by particular team members. Team performance may decrease, and an accidental situation may happen due to inappropriate modification, or the different procedural ways of the implementation among disciplines. The role of knowledge management is crucial in all the steps from acquisition to implementation in order to check whether information interpretation is properly identified or not.

Organizational learning capability which is developed in the knowledge acquiring, generating and sharing or absorbing processes in an organization, plays an important role in improving organizational performance and in achieving organizational goals. Contingency factors, such as power relationship in the organization give crucial effect on organizational performance. It is inevitable that sharing knowledge among multiple disciplines has a pitfall which may lead to performance decrement, incident experience, or accident unless procedural knowledge is properly assured among work performers with different disciplinary mindset. Attention must be paid on this point to prevent performance decrement and accidental occurrences. Some work performers who believe the knowledge established in their disciplinary field to be the best, or who own a protective mindset, are easily caught in a trap. Once they share the procedural knowledge predetermined in their disciplinary field, they readily take the procedure to be the best and then act in a routine manner. Shared procedural knowledge in a particular field was found to be negatively related to team performance (Banks and Millward, 2007). Knowledge processing, such as acquiring, interpreting, implementing, is naturally different among disciplinary fields, and this in turn impacts on the building of necessary data-bases for business and on sharing the knowledge in a heterogeneous organization. The effects of shared knowledge on organizational performance differ in regard to strategic business unit, work team, or disciplinary field.

Social organizations have their visions with organizational and technological constraints as the antecedents and business performance to be achieved as the consequences. As shown in Figure 4, organizations have some advantages and limitations in adapting to the changing society, but the organization which is built in terms of flexibility or resilience has a power of competitive advantage in business. To align and develop organizational competence is to increase adaptability to a dynamic society. Organizational learning capabilities enhanced in recursive processes of

Figure 4. Organizational learning capability model

single-, double- and triple-loop learning, play a critical role in harnessing adaptive potential and in improving organizational performance. Three logical levels in organizational learning are described in the last section of relevance of knowledge management to organizational learning and technology.

ORGANIZATIONAL LEARNING DEVELOPMENT (OLD)

Continuity of Reflexive Organizational Learning for Creating New Values

An organization is a structure formulated as a means to achieve certain goals and to fulfill the enterprise's strategies. Therefore, an organization needs to be continuously redesigned in response to the changes in society. The structure and functions of organizations differ according to organizational goals and strategic visions of the specific enterprise. Organizational performance of inquiring and creating new values can be obtained in the reflexive course of organizational learning in which the disciplinary practitioner is able to act as a professional employee under the constraints of the enterprise, namely, under the limitation of organizational and technological resources. Practitioners including assistant workers as well as professionals are required to be alert and be aware of any changes. They are expected to take appropriate action in the course of reflective organizational learning. New values

Figure 5. New values emerge in the recursive process of organizational learning constrained by individuals, organizationls climate and technologies underpinned by vision/future policy and strategies in the enterprise

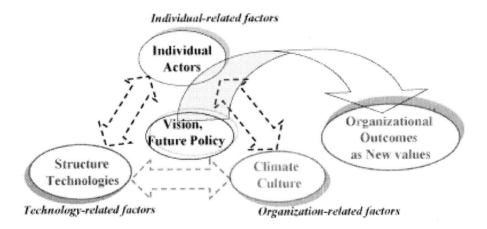

are driven in the continuing process of organizational learning. Three components in any organizations, i.e. individuals as actors, the collective consciousness under the organizational climate and the technologies as the means for taking appropriate and quick action toward realizing organizational goals, are coupled into a creation of new values of organizational performance as shown in Figure 5.

The progress of organizational learning depends on the total management in each practical field constrained by individuals, organizational climate and technologies. Fundamental steps in traditional quality management started by Deming, 1982 were 'plan, do and see' which progressed into four steps, plan, do, check and act (PDCA). In PDCA cycle, the learning process as well as the planning and the operational processes are very important in motivating people and in inducing new ideas in the age of advanced ICT rather than just following the established manuals or just maintaining the rule-based process provided.

Process Models of Organizational Learning

Designing of learning processes in an organization is very important for gaining an insight into various disciplines and into the future. An organization is a complex socio-technical system in which the participants reflect the complexity of the real world by paying attention to the various components in the context of problematic situations. The participants can observe the real world through the reflexive cycle of continuous inquiry. The continuous inquiry leads to progress in practice and serves to foster organizational competence of interpreting the problems, which gradually enables the organization to transform its structure and its functions. The participants know their constraints and potentials which enable new knowledge and values to create in the learning process in the context of the given organization climate. The new knowledge and values form the power of organizational flexibility, resilience or adaptability. The new knowledge that emerged from such a cultural context can be rapidly transmitted and assimilated within the enterprise into another culture.

There are many organizational learning process models reported in the past. Deming (1982) started to progress statistical methods for problem-solving. His original model and its revision to PDCA (plan, do, check and act) cycle are the archetypes in quality control and quality management process. The steps in the approaches to the inquiring and solving of problems are provided in various organizational contexts, and still continue to provide appropriate steps depending upon each problematic situation. In order to set up each step in the process of organizational learning, it is important to read or interpret the future scenario for approaching a desired reality, which is different depending upon the situations of the field; thus the steps in the learning process differ according to the workplace situations.

The models provided with four steps are PDCA(Deming, 1982) as mentioned above, AAAA(appreciate, analyze, asses and act, Minger and Gill, 1996), OADI(observe, asses, design and implement, Kim, 1993, Maruyama, 1992, Schwaninger, 1996 in Cybernetic systems methodology), SECI (socialization, externalization, combination and internalization, Nonaka ,1998). These four-step models are fundamental in solving problems, and appreciation or interpretation in the organizational learning process from the goals to be achieved in the future to the problems to be solved in the present is different dependent upon the situations involved. The following models with six, seven and eight steps described below are examples of enterprises in various fields that have been reported by knowledge management researchers in industry.

The models with six steps are goal setting → analysis → interpretation → control feasibility → strategic treatment → implementation (Ulrich and Probst,1988), plan → align organization →align employees → continuous improvement → analysis → adapt (Kaplan, R.S. and Norton, D.P., 2006).

The models with seven steps are discussions with individuals and groups → perceived world → discourse → created meaning →assemblies of related intentions and accommodations → purposeful action → development of IT-based IS (Checkland, P. 1981, Checkland, P. and Holwell, S. 1998), delimiting the program →establishing the network → apprehending the dynamics → interpreting the behavioral possibilities → determining the control possibilities → shaping the control interventions → further development of the problem solution (Probst, G.J.B. and Gomez, P, 1992).

The model with eight steps are identification of the strategic unit→ developing a vision and defining objectives → business and environment analysis→ developing business strategy→ corporate strategy concept → creation of owner strategy → assessment of strategies → realization and evolution of the strategies (Gomez, 1999).

The learning process of the perpetual step-forward-step-back process in the eight steps (above) reminds us of a diamond cut like model provided with many recursive trials among steps. It is important to note that you do not run in a smooth sequence. The process models of organizational learning are dependent upon organizational visions and organizational culture. Interpretation in each step of the learning process is required if successful outcomes are to be expected. With these continuous inquiries and interpretations, more effective steps of the organizational learning process are designed to achieve the organizational goals.

Figure 6. Organizational learning, information technology and vector of decision-making in knowledge management

Organizational Learning	Technology (IT, ICT)	Managing Knowledge
Triple loop learning (Flood,R and Rom,N.R.A.1996 Jackson,M.2000)	**Cooperation Inducing Tech. for transforming culture/ collective values-action**	Knowledge application for building desired reality in the future
Double loop learning (Argyris,C. and Schon,D.,1978, 2004 Maruyama,M.,1963, 2nd Cybernetics)	**Another Action-Inducing Tech. for both individuals and collectives**	Knowledge interpretation, to create another idea and value
Single loop learning (Wiener,N.,1948)	**Deficiency-Supply Tech. for individual level**	Knowledge acquisition Iteration of knowledge To keep current situation

Knowledge generation and knowledge generalization, i.e. innovation development may be made in the recursive information processing supported by technology, which leads to resilience/flexibility of organization and reduces organizational entropy

RELEVANCE OF KNOWLEDGE MANAGEMENT TO ORGANIZATIONAL LEARNING AND TECHNOLOGY

As shown in Figure 6, three logical levels in organizational learning are 1) single loop learning developed by Wiener, N.1948 which pursues production efficiency by paying attention to the question 'doing things right?' in operational management, 2) double loop learning developed by Argyris and Schon, 1978 which inquires 'doing right things?' in strategic management, and 3) triple loop learning developed by Flood and Rom, 1996, Jackson, 1998 which fulfills overall tasks in long term perspectives. Single loop learning is for routine tasks supported by deficiency-supply technologies. Double loop learning requires another ways or alternatives based on advanced technologies for inducing new values. Triple loop learning requires future development of the organization to enhance organizational competence which then brings enterprise prosperity.

These three logical levels of systemic thinking are all incorporated in the processing of knowledge information, i.e. iteration of information presented in single loop learning, interpretation of the information in double loop learning, and implementation for building a desired reality in triple loop learning. They are for processing information into knowledge creation. Knowledge generation and knowledge generalization, namely, innovation, are made to spread new knowledge beyond boundaries, to develop resilience, flexibility and versatility of organizational fitness to manage the turbulence in society, and to reduce cultural entropy within the organization. An essential element is a robust infrastructure of advanced information technology.

CONCLUSION

Managing knowledge for enhancing the participants in the recursive processes of organizational learning rather than merely following the instructions or the established manuals, leads to the creation of ideas and values. People know that it is not meaningful to extrapolate their future simply from their past. Knowledge management fosters the participants to become cleverer and more talented workers having powerful techniques for transforming themselves, enhancing adaptability or resiliency of the organization. Knowledge management is tantamount to value management or integrated value management which combines the basics established by normal scientific methodology together with whole or holistic systems approaches inquiring to achieve a desired reality in the future. In aligning complex organizations, it is necessary to take strategic action for transforming the organization which can adapt to the field, and also might enjoy business prosperity.

REFERENCES

Argyris, C. (2004). *Reasons and rationalizations: The limits to organizational knowledge.* Oxford University Press.

Argyris, C., & Schon, D. (1978). *Organizational learning.* Reading: Addison-Wesley.

Cameron, K. S., & Quinn, R. E. (1999). *Diagnosing and changing organizational culture.* Jossey-Bass.

Checkland, P., & Holwell, S. (1998). *Information, systems, and information sytems: Making sense of the field.* John Wiley and Sons, Inc.

Deming, E. W. (1982). *Quality, productivity, and competitive position.* MIT Cambridge.

Dolan, S. L., Garcia, S., & Richley, B. (2006). *Managing by values: A corporate guide to living, being alive, and making a living in the 21st century.* Palgrave Macmillan.

EFQM. Retrieved from http://www.efqm.org/

Espejo, R., Schumann, W., Schwaninger, M., & Bilello, U. (1996). *Organizational transformation and learning: A cybernetic approach to management.* Wiley and Sons Inc.

Flood, R., & Rom, N. R. A. (1996). *Diversity management: Triple loop learning.* Wiley and Sons, Inc.

Gomez, P. (1999). *Integrated value management.* International Thomson Press.

Hollnagel, E., Woods, D., & Leveson, N. (2006). *Resilience engineering: Concepts and precepts.* Ashgate.

Jackson, M. (2000). *Systems approaches to management.* Kluwer Academic/Plenum Publishers.

Kaplan, R. S., & Norton, D. P. (2006). *Alignment: Using the balanced scorecard to create cooperate synergies.* Harvard Business School Press.

Maruyama, M. (1963). The second cybernetics: Deviation-amplifying mutual causal processes. *American Scientist, 51,* 164–179, 250–256.

Maruyama, M. (1992). *Context and complexity: Cultivating contextual understanding.* Springer-Verlag.

Minger, J., & Gill, A. (1996). *Multimethodology: The theory and practice of combining management science methodologies.* John Wiley and Sons, Inc.

Nonaka, I., & Nishiguchi, T. (1998). *Knowledge emergence: Social, technical, and evolutionary dimensions of knowledge creation.* Oxford University Press.

Probust, G. J. B., & Gomez, P. (1992). Thinking in networks to avoid pitfalls of managerial thinking. In M. Maruyama (Ed.), *Context and complexity: Cultivating contextual understanding* (pp. 91-108). Springer-Verlag.

Saito, M. (1998). Workers behavior as an active perceiver in job environment: From passive behavior to adaptive action. *The Japanese Journal of Ergonomics, 34*(6), 287–296.

Saito, M. (1998, 2000, 2002). *Job adaptation engineering: Human perception-action coupling* (in Japanese). Nihon Publishing Service.

Saito, M. (2006). Fostering reciprocal mind in information society. *The Japanese Journal of Human Ergology, 85,* 35–37.

Saito, M., Ikeda, M., & Seki, H. (2000). A study on adaptive action development: Interference of mood states with perceived performance and perceived efficacy. In *Proceedings of the 14th International Ergonomics,* San Diego (Vol. 5, pp. 48-51).

Saito, M., & Seki, H. (1998). Intervention study on development of job adaptive resources and enhancement of perceived health level: On cause-effect relationship among structural variables with mediators of job cognition, emotional status, and perceived efficacy. [University of Occupational and Environmental Health]. *Journal of UOEH, 20,* 129–141.

Schwaninger, M. (1996). Status and tendencies of management research: A systems oriented perspectives. In Minger & Gill (Ed.), *Multimethodology: The theory and practice of combining management science methodologies* (pp. 127-151). Wiley and Sons, Inc.

Schwaninger, M. (2000). Managing complexity: The path toward intelligent organization. *Systemic Practice and Action Research, 13*(2), 207–241. doi:10.1023/A:1009546721353

Schwaninger, M. (2006). *Intelligent organizations: Powerful models for systemic management.* Springer.

Todorora, G., & Durisin, B. (2007). Absorptive capacity: Valuing a reconceptualization. *Academy of Management Journal, 44*(5), 996–1004.

Tsai, W. (2001). Knowledge transfer in interorganizational networks: Effect of network position and absorptive capacity on business unit, innovation, and performance. *Academy of Management Journal, 44*(5), 996–1004. doi:10.2307/3069443

Urlich, & Probst. (1988). *Anleitung zum Ganzheitlichen Denken und Handeln, Verlag Paul Haupt,* Japanese version (1991).

Yeung, A. K., Urlich, D. C., Nason, S. W., & von Glinow, M. A. (1999). *Organizational learning capability: Generating and generalizing ideas with impact.* Oxford University Press.

Yossi, S. (2005). *The resilient enterprise: Overcoming vulnerability for competitive advantage.* The MIT Press. Wiener, N. (1948). *Cybernetics.* Paris: Hermann et Cie.

Chapter 3
Permitting the True Potential of Knowledge Assets to be Utilized with KMI[1]

Nilmini Wickramasinghe
Illinois Institute of Technology, USA

ABSTRACT

In order to support a systematic and sustainable approach to knowledge management (KM), innovating organizations must develop an appropriate knowledge management infrastructure (KMI). Such a KMI must support the people, process, and technology aspects of KM, as well as being sufficiently flexible to grow with the changing demands of the organization. This chapter details both the benefits of establishing an appropriate KMI and how to go about this process.

INTRODUCTION

As has already been asserted in several chapters of this book, prudent application of KM is vital to the on going success of any innovating organization. A key question will then be: how can KM become integral to the organization? The key to this question lies in the establishment of an appropriate knowledge management infrastructure.

DOI: 10.4018/978-1-60566-284-8.ch003

ESTABLISHING A KNOWLEDGE MANAGEMENT INFRASTRUCTURE (KMI)

The business world is growing increasingly more competitive, and the demand for innovative products and services has grown greater than ever before. In this period of creativity and ideas, the most valuable resources available to any organization are human skills, expertise, and relationships (Drucker, 1999; 1993; 1988). Knowledge Management (KM) is about capitalizing on these precious assets (Duffy, 2001). Currently, most companies do not capitalize on the wealth of expertise in the form of knowledge scattered across their levels (Gold et al., 2001; Halliday, 2001). However, information centers, market intelligence, and learning are now converging to form knowledge management functions. A KM infrastructure, in terms of tools and technologies (hardware as well as software), needs to be established so that knowledge can be created from any new event or activity on a continual and systematic basis (Duffy, 2000; Wickramasinghe, 2003).

The KM infrastructure forms the foundation for enabling and fostering knowledge management, continuous learning and sustaining an organizational memory (Drucker, 1999; Ellinger et al., 1999; Hammond, 2001; Holt et al., 2000; Lee and Hong, 2002). An organization's entire "know-how", including new knowledge, can only be created for optimization if an effective KM infrastructure is established (Wickramasinghe and Davison, 2004). Specifically, the KM infrastructure consists of social and technical tools and techniques, including hardware and software that should be established so that knowledge can be created from any new events or activities on a continual basis (Duffy, 2001; 2000; Wickramasinghe and Davison, 2004). In addition, the KM infrastructure will have a repository of knowledge, a system to distribute the knowledge to the members of the organization and a facilitator system for the creation of new knowledge (Wickramasinghe and Davison, 2004). Thus, a knowledge-based infrastructure will foster the creation of knowledge, and provide an integrated system to share and diffuse the knowledge within the organization (Srikantaiah, 2000) as well as offer support for continual creation and generation of new knowledge (Wickramasinghe, 2003). A knowledge management infrastructure then contains, at least, the elements displayed in Figure 1.

ELEMENTS OF THE KNOWLEDGE MANAGEMENT INFRASTRUCTURE

The key elements of the KMI depicted in figure 1 will now be discussed in turn:

Figure 1. 5 key elements of the knowledge management infrasture (adapted from Wickramasinghe & von Lubitz, 2007)

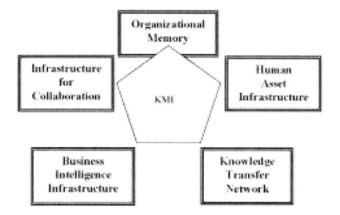

- Infrastructure for Collaboration: The key to strategic competitiveness and improving customer satisfaction lies in the ability of organizations to form learning alliances; these being strategic partnerships based on a business environment that encourages mutual (and reflective) learning between partners (Holt et al., 2000). Organizations can utilize their strategy framework to identify partners, and collaborators for enhancing their value chain.
- Organizational Memory: Organizational memory is concerned with the storing and subsequent accessing and replenishing of an organization's "know-how" which is recorded in documents or in its people (Maier and Lehner, 2000). However, a key component of knowledge management not addressed in the construct of organizational memory is the subjective aspect (Wickramasinghe, 2003).[2] Organizational memory keeps a record of knowledge resources and locations. Recorded information, whether in human-readable or electronic form or in the memories of staff, is an important embodiment of an organization's knowledge and intellectual capital. Thus, strong organizational memory systems ensure the access of information or knowledge throughout the company to everyone at any time (Croasdell, 2001).
- Human Asset Infrastructure: This deals with the participation and willingness of people. Today, organizations have to attract and motivate the best people; reward, recognize, train, educate, and improve them (Ellinger et al., 1999) so that the highly skilled and more independent workers can exploit technologies to create knowledge in learning organizations (Thorne and Smith, 2000). The human asset infrastructure then, helps to identify and utilize the special skills of people who can create greater business value if they and their

inherent skills and experiences are managed to make explicit use of their knowledge.

- Knowledge Transfer Network: This element is concerned with the dissemination of knowledge and information. Unless there is a strong communications infrastructure in place, people are not able to communicate effectively and thus are unable to effectively transfer knowledge. An appropriate communications infrastructure includes, but is not limited to, the Internet and intranets for creating the knowledge transfer network as well as discussion rooms, bulletin boards for meetings and for displaying information.

- Business Intelligence Infrastructure: In an intelligent enterprise various information systems are integrated with knowledge-gathering and analyzing tools for data analysis, and dynamic end-user querying of a variety of enterprise data sources (Hammond, 2001). Business intelligence infrastructures have customers, suppliers and other partners embedded into a single integrated system. Customers will view their own purchasing habits, and suppliers will see the demand pattern which may help them to offer volume discounts etc. This information can help all customers, suppliers and enterprises to analyze data and provide them with the competitive advantage. The intelligence of a company is not only available to internal users but can even be leveraged by selling it to others such as consumers who may have an interest.

KNOWLEDGE MANAGEMENT INFRASTRUCTURE DESIGN

Knowledge management facilitates the following processes (Marshall & Prusak, 1996; Wickramasinghe, 2003; Alavi and Leidner, 1999): 1) generation of knowledge: - creating new, tacit knowledge, 2) access of knowledge: - accessed easily by people inside or outside the firm, 3) transfer of knowledge: - transferred formally through training or informally through social contact, 4) representation of knowledge: - represented by recorded, explicit knowledge that is easy to utilize, 5) embedding of knowledge: - automating the use of knowledge in a decision making process,6) facilitation of knowledge: - developing cultures and policies that support knowledge sharing. It is important that management reviews the knowledge processes to determine which is the best one suited to the company's business strategy since not all processes are as important or relevant to every KM initiative. We shall now examine more closely the technologies and technological infrastructure issues that support each of these processes. We emphasize though that technology should not be viewed in isolation rather it is important that both technological and organizational considerations are made in tandem when developing an appropriate KM infrastructure.

Table 1. Key knowledge management processes and related infrastructures

KM Process	Information Technology Infrastructures	Organizational Infrastructures

generation of knowledge	• electronic networking
	  • internet
	  • intranets
	  • extranets
	• groupware
		• human experts and knowledge workers

access of knowledge	• data warehouses • online databases • knowledge repositories • expertise directories	• accessibility of human experts
transfer of knowledge	• data mining • OLAP	• formal training • apprenticeships • informal socialization • formal socialization
representation of knowledge	• knowledge maps	• knowledge centers • document management centers
embedding of knowledge	• decision support systems • intelligent agents	
facilitation of knowledge flow	• electronic networking • groupware	• top management leadership • rewards and incentives • succession policies

In choosing and designing a knowledge management infrastructure, an important consideration is to first address the organization's process needs: generation of knowledge, access of knowledge, transfer of knowledge, representation of knowledge, embedding of knowledge, and facilitation of knowledge (Duffy, 2000; Orlikowski, 1992; Schultz, 1998; Swan et al., 1999; Davenport and Klahr, 1998). From this the next steps should concentrate on identifying the necessary technological and organizational infrastructures that will support these processes. Table 1 summarizes these major infrastructures that support knowledge management.

INFRASTRUCTURES THAT SUPPORT THE GENERATION OF KNOWLEDGE

Technology assists in the generation of knowledge by allowing people to freely exchange ideas by using tools such as electronic networks and groupware. Marshall and Prusak (1996) explain that the generation of new knowledge takes place in a social setting where people can openly discuss, argue, and challenge prevailing theories. Technology tools that support the generation of knowledge revolve around expediting communication. For example, a new product development team needs to facilitate communication among many different departments including research, engineering, marketing, and finance.

Electronic networking is perhaps the greatest tool for generating knowledge (Kanter, 1999). The Internet allows geographically distant people to communicate and share information easily and cheaply by using standard protocols. Intranets on the other hand, allow the effortless sharing of confidential information among employees and security levels can be easily set for each employee allowing access only for those who need to know or for all employees. Some of the most useful application of intranets has been to support and encourage peer-to-peer knowledge sharing and its applications (Dixon, 2000). Companies can also use extranets, which are designed to offer clients or suppliers access to company information whenever needed. In an increasingly linked and just-in-time environment, accurate and timely information sharing among partners is increasingly important to support rapid decision making.

Another popular communication tool is groupware, software specifically designed to support team work. In an university setting for example, WebCT offers a portal for students and instructors to access documents quickly and communicate through email and bulletin boards. Key features of groupware that make it particularly useful for supporting the KM steps are that it allows every team member to have access instantly to the same body of information and that it is possible to support each other as well as support simultaneous changes made to this information.

INFRASTRUCTURES THAT SUPPORT THE ACCESS OF KNOWLEDGE

KM companies assist employees in accessing knowledge. Knowledge access is often facilitated by technology, including data warehouses, online databases, and knowledge repositories. In large companies, knowing every employee and his or her specialty is near impossibile. Designing a space in which employees may seek the specific knowledge that they require is the goal of creating access. The physical librarian at the reference desk was once the starting point for many research questions. Today, much of the librarian's job as the key to knowledge and the library's function as a warehouse of information is automated.

Data warehouses have contributed greatly to the knowledge management movement. They store snapshots of operational data such as sales, inventory, and customer information. Many larger companies now have ten to twenty years of transactional data with which they can assess their relative current position or upon which they can build future models. For example, Tandem Computers has designed a data warehouse to which many systems can report, making it possible to assess key numbers, e.g. sales data and financial data that come in from disparate locations, to the one place (Marshall & Prusak, 1996).

Online databases often refer to external information databases such as Lexis-Nexis, which provides access to published news and research. However, online databases may also refer to internal databases. A best practices database can offer solutions to common and not so common problems. For instance, help desks often create best practice databases to better serve customers.

Knowledge repositories usually refer to postings of reports on past projects. The large consulting firms develop repositories of client proposals, leads, white papers, presentations, and many other documents that consultants all over the globe produce (Kanter, 1999).

Though much of the knowledge management literature refers to accessibility of knowledge through technology, the accessibility of human experts is also of critical importance. Cross, Parker, Prusak, and Borgatti (2001) explain that knowing who knows what, gaining timely access, willingly sharing knowledge rather than dumping information, and feeling safe in asking for information facilitate the access of tacit knowledge, knowledge in the expert's head. Companies often create electronic expertise directories to help employees find needed contacts and mentors.

INFRASTRUCTURES THAT SUPPORT THE TRANSFER OF KNOWLEDGE

Transferring knowledge usually begins with the distribution of written reports. Transferring knowledge also includes training employees to interpret the reports and educating employees about the structure of the organization and to whom they should go for specific knowledge (Marshall & Prusak, 1996). Transferring data may also include techniques for transforming inert data into usable information.

Data mining and OLAP (on-line analytic processing) permit companies to analyze the jumble of data stored in data warehouses. For example, grocery stores use rule induction to produce information on who buys what and what products are purchased together. Information is gathered via a shopping card. Information based on shopping card usage may be used to target promotional offers (e.g. coupons given to customers at the register) to particular customers. Mathematical models and cheap computing power allow quick, in-depth analysis of large volumes of historical data.

Many more organizational, rather than technological, structures facilitate the transfer of knowledge. Formal training and apprenticeships are a tried and true method of transferring knowledge to new employees or to employees who are working towards a promotion. New KPMG employees undergo rigorous training in the Internet and KPMG's internal knowledge web (Kanter, 1999).

Informal socialization includes discussions at the water cooler, casual exchanges over lunches among colleagues, and any other unstructured event that allows the sharing of ideas. With the demand for increased output and the globalization of many businesses, fewer opportunities exist for serendipitous information exchange.

Formal socialization attempts to create opportunities for knowledge exchange may include group meetings or knowledge fairs. A common knowledge fair might include employees from research and development and from marketing with the expectation that their knowledge would combine with synergy to create new product ideas.

INFRASTRUCTURES THAT SUPPORT THE REPRESENTATION OF KNOWLEDGE

Representation of knowledge is often determined by a department that organizes and sets standards for what knowledge is retained and in which format it is to be retained. Often a knowledge center or a document management center will oversee the presentation of knowledge. First, the company faces a policy choice of which knowledge is important and worth storing. Second, the knowledge center must decide on the best way of presenting information (e.g. a text document, a database, a media clip, a hyperlinked document). Third, the knowledge center should consistently manage its documents to eliminate obsolete documents and create ease of use. Access to these documents is often through a document repository.

Companies with large numbers and varieties of documents may design knowledge maps (Kanter, 1999). A knowledge map is a visual display of captured knowledge that allows an information seeker to follow paths from one source of stored information to another. Often a knowledge map is a hyperlinked hierarchy of topics that represents documents residing on a server.

INFRASTRUCTURES THAT SUPPORT THE EMBEDDING OF KNOWLEDGE

Infrastructures that support the embedding of knowledge are primarily technological. These tools are complicated, computerized checklists and decision trees that aid in decision making. Marshall and Prusak (1996) explain that automating knowledge in the form of computerized controls works best when the inputs and outputs are factual and not based on biases or uncertain interpretations. When knowledge facts are embedded in an automated check list, front line employees can use the experience and knowledge of their peers. However, facts do change; management should take care to keep the facts that aid decision making current.

Decision support systems are designed to help decision makers make an informed choice based on the outcomes of past decisions. For example, Partners HealthCare designed a decision support system to help doctors prescribe the best medication to its hospital patients (Davenport and Glaser, 2002). In this case, the decision support system accessed patient records and databases of drug characteristics to suggest the drug and dosage that best helped the patient and best lowered hospital costs. The 700 bed hospital estimates that it saved $1 million by preventing adverse drug reactions in patients.

Intelligent agents are software packages that save time and effort by embedding commands or knowledge in computer processes. A simple example is sophisticated email software. The software may allow the user to create rules for directing mail to different folders or automatically scheduling meetings based on the information in the email message (Kanter, 1999). Spreadsheets are another example of embedded knowledge. Excel's statistical package can calculate in seconds what it would take a person, days to calculate.

INFRASTRUCTURES THAT SUPPORT THE FACILITATION OF KNOWLEDGE

The facilitation of knowledge is primarily supported by culture, top management leadership, and rewards and incentives. The culture of a company is the primary social infrastructure for the sharing of knowledge. In a knowledge management environment a sharing culture should be cultivated. Competitive environments often prevent the sharing of knowledge. Some highly competitive firms are endeavouring to change their cultures. For example, Salomon Brothers has asked its stock traders to think more like a stock holder than a stock trader. Top management leadership and human resource policy have the most influence on a company's culture.

Top management leadership, primarily leadership by example, can be a strong influence on the exchange of knowledge. Do the top leaders themselves share information throughout the company? Does the company have an open-book policy? Jack Welch is known for his policy on being number one or two in the market and for his policies on promotion, including his emphasis on the criteria that an employee must demonstrate being a team player before he/she can warrant promotion (Slater, 1999).

Rewards and incentives support behavior and companies should oversee compensation systems to influence positive behavior (Davenport and Prusak, 1998). For instance, stock traders who are paid based on the volume of trades, in general, focus on increasing volume rather than on what would benefit the company or the customer. In such scenarios, companies should also consider implementing policies that compensate employees for sharing usable knowledge. Perhaps an employee could earn a small bonus every time a document he or she posted is accessed.

In a knowledge company, developing succession policies becomes crucial for knowledge retention. When an employee retires or is down-sized, the company usually loses the tacit knowledge that is only known by the individual. Lesser and Prusak (2001) suggest four tactics for minimizing the loss of departing employees: 1)When layoffs are under consideration, think instead about reducing the salary of all employees. 2) Devise practices to capture the knowledge of employees on the verge of retirement, 3) Pay departing employees a bonus for training their replacement and 4) Encourage experienced employees to work with new employees.

METRICS

The various infrastructures that support knowledge have been grouped in this chapter into two major categories: technical infrastructure (information technologies) and organizational infrastructures (including human elements, rewards and incentives, formal processes and other structural and process dimensions). These two categories of infrastructure interact in several ways, and these interactions in effect dictate the kind of metrics we would use to measure their effectiveness in facilitating knowledge development.

The information technologies and other technical dimensions of the infrastructures are composed of techniques, systems, repositories, and networks. These in turn are embedded in organizational infrastructures. The more formal and standardized the technical infrastructures in the organizational structures and processes, the more they facilitate the generation, access, transfer, representation and flow of knowledge in the organizational framework. This means that such elements of the technical infrastructures such as data mining, knowledge maps and databases can become a standard feature of the organization, thereby providing organizational members with an embedded system that allows them to create and to exchange knowledge.

The measurement of the performance and success organizations have in creating and exploiting knowledge would depend on the formality of existence of technology infrastructures within the organization. There are three such modes:

1. Metrics of the *human* abilities and performance in creating and exchanging knowledge. This means that we measure elements of the interaction between databases, decision support systems and networking (among others)—as they

are used by human experts and knowledge workers. The metrics we would use are degree of use of the technology infrastructure (such criteria as frequency of use; level of usage, etc.) and the success with which such use occurs (such criteria as creation of new knowledge and success in transferring it from the knowledge repositories to the human experts). In a way, we are measuring here the human experts' abilities to generate, access, transfer, represent, embed and facilitate the flow of knowledge.

2. The metrics of *organizational* aspects of knowledge include measures of the degree to which knowledge becomes embedded in organizational infrastructure, such as structural dimensions and processes. For example, we can measure the degree to which knowledge from the technology infrastructures (knowledge maps, decision support systems, data mining, etc.) becomes an integral part of the processes of organizations. Examples of these processes are the system of rewards and incentives, succession policies and the strategic decisions made by senior management. The more knowledge is embedded in the structure and processes of the organization, the better we are equipped to successfully carry out these tasks in the organization. Thus, formal training and socialization of new members, for example, greatly benefit from embedded knowledge which allows members to rapidly curtail the "learning curve" they need to adapt to organizational realities. This is because once knowledge is embedded in these training and development programs, there is a rapid learning process, gaining from the embedded knowledge.

3. Another set of metrics would encompass the metrics geared towards answering the question: why do we measure? What are the reasons we use metrics to assess the ways in which knowledge contributes to the organization and its members. We measure because we wish to evaluate the degree to which knowledge contributes to the goals and objectives of organizations and their members. There are various groupings of these goals and objectives: economic, personal, organizational, and social. *Economic* goals include the desire of organizations to succeed in the marketplace and for members to do well financially from their membership in the organization (via salaries, stock options, etc.). This can be extended to all the stakeholders of the organization, such as vendors, customers, and stockholders. *Personal* goals include those goals of individuals to do well in their careers and to expand their individual horizon. Knowledge allows them to do so, by contributing to their advancement in the organization. *Organizational* goals include the entity's desire to succeed, to compete and to survive. Embedded knowledge allows the organization to gain momentum in the marketplace and to gain advantage over less knowledgeable organizations against which it competes.

Finally, social goals include the desire of organizations and members to be good "citizens" of their society and their political system. These goals include the desire to maintain good relations with other social systems, to do little harm to the environment, and to serve the causes and needs of their society.

We develop metrics of knowledge by relating them to the degree to which such goals and objectives are being accomplished. Clearly, some of these metrics categories will not allow for combinations or conjoining, and some may even be in conflict with other metrics. Our task is to sift through the available metrics and to select those that best represent the key dimensions of knowledge creation and transfer in organization. We also need to make sure that we balance the human and organizational aspects of metrics, and to account for metrics of the economic, social, organizational and personal modes of measurement

CONCLUSION

For Innovating organizations to realize the full potential of KM it is vital that a suitable KMI (knowledge management infrastructure) is established. This requires careful consideration be given to people, process and technological issues as well as having an appropriate system to measure these components. In order to address this, the chapter has outlined the necessary components that any KMI must have as well as a suitable metric system so that the benefits of the respective attributes of the KMI can be measured.

REFERENCES

Alavi, M. (1999). *Managing organizational knowledge*. Working Paper.

Alavi, M., & Leidner, D. (1999). Knowledge management systems: Issues, challenges, and benefits. *Communications of the Association for Information Systems*, 1, paper no. 5.

Boland, R., & Tenkasi, R. (1995). Perspective making perspective taking. *Organization Science, 6*, 350–372. doi:10.1287/orsc.6.4.350

Croasdell, D. C. (2001). IT's role in organizational memory and learning. *Information Systems Management, 18*(1), 1–4. doi:10.1201/1078/43194.18.1.20010101/31260.2

Cross, R., Parker, A., Prusak, L., & Borgatti, S. P. (2001). Supporting knowledge creation and sharing in social networks. *Organizational Dynamics, 30*(2), 100–120. doi:10.1016/S0090-2616(01)00046-8

Davenport, T., & Prusak, L. (1998). *Working knowledge.* Boston: Harvard Business School Press.

Davenport, T. H., & Glaser, J. (2002, July). Just-in-time delivery comes to knowledge management. *Harvard Business Review, 80*(7), 107–112.

Davenport, T. H., & Hansen, M. T. (1999). Knowledge management at Andersen Consulting. *Harvard Business School Case,* 9-499-032.

Davenport, T. H., & Klahr, P. (1998). Managing customer support knowledge. [not in text]. *California Management Review, 40*(3), 195–208.

Drucker, P. (1993). *Post-capitalist society.* New York: Harper Collins.

Drucker, P. (1999, October). Beyond the information revolution. *Atlantic Monthly, 284*(4), 47–57.

Drucker, P. F. (1988, January-February). The coming of the new organization. *Harvard Business Review, 66*(1), 45–53.

Duffy, J. (2000). The KM technology infrastructure. *Information Management Journal, 34*(2), 62–66.

Duffy, J. (2001). The tools and technologies needed for knowledge management. *Information Management Journal, 35*(1), 64–67.

Ellinger, A. D., Watkins, K. E., & Bostrom, R. P. (1999). Managers as facilitators of learning in learning organizations. *Human Resource Development Quarterly, 10*(2), 105–125. doi:10.1002/hrdq.3920100203

Fadlalla, A., & Wickramasinghe, N. (2005). Realizing knowledge assets in the medical sciences with data mining: An overview in creating knowledge-based healthcare organizations (pp. 164-177). In N. Wickramasinghe, et al. (Eds.), *Creating knowledge-based healthcare organizations.* Hershey, PA: Idea Group Inc.

Gold, A. H., Malhotra, A., & Segars, A. H. (2001). Knowledge management: An organizational capabilities perspective. *Journal of Management Information Systems, 18*(1), 185–214.

Halliday, L. (2001). An unprecedented opportunity. *Information World Review,* (167), 18-19.

Hammond, C. (2001). The intelligent enterprise. *InfoWorld*, *23*(6), 45–46.

Holt, G. D., Love, P. E. D., & Li, H. (2000). The learning organization: Toward a paradigm for mutually beneficial strategic construction alliances. *International Journal of Project Management*, *18*(6), 415–421. doi:10.1016/S0263-7863(99)00066-6

Kanter, J. (1999). Knowledge management practically speaking. *Information Systems Management*.

Lee, S. M., & Hong, S. (2002). An enterprise-wide knowledge management system infrastructure. *Industrial Management & Data Systems*, *102*(1/2), 17–25. doi:10.1108/02635570210414622

Lesser, E., & Prusak, L. (2001). Preserving knowledge in an uncertain world. *MIT Sloan Management Review*, *43*(1), 101–102.

Marshall, C., & Prusak, L. (1996). Financial risk and the need for superior knowledge management. *California Management Review*, *38*(3), 77–101.

Orlikowski, W. (1992). The duality of technology: Rethinking the concept of technology in organizations. *Organization Science*, *3*(3), 398–427. doi:10.1287/orsc.3.3.398

Schultz, U. (1998, December). *Investigating the contradictions in knowledge management.* Presentation at IFIP.

Srikantaiah, T. K. (2000). Knowledge management for information professional. ASIS Monograph Series, *Information Today*, Inc.

Swan, J., Scarbrough, H., & Preston, J. (1999). Knowledge management–the next fad to forget people? In *Proceedings of the 7th European Conference in Information Systems.*

Thorne, K., & Smith, M. (2000). Competitive advantage in world class organizations. *Management Accounting*, *78*(3), 22–26.

Weill, P., & Broadbent, M. (1998). *Leveraging the new infrastructure.* Cambridge: Harvard Business School Press.

Wickramasinghe, N. (2003). Practicing what we preach: Are knowledge management systems in practice really knowledge management systems? *Business Process Management Journal*, *9*(3), 295–316. doi:10.1108/14637150310477902

Wickramasinghe, N., & von Lubitz. (2007). *Knowledge-based organizations: Theories and fundamentals.* Hershey, PA: IGI Global.

Wickramasinghe, N., & Davison, G. (2004). Making explicit the implicit knowledge assets in healthcare. *Health Care Management Science*, 7(3), 185–196. doi:10.1023/B:HCMS.0000039381.02400.49

Wickramasinghe, N., & Lichtenstein, S. (2006). Supporting knowledge creation with e-mail. *Int. J. Innovation and Learning*, 3(4), 416–426.

Wickramasinghe, N., & Mills, G. (2002). Integrating e-commerce and knowledge management-what does the Kaiser experience really tell us? *International Journal of Accounting Information Systems*, 3(2), 83–98. doi:10.1016/S1467-0895-(02)00037-4

Wickramasinghe, N., & Schaffer, J. (2006). Creating knowledge driven healthcare processes with the intelligence continuum. [IJEH]. *International Journal of Electronic Healthcare*, 2(2), 164–174.

ENDNOTES

[1] This chapter includes a distillation of material from previous IGI publications by the author namely: Wickramasinghe, N. 2007 "Knowledge-Based Enterprise: Theories and Fundamentals" with D. von Lubitz Idea Group, Wickramasinghe, N 2004 "Incorporating the People Perspective in Data Mining" in Ed. J. Wang *Encyclopaedia of Data Warehousing and Mining* Idea Group, Hershey and Wickramasinghe, N. 2006 "Creating Superior Knowledge Discovery Solutions" in press in Ed Medhi, *Encyclopaedia of Information Science and Technology*, 2nd Edition IDEA Group, Hershey.

[2] Knowledge as a subjective component primarily refers to an ongoing phenomenon of exchange where knowledge is being shaped by social practices of communities (Boland & Tenkasi, 1995), in the tradition of a Hegelian/Kantian perspective where the importance of divergence of meaning is essential to support the "sense-making" processes of knowledge creation (Wickramasinghe & Mills, 2001).

Chapter 4
Normal Science and Post–Normal Sciences

Elie Geisler
Illinois Institute of Technology, USA

ABSTRACT

This chapter describes the key attributes of normal science and the recently heralded post-normal science. Drawing from the philosophy of science and other literatures, the chapter argues that the subjugation of post-normal science to the social and economic urgencies and exigencies is only a matter of degree, since such relationship has existed ever since science had become "big science," nurtured by society through public funding. The chapter provides examples from the healthcare sector. These examples show the confluence of topics and ailments that are given priority in research as those same areas considered urgent by the social and economic elites who influence the funding of science in healthcare and medicine.

INTRODUCTION

The discourse on how knowledge progresses and how science evolves has been a contentious exercise by scholars and philosophers for over a century. There are two major periods that distinguish the search for answers to these fundamental issues of knowledge creation.

DOI: 10.4018/978-1-60566-284-8.ch004

The first period involved the proposing of theories and methods of how scientific research is carried out and how knowledge is therefore generated. In this context it is useful to list two diverse philosophies of science. Karl Popper (2002) had argued that science progresses through the advancement of conjectures about nature, followed by attempts to refute such conjectures. In Popper's view, the focus is on each proposition or hypothesis that offers a conjecture, and the individualized attempt to refute it. Scientific inquiry thus becomes a constant effort in which conjectures are proposed and refutations are exercised. Any knowledge generated from such conjectures is temporarily accepted—until such time as it can be refuted or shown to be false. In this framework knowledge is the sum total of the conjectures which we temporarily accept (or not reject). The process or method by which we generate this scientific knowledge is, as much as possible, objective and methodical. We put the conjecture to the test of empirical testing, thus obtaining the result of refutation or temporary acceptance. This also means that the knowledge thus acquired is not necessarily the "truth," since the scientific method of testing and refutation is not geared towards discovering the "truth," rather it is aimed at refuting a particular conjecture via strictly defined empirical tests.

Popper's method has been the target of several distinct criticisms. Imre Lakatos (1980) has argued that the growth of science should be examined not in the microscopic lens of individual conjectures but through the prism of a continuity that is to be found in what he called "genuine research programs." These programs are to Lakatos the focus of exploration of how knowledge is gained in scientific research. He proposes the example of Newton's gravitational theory to illustrate his model. Upon its introduction into the scientific community, Newtonian theory was opposed with several observational theories. Yet, Lakatos argued that Newton's theory was a program and those who participated in it have been able to provide counter-examples and counter-arguments, until they were at the point of converting the opponents to their side—hence the manner in which science progresses and new knowledge is gained. Research or scientific programs are thus tenacious endeavors in which arguments and counter-arguments continually collide. This approach differs from Popper's refutation of singular conjectures in that it is predicated on the continuity of testing counter examples and what Lakatos and Kuhn (1967) described as "anomalies" or exceptions to the core model in the program, yet not powerful enough to nullify or refute the core model.

PARADIGMS AND NORMAL SCIENCE

Thomas Kuhn was another scholar in this first period whose work helped to coin the concepts of "paradigm" and "normal science." Kuhn had argued that scientific progress is as much a social phenomenon as it is the rigorous and objective examination of observational data according to a proposed model. He suggested that scientific disciplines have a distinct historical development. Key progress from the pre-paradigmatic stage to the paradigmatic (or "normal" stage), and finally to the revolutionary stage (in which the discipline transitions from one paradigm to another through a crisis that develops in the degree to which scholars in the discipline have faith in the ability of the paradigm to solve the problems of the discipline).

Kuhn argued that when a paradigm is accepted by the disciplinary scientific community, it is practical as "normal science." A paradigm start as a set of promises that a line of research and a proposed set of scientific models, assumptions, and methods will lead to new solutions to the problems posed by the discipline. When this paradigm takes hold, it assumes more rigorous lines and methods of inquiry, and its adherent begin to establish and to rely on a 'tradition" in the conduct of research and discovery in such a disciplinary paradigm.

The paradigm is the core of normal science. Within its framework there are established criteria for which problems are to be the object of inquiry, which models and methods are to be used, and which solutions and discoveries are to be accepted by peers in the disciplinary community.

Because scientists within the paradigm control these issues and have the power to constrain the acceptance of theories that contradict or that are not in agreement with the existing paradigm, normal science is restrictive and highly resistant to changes and to novel ideas. In Kuhn's words: "Novelty emerges only with difficulty, manifested by resistance, against a background provided by expectation."

Therefore, Kuhn postulated that new theories can only supplant "normal science" by a process imbued with revolutionary manifestation of one new paradigm replacing the reigning paradigm in a discipline. *Normal* science gives way to a revolutionary new theory which, once taking over the traditional paradigm, will itself develop into a paradigm and so on.

Kuhn has effectively extended Lakatos' framework of the progress of science viewed as a coherent program with continuity in verification and in cleaning-up anomalies. In Kuhn's framework there is a point where such anomalies can no longer be explained by the current paradigm—hence a crisis emerges and a new paradigm may be in line to replace the "normal science."

Kuhn also criticized Popper's philosophy of science. Kuhn argued that paradigmatic subjectivity allows for anomalies, beliefs of scientists, and the disciplinary patterns that characterize a paradigm. Hence, there is no room in normal science for the rejection of individual conjectures or theories simply because the examined data fail to "fit" the theoretical model. Popper's rigid application of the conjecture-refutation principle would, in Kuhn's view, lead to the point where no theory would be accepted into the paradigm. For Lakatos, acceptance of theories is a programmatic event—for Kuhn it is also a social/group event where a community of disciplinary scientists forms a paradigm and effectively "rules" within its boundaries.

POST-NORMAL SCIENCE

The second major period that emerged in the latter part of the twentieth century was an extension of the Lakatos-Kuhn view of how science progresses and scientific knowledge is created. The concept of "post-normal" science was introduced by Funtowicz and Ravetz (1993, 1994). They considered two conditions or circumstances in which the Lakatos-type "program of science," Kuhn's "paradigm," and a community of scientists in a disciplinary area can be extended and assessed from a much wider perspective.

The first condition is the belief that the process of scientific inquiry is enmeshed in social values and driven by social, political, and economic issues of concern. This entails the circumstances where scientific choices are influenced by social and political values rather than by rigorous and objective methodologies. Scientific inquiry thus becomes an instrument of social policy. Rather than searching for solutions to well-defined scientific queries, the focus shifts to inquiries of uncertain, value-laden and, in many instances, controversial issues. Much of the objectivity of "normal science" pursuit is replaced by subjective and ambiguous topics in the public arena where conflicts and disputes are the norm and consensus is reached to arrive at some middle-of-the-road solutions.

Another condition is the expansion of the scientific community in the discipline to a much wider population of all the stakeholders who are influenced by the social topics, participate in their selection and in their definition, but are *not* scientific. These diverse groups view scientific inquiry as a tool in the pursuit of their social and political agendas, and in advancing their subjective philosophies, opinions, and models of the physical as well as the social worlds they all inhabit.

This so-called "post-normal science" is therefore concerned with the process of scientific inquiry as it is embedded in the social agenda. This entails the analysis of how topics for research are selected, how they are funded and by whom, how are the methodology and the quality of such research evaluated, and how the topics thus selected and the results of the research relate to the social issues and to the political agenda of the constituents of the scientific effort.

A favorite example, used by both proponents and detractors of "post-normal science," is the issue of global warming. Heralded by some as an urgent problem of worldwide environmental changes, global warming is viewed by other groups as a very long-term phenomenon (Avery and Singer, 2007). In the dispute about the severity and the urgency of this phenomenon, both sides marshal scientific inquiries and findings to help support their position and theory of the phenomenon. This new form of the mixing of science and social issues is open to all those who wish to participate—regardless of their scientific training or knowledge—as long as they care about and wish to influence the process of policy-making. This much expanded community of peers, who are not peers in the strict disciplinary terms, tends to intensify the level of the dispute and to raise the level of discussion to anything but the normal perspective of scientific inquiry and the creation of knowledge (Michaels, 2005).

Due to the uncertainty of the facts and the polarization of the political discourse, some groups go to the length of hotly disputing the use of scientific findings in this post-normal science by suggesting that such actions undermine science itself (Shulman, 2007). This is a double-edged sword, since such arguments try to endow political ideologies with the mantra of science—tantamount to evoking "normal" science to corroborate or support the assertions of "post-normal" science, the latter of a more social and subjective nature (Dennett, 2006).

One inherent problem with "post-normal" science is that it transcends even Lakatos' framework of the community of scientists within a disciplinary program. These scientists explore scientific problems in a way that would continually demonstrate that anomalies or empirical results that do not support the theory embraced by the program can be explained by some aspect of this theory. In "post-normal" science, however, the focus is not on the exploration of *scientific* findings, but on *political* and *social* opinions and solutions to political and social problems—as they are *defined* by the rival constituencies.

EXAMPLES FROM THE HEALTHCARE SECTOR

Few sectors offer such a salient illustration of the working of "post-normal" science as healthcare policy. There are several concepts that have been coined in the often contentious debate over health care, especially in the public arena in the United States (Weissert and Weissert, 2006). These concepts include health care *availability*, *accessibility*, and *affordability*. The precise definitions of these terms are fuel for heated debates and for conflicting ideologies and social-political actions.

How much health care should be available, accessible, and affordable? Who should pay for it? What should be the quality of such care, and in which directions should scarce resources be invested? These are some of the questions involved with setting the popular agenda in the discussion over healthcare delivery.

Furthermore, in order to refine these terms and to define them in a manner that will support the given social position, there is a tendency by social activitists to engage scientific research for the rescue of their social and political agenda.

The more precise employment of "post-normal" science occurs in relation to large-scale, multi-year research programs in health care. Driven by social and political issues, certain diseases are given preference in the public debate, and massive resources are then divested towards research that may lead to cures.

In the 1970s, President Richard Nixon heralded the "war on cancer," in which federal investments were earmarked to discover the causes and the cures for the disease. In the 1980s, Acquired Immune Deficiency Syndrome (AIDS) dominated the public debate, and government funding was poured into research on its diagnostics and therapeutics. In the decade of the 1990s there was a voice given to diseases particular to women (such as breast cancer). In the decade that follows, the current focus in the social and political debate is obesity and chronic diseases such as diabetes (Mason, Leavitt, and Chaffee, 2006).

When scientific inquiry is subjugated to social, economic, and political constituents and positions, there is a certain loss of objectivity and even the lessening of the strong confidence that the public has in scientific research. In the case of climate change there are open discussions and even public clashes between scientists and other institutions, such as governmental institutions. In meetings of the Intergovernmental Panel on Climate Change (IFCC) in April 2007, many scientists clashed with government officials over the exact wording of the climatic threat being of "very high confidence" that such changes are indeed currently affecting the world (Reuters, 2007).

Similar clashes and debates abound in the case of healthcare delivery. Issues range from how much funding should be allocated to which area of research, to which disease, or to research that will ultimately benefit which segment of the population (women? children? the elderly?).

Science is invariably brought into the debate as the arbiter with the presumed aura of objectivity. Even science that has been conducted under biases of resources allocation by social preferences is nevertheless considered a rigorous and objective inquiry and its results are viewed as weighty argument for or against a certain viewpoint.

KNOWLEDGE GENERATION AND POST-NORMAL SCIENCE

How is knowledge generated in this value-laden and socially-driven post-modern science? What is the value of such knowledge, and is it equivalent to knowledge created from "normal" science? Supporters of post-normal science argue that there is little, if any, loss of objectivity or value in the knowledge thus created. The key difference between normal and post-normal science is in the criteria and the process of allocating resources to scientific problems that are "worthy" of inquiry. This, they argue, will not detract from the manner in which these studies are conducted, as scientists will continue to be empirically objective and rigorous.

Opponents argue that such knowledge is tainted because when social or political activists are those who ultimately determine which problems will be selected for research and which programs will be funded, such decisions are no longer made within the scientific community. Hence, they argue, the research will invariably yield the desired outcomes to support the funder's position.

For example, when proponents of policy changes aimed at increasing availability and affordability to the under-insured or the un-insured in the United States, they rely on studies of the cost of treating these segments in the emergency departments of hospitals. Data from these studies are used to support the policy—since there is a cost being expended anyway, why not divert such resources to insure these groups?

Opponents rely on studies that purport to generate knowledge about how households in these segments of the population make decisions on the purchasing of health insurance. These studies are then utilized to support arguments that many households select not to purchase health insurance and use these funds for other purposes, while relying on care services offered by the emergency departments of mostly urban hospitals.

CONCLUSION

Post-normal science is a term that applies to a well-known phenomenon of what Derek DeSolla Price called "Little Science, Big Science" (1965). When public institutions such as the government and large foundations decide to enter the arena of funding scientific activity, the opinions, biases, and policy preferences follow the money and create the basis for the allocation of such resources. "Big Science" is possible because of such massive funding. Resources can be expended on lavish laboratories and expensive equipment, so that scientific problems hitherto considered impossible to study suddenly are within reach and can be investigated.

The rigorous methods directed by philosophers of science are still valid even in this new period where science has moved from the workshop of eccentric and curious scientists of the last 300 years to the massive laboratories and research institutes now employing thousands of scientists and engineers.

In my view the concept of post-normal science fails to describe a brand new phenomenon, typical of the early years of the 21st century. Rather, it describes a pattern to which we have been accustomed since the end of the Second World War when governments had concluded that science is an activity with benefits to society and the economy—thus should be funded from the national treasury.

Although there is not much that is new in this concept, it is worrisome that the scientific community is subjugated to the topics and the preferences of the social and political elites. In "big science" the cost of inquiry exceeds any person's ability to bear the burden, hence the need to appeal to the public coffers, and by so doing, to comply with the public choices and inherent biases.

Assuring that the methodology employed in scientific research is rigid and uncompromising is now the key criterion to objectivity in the current state of science. The focus should not be on who selects the topics, how they are funded, and who will own the results—rather, for the sake of credible knowledge thus generated the focus should be on *how* to carry out the research. This will allow the "priesthood" of the scientific community to maintain the burning fires of the temple and to keep them out of reach of external interference.

REFERENCES

Avery, D., & Singer, F. (2007). *Unstoppable global warming: Every 1,500 years.* London: Rowman & Littlefield Publishers.

Dennett, D. (2006). *Breaking the spell: Religion as a natural phenomenon.* New York: Penguin Books.

DeSolla Price. (1965). *Little science, big science.* New York: Columbia University Press.

Funtowicz, S., & Ravetz, J. (1993). Science for the post-normal age. *Futures, 25*(3), 735–755.

Funtowicz, S., & Ravetz, J. (1994). The worth of a songbird: Ecological economies as a post-normal science. *Ecological Economics, 10*(3), 197–207. doi:10.1016/0921-8009(94)90108-2

Kuhn, T. (1962). *The structure of scientific revolutions* (second ed.). Chicago: University of Chicago Press.

Lakatos, I. (1980). *The methodology of scientific research programs: Philosophical papers.* New York: Cambridge University Press.

Mason, D., Leavitt, J., & Chaffee, M. (2006). *Policy and politics in nursing and healthcare.* Los Angeles, CA: Saunders Press.

Michaels, P. (2005). *Shattered consensus: The true state of global warming.* London: Rowman & Littlefield Publishers.

Popper, K. (2002). *Conjectures and refutations: The growth of scientific knowledge.* London: Rutledge.

666Reuters. (2007). *Scientists, governments clash over warming report.* Retrieved on April 6, 2007, from www.news.yahoo.com

Shulman, S. (2007). *Undermining science: Suppression and distortion in the Bush administration.* Sacramento, CA: University of California Press.

Weissert, C., & Weissert, W. (2006). *Governing health: The politics of health policy.* Baltimore, MD: John Hopkins University Press.

Section 2
Approaches to Healthcare Operations Management

This section presents six chapters as follows: Chapter 5, "Whole Systems/Holistic Approaches to the Continuation of Organizational Transformation," by Saito. Chapter 6, "Knowledge Information Processing Levels and Knowledge Information Interpretation," by Saito. Chapter 7, "The Intelligence Continuum and Emergency and Disaster Scenarios," by Wickramasinghe. Chapter 8 "Evaluation of Human Action: Foucault's Power/Knowledge Corollary," by Wickramasinghe. Chapter 9, "Key Considerations for the Adoption and Implementation of Knowledge Management in Healthcare Operations," by Wickramasinghe and Geisler, and finally Chapter 10, "Realizing the Healthcare Value Proposition: The Need for KM and Technology," by Wickramasinghe.

As already discussed in the preface, integral to the presentation of knowledge management issues in this book is the embracing of the sociotechnical perspective; a perspective that takes into consideration both human and technology issues that must complement and coordinate if superior operations are to be effected. In order to develop a full appreciation of the importance of such a sociotechnical perspective to facilitate ones understanding of the role of knowledge management in redesigning innovative healthcare organizations, it is vital to first investigate key concepts, including whole systems and holistic approaches, as discussed in Chapter 5, the knowledge-information processing dynamic presented in Chapter 6, as well as the dynamics of intelligence both human and machine (or artificial) as presented in Chapter 7, and finally and often one of the most daunting aspects in the application of knowledge management initiatives, namely that of the power dynamic, which is presented in Chapter 8. Chapters 9 and 10 then begin to focus explicitly on healthcare contexts and present key issues concerning the adoption and implementation of KM, as well as the role of KM for realizing the healthcare value proposition. Taken together, Sections 1 and 2 provide the fundamental principles of KM and human action. In Sections 3 and 4, instances of these key aspects are highlighted in various healthcare contexts.

On the completion of this section, the reader should be well equipped to understand most, if not all, the key aspects of sociotechnical dynamics.

Chapter 5

Whole Systems/Holistic Approaches in Individual and Collective Levels

Murako Saito
Waseda University, Japan

ABSTRACT

In managing complexity and ambiguity, we need holistic or whole systems approaches. Complementary systemic approaches to integrate some separate systems are needed for fostering organizational adaptability or organizational flexibility in the changing social environment. It is not sufficient simply to keep in line with the standards established in the past by a particular discipline, but it is important to encourage the participants to progress for coping with the changes in society. Cognitive misfits between individual and organizational levels result in a decrement of quality of service which actually leads to the decrement of business performance. Conceptual frameworks of whole systems of human society, namely conceptual frameworks of human cognition and action in individual and collective levels are introduced for discussing the alignment of cognitive misfits and transformation of organizational culture. Classifications and categorizations are also introduced for further analysis of human cognition-action coupling process in individual and collective levels. Typology of the methodologies for intervening into complex social systems is discussed in the latter part of this chapter for pursuing the assessment and control of various method biases and also for determining the axes in mapping cognition-action in the actual fields. Continuous inquiry into the good and intervention to complex social systems play crucial roles in the approaches toward effective organizational transformation.

DOI: 10.4018/978-1-60566-284-8.ch005

INTRODUCTION

In managing complexity and ambiguity, we need holistic or whole systems approaches. Complementary systemic approaches to integrate some separate systems are needed for fostering organizational adaptability and flexibility for coping with the changes in the social environment. It is not adequate to keep in line with the standards established by a particular discipline in a piece meal fashion, but to challenge the participants to pay attention to the changes in various fields and progress toward their desired reality. You can not extrapolate the future simply from the past.

It is difficult for us to go beyond cognitive barriers, and it is not easy for us to enhance an appropriate collaboration among multi-disciplinary fields. Holistic approaches which embrace various possibilities of aligning different cognitions in different disciplinary fields are necessary for developing work performance both at individual and collective levels. Collaboration beyond cognitive barriers will be enhanced more by working together with different disciplines in order to understand and to share various paradigms and future perspectives among disciplines rather than by simply complying with the rules and regulations established in the past without appropriate appreciation.

Conceptual frameworks of human systems, some categorizations and classifications of human cognition-action coupling in individual and collective levels, and typology in the methodologies for intervening in complex social life, are described in this chapter for healthcare research development in the future. This chapter provides some holistic approaches to human action in order to increase individual work performance and organizational performance achieved in the recursive process of organizational learning.

CONCEPTUAL FRAMEWORK OF HOLISTIC OR WHOLE SYSTEMS OF HUMAN ACTION

Two conceptual frameworks of holistic or whole human systems are introduced. One is the concept of human systems developed by Wilber, 2000 which is well known in the field of Cognitive Sciences and has been frequently applied in aligning collaboration with multiple disciplines. The other is the concept of dynamic and resilient organizational systems developed by Schwaninger, 2000, 2006; called an intelligent organization of which structure is an icosahedron.

Conceptual Framework of Human Systems

The alignment of cognitive misfit between individuals and groups plays a critical role in improving human performance by motivating employees. Cognitive alignment is, therefore, necessary to enhance collaboration of multi-disciplinary teams. Aligning cognitive misfit or decreasing the degree of mismatch between the individuals and collectives or organizations is of crucial importance in creating business and economic value as well as ethical and social value.

As reported by Wilber, 2000, two kinds of alignment between cognition and action at the individual and collective levels depicted in a horizontal direction (as shown in Figure 1) have been studied; mainly in the areas of psychology, group dynamics, social psychology. The studies regarding two other kinds of alignment of cognitive fit between individuals and collectives and the alignment of performance between individuals and collectives (as shown in Figure 2) in a vertical direction have been carried out, and the development of the studies in the latter are expected in the future. The study on cognitive alignment between individuals and collectives requires new scientific perspectives of post normal science. Orchestration under excellent conductors instead of the leaders in a particular disciplinary area plays an important role for aligning cognitive differences among individuals and collectives. Organizational culture as a collective entity may be decreased by the lack of the alignment between individual and collective cognition-action, and inversely cultural entropy in the organization is increased.

Cognitive/value congruence in individuals and organizational perspectives is a valid predictor of satisfaction, commitment and actual turnover (Schmitt, and

Figure 1. The relationship of cognition with action in individual and in collective levels

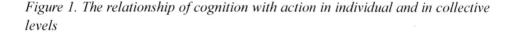

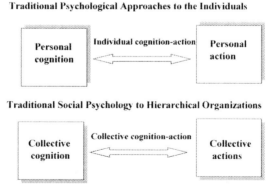

Figure 2. Cognitive/value alignment and performance alignment between individuals and collectives

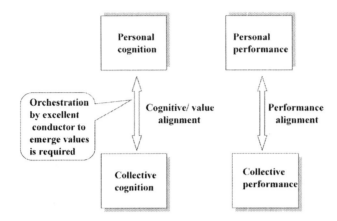

Chan, D. 1998), and is of importance in improving organizational performance. One of the management problems in the healthcare sector in Japan is shortage of manpower, especially excellent workers. There is a movement toward an industrial market. Turnover of nurses from hospitals to industries has been increasing. For pulling excellent employees into the healthcare sector, traditional human resource management is not adequate, rather new management perspectives are required. Instead of human resource management, human capital or asset management becomes valid in the ICT age, and necessitates the alignment of cognition misfit between individual and collective levels and among multiple paradigms in disciplinary fields. Addressing the lack of personal alignment, lack of group structure alignment, lack of value alignment, lack of mission alignment are crucial in the improvement of business performance and in trying to attain a competitive advantage for the future.

In the future, research focus should be placed on cognitive/values alignment between the individual and collective levels and on complementary approaches between task performance and contextual performance in multi-disciplinary work team level and in organizational culture level. Organizational culture is able to be transformed by the perspectives and insight of people who participate and are able to share visions and missions of the organization. The prospective values in the future are more powerful to change organizational climate and to increase flexibility and resiliency of the organization in a changing society. Integrated value management in complementary approaches to complex organization, therefore, plays a crucial role in pursuing organizational visions and in transforming organizational culture to tide over the turbulence in the external environment.

Intelligent Organization as a Polyhedron

The Framework of cybernetic management or systemic management was developed by European researchers (Beer, 1979, Ulrich, 1996, Flood and Rom,1996, Jackson, 2000, Espejo, Schumann, Schwaninger, and Bilello, 1996, Schwaninger, 2000, Schwaninger, 2006). The framework of intelligent organization was focused in this chapter for discussing holistic or integrated social systems. The participants of intelligent organization which is structured as a polyhedron as shown in Figure 3, are expected to act as professional workers. Their positions in a polyhedron make them reframe their insights on new actions, revitalize organizational capabilities enabling the participants which enhance action development through synergetic interaction among the participants and collaborative generation of knowledge among different disciplines. Knowledge conversion, explicit versus implicit in information processing, and knowledge generation are harnessed in the process of interpersonal cohesion in the climate of an intelligent organization. Spreading and generalizing knowledge is also driven in such a cultural atmosphere as in an intelligent organization. The framework for an intelligent organization is similar in its perspectives and insights with the organizational context in which new values emerge in recursive process of organizational learning as described in Chapter 2. In dealing with complex social systems, reflexive/recursive processes of organizational learning, embracing the constructs on three levels of organizational learning, such as single, double and triple loop learning as described in Chapter 2, and the

Figure 3. Image of polyhedral structure

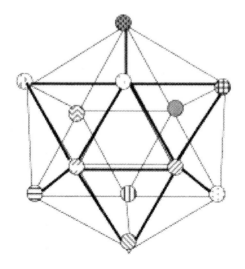

constructs of organizational structure which dissolve traditional hierarchy of top versus bottom, or centrality versus peripherality, play crucial roles for the alignment of cognitive misfit. People who participate and work in a polyhedral structure of organization never feel peripheral, but rather autopoietic. They are able to act as a central actor. The participants are motivated to work and to contribute to create new values and knowledge.

CLASSIFICATION, CATEGORIZATION OF HUMAN COGNITION-ACTION COUPLING IN INDIVIDUAL LEVEL

Classification of human competence of cognition-action coupling in the individual level which is useful in assessing complex society, is described in the following sections. Being an individual is an individual participating in society, not a segregated individual in a laboratory.

Foucault's Categorizations of Human Cognition-Action Coupling Techniques

Four techniques are provided for understanding human cognition-action coupling, i.e. techniques of production that allow us to manipulate objects, technologies of sign that allow us to communicate, technologies of power that control us to conduct with respect to others, and technologies of the self that are used for self-transformation (Foucault, M. 1988). Human cognition-action is able to enhance power and knowledge conditioning the formation of the self, as Foucault (1988) stated. People are required for enhancing interpretation competence and techniques for symbols in the cognition level as well as signals in the perception level and signs in the reaction level, which allow them to be alive in a critical manner in three worlds, physical, personal and social worlds of Habermas's tricotomy (Habermas, 1978, 1984). Human nature constantly struggles with the constraints of one's own subjectivity, or one's personal world view. People strive to know practical mechanisms of power and resistance, and to design their own life style. Critical social intervention is no longer for the discovery of universal knowledge, but for an exploration of contingency and plasticity of the constraints and the boundaries. Four effective techniques as indicated by Foucault, 1988 in addition with innate ability are leveraged for developing human power and for exploring the contingency in human life. Most of the employees working in manufacturing plants in the 20th century were forced to concentrate on routine work for keeping the operation standards of machines. They were just treated as robots without work discretion or autonomy and were controlled without human respect. Techniques of power which control them in conduct with respect to others and the techniques of self that are used for transforming themselves, as Foucault stated, are of importance for enhancing human cognition-action coupling competence and for taking action as professionals and respectable individuals.

Conceptual Framework of Care

Medical cure and healthcare have been considered to be medical and health service given by medical professionals. The traditional style of the asymmetrical relationship between care-providers and care-recipients has been widely discussed both within the healthcare sector as well as general public areas. Recent arguments suggest that the relationship of power between supply side and demand side should be balanced and managed in an appropriate manner for all the stakeholders. Social inquiries into these aspects are needed if the alignment of cognitive misfits between care-providers and care-recipients is to be corrected.

We have tried to classify the concept of care into four types, such as egoistic type, bureaucratic type, specialist type and dynamic collaboration type of care by using two axes, one is the axis of the degree of care, the other is the axis of group level, as shown in Figure 4. Our studies suggested that dynamic and collaboration type of care played a great role in improving team and organizational performances (Saito, Watanabe, Murakami, Karashima, 2005, Saito, Murakami, Karashima, 2007). Collaboration type of care was more influential and effective than the other three

Figure 4. Typology of cognitive capitals by two axes of care and group level

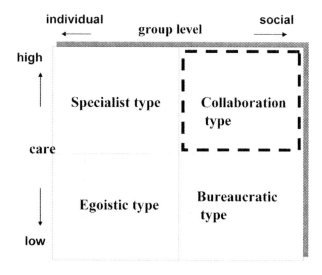

types of care, egoistic, specialist and bureaucratic types of care in improving orga-nizational performance. Leadership for enhancing teamwork composed of multiple disciplines plays an important role in providing collaboration type of care and affects the professional staffs' satisfaction which in turn drives clients' satisfaction as well as all other stakeholders' satisfaction. The results of our studies on the causation of driving cognitive or value chain of care-providers and care-recipients give us an insight into redesigning the organization by appropriate application of knowledge management in order to improve organizational performances and to ensure business prosperity in service enterprises as well as in manufacturing industry.

Care is fundamentally reciprocal (von Krogh, 2000, 2001). We care for others, and the others care for us. Care plays a pivotal role in organizational knowledge development at the individual and organizational levels. Caring has an influential quality of power in enhancing interpersonal relationship and in creating organiza-tional climate. Organizational knowledge which is essential in service industries is developed in the recursive learning process of explicit knowledge and tacit knowl-edge. People need a collaborative type of care shown in the upper right quadrant. Collaborative care-providers, not individualistic types like specialist, egoistic, or bureaucratic, are needed for coping with complex and changing society.

Nishida's Inquiry into the Good

Inquiry into the good (Nishida, 1911, 1990) is widely known as a representative way of thinking in Japan. Nishida is one of the representative Japanese philosophers on human cognition and action in society. What is good is to take action in keeping with a good balance with outside society. For this purpose, you need to be aware of the fact as it is in a practical field and to pay attention to what is going on and what does it mean for yourself and other people. Being aware of the fact as it is in society which is called " pure experience or direct experience". Pure or direct experience signifies self-awareness, self-awakening and unifies both the knowledge acquired and practical experiences. Without pure experience in the actual field which comes first as direct experience before indirect experiences based on objective logic, any indirect experience does not truly assist when you want to coordinate and collabo-rate with people in the society. You can not manage only with indirect experience, rather you need both pure and indirect experience. Indirect experiences are essen-tially explicit knowledge. Continuous inquiry into the good mentioned by Nishida develops reciprocal relationships, alignment of people to share visions, building strategic alliances which keep intermediate system balance and confirmation of being one elemental existence in a social system.

The good inquired by Nishida is still new and influential even after almost a hundred years, because it is structured by an holistic view of human systems, complementary view beyond the simple sum of the parts, beyond particularity in normal scientific logic. An inquiry into the good guides us to develop human works and to enhance organizational competence. His philosophy leads us to take a good balance in the process of human cognition-action coupling which is originally undifferentiated and inseparable, and is ever challenging. Good balanced human cognition-action coupling leads us to raise the quality of social being. His philosophy contributes to the current argument on the alignment of cognitive misfit and suggests how to integrate into a cognitive congruence which stems from understanding Nishida's key word, pure experience.

CLASSIFICATION, CATEGORIZATION OF ORGANIZATIONAL CULTURE IN COLLECTIVE LEVEL

Alignment of collective cognition-action is discussed by selecting two assessments, cultural value assessment by Barrett (1998, 2000) and diagnosing organizational culture by Cameron and Quinn (2006) in the following section.

Cultural Value Assessment in Collective Levels

This tool of cultural value assessment (CVA) was provided by Barrett (1998, 2006) as one of the cultural transformation tools (CTT). Cultural values in the individual, group and organizational values in the present and future are able to be identified by using the CTT. Barrett (2006) stated "culture is a source of competitive advantage which devotes its resources to implementing cultural transformation program and value management". Seven collective values or seven levels of consciousness in group and organization were prepared by Barrett (2006). Level 1 is survival consciousness, financial stability and safety for the group and organization. Level 2 is relationship consciousness, building harmonious internal relationship to create a sense of belonging. Level 3 is self-esteem consciousness, creating the order of effective performance that engenders respect and pride. Level 4 is transformation consciousness, involving group members and giving them a voice in decision-making. Level 5 is internal cohesion, aligning group members around a shared vision, mission and values. Level 6 is making a difference consciousness, cooperating with and forming alliance with other groups. Level 7 is service consciousness, caring for humanity, future generation and the planet. The upper three levels of 7, 6, and 5 represent a common good which has similar meaning to the good explained by Nishida (1911, 1990), intermediate level 4 represents transformation, and the lower three levels 3, 2, 1 represent self-interest. Each value measured is mapped to compare the difference of organizational culture. Problematic situations in organizational environment are disclosed and are focused by mapping and by comparing seven levels of organizational consciousness.

Classification of Organizational Culture by Four Quadrants

Four-quadrant classification was provided by Cameron,K.S. and Quinn,R.E.2006, Cameron,K.S., Quinn, Degraff,R.E.J. and Thakor,A.V. 2006). The reason why they developed this classification was that most common methodologies, such as TQM, down-sizing and reengineering had not brought the expected outcomes to enhance business effectiveness, although they have been effective for some particular purposes, for instance, line operational efficiency, shortage of leading time, in manufacturing operation. Most of the fields which implemented these methodologies had fallen short and were required to take another action for successful outcomes. Cameron reported that the endeavors in over 40 percent of the fields implemented had been a complete failure. Why does this implementation of quality management which has been commonly accepted have to end in failure? This is because of the negligence of organizational climate or culture. Diagnosing and changing organizational culture is needed for identifying current situations of organization and for continuing trans-formation of organizational culture, which leads to enhancement of organizational competence coping with the turbulence of the social environment.

Our studies also suggested that organizational culture plays a decisive role in reducing human errors and erroneous actions and in improving team reciprocity and organizational performances (Saito, Inoue, Seki, 2005; Murakami, 2005; Murakami, Inoue and Saito, 2007). Most accidents recently reported, such as automobiles, airplanes, or surgical operational errors, are found to be a system error or an organi-zational accident stemming from a concealing atmosphere of organizational culture controlled by a few at the TOP. These accidental events bespeak an important role of organizational culture for safety control. You will see some empirical evidence in Chapter 11 and 12.

The methodology for creating values in organizations was developed by preparing four quadrants for clarifying the meaning of values (Cameron, Quinn, 1999; Cameron, Quinn, Degraff and Thakor, 2006). Four quadrants which were made by two axis, flexibility-control and internal-external, were defined to be 'collaborate' in a clan climate, 'control' in hierarchy climate, 'compete' in market climate and 'create' in adhocracy climate. Two diagonal axes, the axis of transformation and the axis of agility provided diagonal quadrants; the direction of changing organizational climate toward adhocracy or controlled, and the direction of changing fast or slow were also applicable for changing organizational culture. Alignment across the quadrants in accordance with the problematic situation leads to an effective organizational transformation. In complex and dynamic society, there must be some other type of culture in addition to the four types of organizational culture reported by Cameron, however, the four quadrant method assists in the understanding and classifying of organizational culture. We have to keep our eyes on the facts we encounter in the field, and to decide which way and how fast to go by depicting the four-quadrant diagram. The necessary steps are identified by diagnosing organizational culture, and are confirmed by all the stakeholders before taking action.

TYPOLOGY IN THE METHODOLOGIES FOR INTERVENING COMPLEX SOCIAL SYSTEMS AND FOR CHANGING ORGANIZATIONAL CULTURE

Three matrix types of methodology introduced here-in-after are multi-methodology by Minger and Gill, 1997, means-ends hierarchical workspace by Rasmusen, Pejtersen and Goodstein, 1994 and installment matrix for future research in healthcare sector by Saito, M. 2001. Typology in the methodologies for intervening complex social systems is discussed for determining the axes in mapping cognition-action in the actual working fields, and for developing the assessment and control of various method biases.

Multi-Methodology Structured by Habermas' Trichotomy and Intervention Steps

The matrix of multi-methodology developed by Minger,J. Gill,A. 1997 is structured by two axes, namely; the axis of the intervention phases in organizational learning in the horizontal direction and the axis of Habermas's three worlds (Habermas, 1984, 1987) in the vertical direction. The four intervening steps in multi-methodology are appreciation, analysis, assessment and action, which are similar to the steps of plan, do, check and act. Habermas's three worlds are material, personal and social. The four steps by three worlds (4 X 3) provides 12 sections. Most of the traditional models reported in the past are in the material world and in the personal world and few are in the social world. The four steps in the material world are frequently used in the fields of Science and Engineering, the four steps in the personal world are used in psychology while the four steps in the social world are used in the field of social sciences. The focus in each academic field is limited to a particular area of the 12 sections of multi-methodology. However, whole systems/holistic approaches require a complete view of multi-methodology and include future scenarios toward the goals for intervening complex social systems and for changing organizational culture.

Method is to be selected and adopted in accordance with the purposes of the survey, and the goals to be achieved, as well as with the reasons why and what problems have to be adopted and changed. Most of the criteria in the material world are concerned with efficiency in production, or in designing production systems. Most of the criteria in the personal world are concerned with self-transformation, personal ethics, while those in the social world are concerned with the transformation of organizational culture for enhancing the participants to be in vivid and vigorous moods for enhancing organizational competence.

Multi-methodology is not adequately developed from the viewpoint of categorization-based approaches, because in the classification of multi-methodology, the importance of semantic knowledge and feed-forward knowledge as implicit knowledge is not considered. Lack of multiple causation in real world limits the assessment of human action subsumed into a hierarchy of causation, even though declarative knowledge, feedback knowledge as explicit knowledge is adopted. Approaches to holistic or whole systems like our society are needed to develop the models which clarify the pattern of causal relationship in complex society.

The approaches structured by different axes representing means-ends and whole-part for analyzing actual work spaces, office work and surgical operation room, are described in the following section.

Worker's Navigation in Work Space by Two Axes of Means-Ends, Parts-Whole

Conceptual worker's navigation in work space by two axes representing means-ends relation in vertical axis and decomposition of part-whole relation of work organization in horizontal axis was developed for work domain analysis (Rasmussen, Pejtersen and Goodman, 1994, Rasmussen and Pejtersen,1995) In the vertical axis of means-ends relation, "What should be done" is considered as the work function in level 1. "Why to use it" as the ends of level 1 is level 1 + 1 in higher level. "How to do it" as the means of level 1 is level 1 - 1 in lower level, as shown in Figure 5. Mapping of worker's navigation by using worker' navigation matrix enables the observer to assess and compare for the identification of the most effective achievement among navigator's actions.

A conceptual navigation space in the surgical operation room as an application of workers' navigation principal developed by Rasmussen was shown in Figure 6. Characteristic navigation space was depicted by each professional, such as surgeons, anesthetists, pathologists and nurses. The main territory of each staff is characteristically occupied in comparison with the mapping pattern of four kinds of staff navigation. The most efficient action to be taken in each profession and the most effective teaming can be found on the mapped territory patterns in the work space made by

Figure 5. What, What and How levels in hierarchical organization by two axes of the means-ends and whole parts

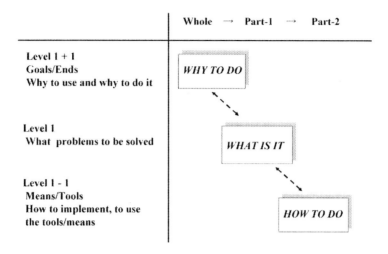

two axes, the axis of the levels of functional abstraction on operation work and the other axis is the levels of decomposition of whole body into parts of the body. The most efficient and effective surgical operation could be identified from the mapping method which gives us some ideas regarding the redesign of the operation teaming and territory alignment including total operation room climate.

Mapping Future Research in the Healthcare Sector by Healthcare Demand and Lifestyle

In managing collaborative work carried out, 2001-2005, in Institute on Health Sciences and Engineering, Waseda University, future researches dealing within the Institute were mapped by two axes of healthcare demanded and lifestyle as shown in Figure 7 (Saito,2001). Interdisciplinary researchers came together from various faculties, Science and Engineering, Education, Human Sciences, Culture and Arts, etc. to put forward our project plans and to achieve the goals. It was not easy to align cognitive misfit among researchers with different paradigms. Without mapping different themes and methods, researchers are apt to concentrate only on their academic disciplines or a particular area, and they did not transcend the established boundaries of each discipline and take enough time to investigate the interaction of technology and human systems. An established particular discipline is stimulated with revolutionary perspectives and many new insights offered from the other disciplines related in the installment matrix.

Figure 6. Conceptual navigation of surgeons, anesthetists, pathologist, and nurses during surgical operation

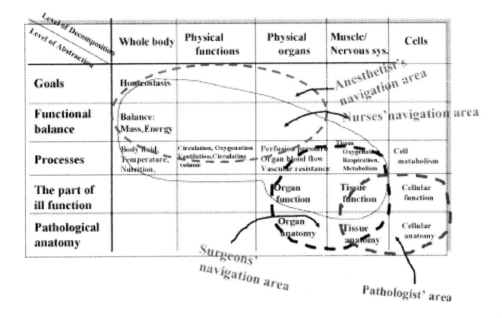

The vertical axis is a combined axis of activity of daily life (ADL) and social economic status (SES) and has four levels of daily life-social economic status, such as low-poor, low-good, high-poor, and high-good. The horizontal axis represents four kinds of clients' lifestyle, such as hospitalization, commuting hospital, working life managed by industrial care-providers and the status that enables one to take care of yourself keeping an autonomous life style. Three territories were provided for the researchers engaging in the project, 1) physical work environment, safety systems engineering, policy engineering as territory 1, 2) quality of care, human relation, community health based on cognitive psychology, social psychology, tele-health care system, as territory 2, and 3) organizational resigning, integrated value management based on social sciences and industrial systems management as territory 3. This installment matrix gives us an effective linkage among interdisciplinary researchers in exploiting and exploring the problems not only in a specific discipline, but also an interdisciplinary point of view.

The primary focus in future studies is to be placed on the alignment of cognition/ values among individuals and collectives, in fact, among all the stakeholders, and placed on the preparation of complementary approaches between task performance and contextual performance in multi-disciplinary work team/group level and or-

Figure 7. Installment matrix of healthcare demands/needs type in vertical axis and the type of life style in horizontal axis

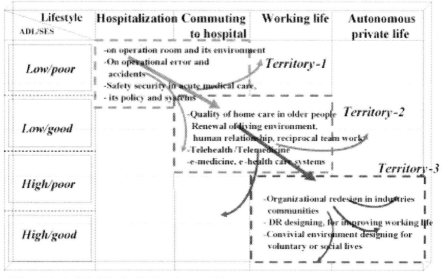

ADL=Activity in Daily Life, classified into low and high
SES=Social Economic Status, classified into poor and good

ganizational culture level. Organizational culture is able to be transformed by the perspectives and insights of people who participate and share visions and missions of the organization. The perspective values in the future, directed by knowledge management are more powerful in changing the organizational climate and increasing the organizational competence in changing society. Knowledge management or integrated value management, therefore, plays a crucial role in pursuing organizational visions and achieving organizational performances and missions, and of transforming organizational culture to tide over the turbulence in the external environment.

CONCLUSION

Alignment of Cognitive Incongruence or Misfit

Alignment of cognitive incongruence between different levels of organization by integrating hierarchical boundaries and among different disciplines by coordinating disciplinary boundaries in the same level is imperative for empowering the participants to take action in a discretional manner. Development of alignment methodology is urgently required for enhancing organizational performance and organizational competence to be a holistic or whole system coping with changing social environment. Concepts and classification of complex human systems described in this Chapter were introduced for aligning cognitive misfit among the participants to the organization. Intelligent organization as a polyhedron type of organization in which the participants can act as professional staff with a discretional manner, is expected to play a role in enhancing organizational flexibility and adaptation.

Continuous Inquiry into the Good by the Participants

Pure or direct experience in the field comes first before indirect experiences obtained by text or books written by specialists or authorities in a particular discipline. Pure/direct experience is a consciousness of self-awareness, self-awakening and unifies knowledge acquired with the experiences of oneself in a practical field. Continuous inquiry on the occasion of pure experience enables us to manage ourselves to attain self-sufficiency and simultaneously others' sufficiency for keeping a good balance to work together and to amplify together in approaching a desired reality. The participants of the organization are the most important assets of the organization, and they manage themselves by continuous inquiries into the good, or into the values and the ideas emerging in the innovative process of a learning organization. Whole or holistic systems approaches by using classification, categorization or typology in multiple methodology help the participants change their organizational environment and enhance organizational competence.

REFERENCES

Barrett, R. (1998). *Liberating the corporate soul: Build a visionary organization.* Butterworth-Heinemann.

Barrett, R. (2006). *Building a value-driven organization/a whole system approach to cultural transformation.* Elsevier.

Beer, S. (1979). *The heart of enterprise.* Wiley and Sons, Inc.

Borman, W. C., & Motowidlo, S. J. (1997). Task performance and contextual performance: The meaning for personnel selection research. *Human Performance, 10,* 99–110. doi:10.1207/s15327043hup1002_3

Cameron, K. S., & Quinn, R. E. (1999). *Diagnosing and changing organizational culture: Based on competing vcaues framework.* Jossy-Bass, Wiley imprint.

Cameron, K. S., Quinn, R. E., Degraff, J., & Thakor, A. V. (2006). *Competing values leadership: Creating value in organization.* Edward Elgar.

Espejo, R., Schumann, W., Schwaninger, M., & Bilello, U. (1996). *Organizational transformation and learning: A cybernetic approach to management.* Wiley and Sons Inc.

Flood, R., & Rom, N. R. A. (1996). *Diversity management: Triple loop learning.* Wiley and Sons, Inc.

Foucault, M. (1988). *Politics, philosophy, culture.* Routlege.

Habermas, J. (1978). *Knowledge and human interests.* London: Heinemann.

Habermas, J. (1984). *The theory of communicative action, vol.1, reason and the rationalization of society.* London: Heinemann.

Hollnagel, E. (1998). *Cognitive reliability and error analysis method: CREAM.* Elsevier. Jackson, M. (2000). *Systems approaches to management.* Kluwer Academic/Plenum Publishers.

Holnagell, E. (1993). *Human reliability analysis: Context and control.* Academic Press.

Minger, J., & Gill, A. (1997). *Multimethodology: Theory and practice of combining management science methodologies.* John Wiley and Sons, Inc.

Murakami, G. (2005). *A study on care cognition and performance reliability in team nursing.* Dissertation abstracts for master's degree, Waseda University (in Japanese, pp. 245-248).

Nishida, K. (1911). *An inquiry into the good* (in Japanese). Iwanami Publisher.

Nishida, K. (1990). *An inquiry into the good* (in English). Translated by M. Abe & C. Ives, Yale University Press.

Nonaka, I., & Konno, N. (1998). The concept of 'ba': Building a foundation for knowledge creation. *California Management Review, 40*(3), 1–15.

Nonaka, I., & Nishiguchi, T. (2001). *Knowledge emergence: Social, technical, and evolutionary dimensions of knowledge creation.* Oxford University Press.

Rasmussen, J., & Pejtersen, A. M. (1995). Virtual ecology of work. In J. Flach, P. Hancock, J. Caird & K. Vicente (Eds.), *Global perspectives on the ecology of human-machine systems, vol.1* (pp. 121-156). LEA.

Rasmussen, J., Pejtersen, A. M., & Goodman, L. P. (1994). *Cognitive systems engineering.* John Wiley and Sons, Inc.

Saito, M. (2001). *Installment matrix for future research themes.* Reports in the Institute of Health Sciences and Engineering, Waseda University.

Saito, M., Inoue, T., & Seki, H. (2005). Organizational control mode, cognitive activity, and performance reliability: The case of a national hospital in Japan. In N. Wickramasinghe, J. N. D. Gupta & S. K. Sharma (Eds.), *Creating knowledge-based healthcare organization* (pp. 179-192). Hershey, PA: Idea Group Publishing.

Saito, M., Murakami, G., & Karashima, M. (2007). Effect of communication and emotional types on team reciprocity in healthcare organization. *International Journal of Healthcare Technology and Management, 8*(3/4), 196–208. doi:10.1504/IJHTM.2007.013160

Sakurai, Y. (1996). *Foucault: Power and knowledge* (in Japanese). Kodansha.

Schmitt, N., & Chan, D. (1998). *Personal selection: A theoretical approach.* Sage Publications.

Schwaninger, M. (2000). Managing complexity: The path toward intelligent organization. *Systemic Practice and Action Research, 13*(2), 207–241. doi:10.1023/A:1009546721353

Schwaninger, M. (2006). *Intelligent organization: Powerful models for systemic management.* Berlin: Springer.

Ulrich, W. (1996). Critical systems thinking for citizens. In R. Flood & N. R. A. Rom (Eds.), *Critical systems thinking: Current research and practice* (pp165-178).

von Krogh, G. (2000). *Enabling knowledge creation: How to unlock the mystery of tacit knowledge and release the power of innovation.* Oxford University Press.

von Krogh, G., Ichijo, K., & Nonaka, I. (2001). Bringing care into knowledge development of business organization. In Nonaka & Nishiguchi (Eds.), *Knowledge emergence: Social, technical, and evolutionary dimensions of knowledge creation* (pp. 30-52). Oxford University Press.

Wilber, K. (2000). *A brief history of everything.* Gateway.

Chapter 6

Conceptual Levels of Information Processing and Information Interpretation in Knowledge Management

Murako Saito
Waseda University, Japan

ABSTRACT

In managing knowledge, conceptual confusion on information arises frequently among researchers in different disciplines. The term of information is defined at least into four: data, information, knowledge, and wisdom. Procedural ways of information are different among disciplines even when the definition is similar. Interpretation of information varies in accordance with its meaning or its value for the receivers. Most of the misalignment in the field stems from different interpretations and the different procedural ways of the information presented. In this chapter, first, information processing levels in knowledge management and second, three levels in cognition-action reflective process are described. Thirdly, information interpretation in internal world, and finally juxtaposition of scientific and interpretive perspectives are discussed for developing organizational learning and organizational resilience and for building common ground for productive and constructive dialogue between and within disciplinary fields.

DOI: 10.4018/978-1-60566-284-8.ch006

INTRODUCTION

It is rarely recognized, although it occurs frequently, that the way of knowledge information processing differs among different disciplinary areas. Specifically, the procedural ways of the information differentiates among academic disciplines in comparison with declarative or generalized knowledge. Even though people in the field could understand the information presented in a feed-back process, the procedural way of the information is not necessarily similar, nor confirmed among disciplines. People follow the procedures they get used to or are trained in, in their disciplinary fields. Human errors in information processing frequently occur due to the specific procedures used in a particular discipline. The procedures in a particular area differ from the ones used in other disciplinary fields. The procedural way in the feed forward process of information acquired is very important for team members in multiple disciplines to deliver services to end-clients.

In this chapter, multiplicity of knowledge-information processing, and the three levels in cognition-action coupling process, feed-forward processes of knowledge information, holistic principles for developing stakeholders' action in organization and information interpretation in the internal world are described for understanding the development of organizational learning and organizational resilience and also for the argument in aligning the misfits among disciplines and between human cognition and action in operations management.

INFORMATION PROCESSING LEVELS IN KNOWLEDGE MANAGEMENT

In managing knowledge, conceptual confusion on information arises when we collaborate with researchers in different disciplines. The term of information has been defined into four meanings, data, capta, information and knowledge (Checkland and Holwell, 1998). Conceptual levels of information in the author's classification which is shown in Figure 1 are 1) information as data in physical and reaction level or in operational management level, 2) perceptual information in response-behavior level or in strategic management level, 3) knowledge in cognitive-action level or normative management level, and 4) wisdom in integrated and acculturated action level in the long span, which leads people to realize their healthy and purposeful lives and to accelerate global health. In the upper two levels of wisdom and knowledge, information processing is dealt with consciously by point-to-point liner processing, while in the lower two levels, routine work as a daily duty is dealt without profound consideration on each work. Most workers treat routine work unconsciously by treating them as parallel distribution processing; moreover, they behave as they are trained. The concepts which define meanings of information in every level are to be shared among different disciplinary workers in developing collaboration work. Organizational learning comprises all the levels of information from accumulating data and mining data in perceptual levels, to modifying or interpreting information in cognitive and integrated action levels, and continues to run through all the levels for confirming that the information acquired gives some meaningful ideas and value to the organization, why and how the meaningful ideas are to be implemented.

For instance, clinical path (CP) which is frequently applied as one of the effective tools in the healthcare sector is generally designed for clinicians to do their job in considering clients' needs in providing efficient care. Few cases in CP are designed by comprising information in all its levels, by considering patients' and their family's needs and values, especially in the cases of aged patients. The CP is to be designed by considering a value chain of the clients' lives including all the process of internal and external organizational learning. Knowledge enables us to acquire the information we require, but you have to decide for yourself whether the information is in fact informative to you or not, before taking action. It is very important that information resource management leads to the creation of knowledge and integration of knowledge, which is inevitably dependent upon the degree of your understanding and interpretation of the information you have acquired.

At least 2 or 3 levels, plural conceptual levels of knowledge, are required to consider and assess in evaluating human action. Multiplicity and hierarchy of

Figure 1. Conceptual levels of data, information, knowledge and wisdom which are featured by human cognition-action coupling

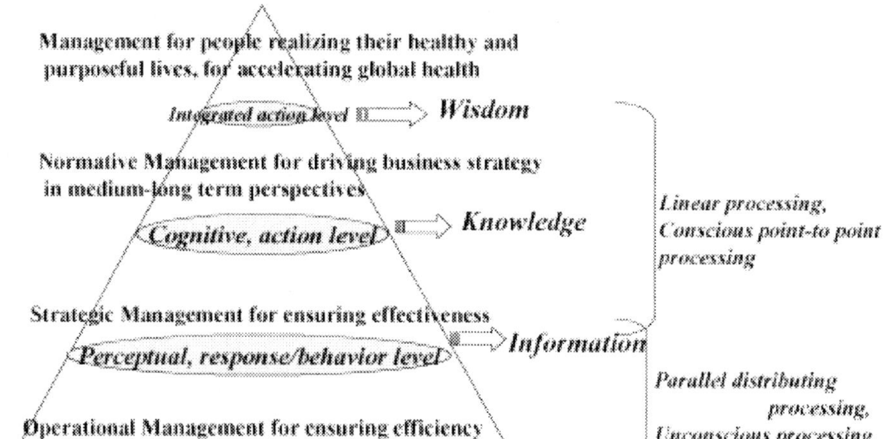

human actions has to be considered in evaluating the outcomes. Inseparability of stimulus and response, inseparability of perception and behavior, and inseparability of cognition and action coupling, in which coupling processes some moderators and mediators play their roles as a catalyst or leverage and thus have to be considered in assessing and evaluating human actions in the fields. Our studies suggest mood states at work, interpersonal relation, organizational learning and leadership, play crucial roles as moderators or mediators (Saito, Ikeda and Seki, 2000, Saito, Inoue and Seki, 2005, Saito, Murakami and Karashima, 2007, Bass,1999). These case studies are described in Chapter 12, 13 and 14.

THREE LEVELS IN COGNITION-ACTION COUPLING PROCESS OF HUMAN ACTION

Basic Three Levels of Information Processing in Ergonomics

A simplified basic three-level model on human action, 1) skill-based behavior which is automated response to the signals given, 2) rule-based behavior which is associated behavior with stored rules and tasks for the signs presented, and 3) knowledge–based behavior which is planned for decision making tasks for the symbols provided, was reported by Rasmussen (1974). The three levels are shown in Figure 2. This basic three-level model of human action was developed into the Step Ladder Model (SLM) (Rasmussen, 1986; 1994; 1995). Human action is made through the recursive process of organizational learning, at least in three levels of information processing, which is figured out skill-based (SB), rule-based (RB) and knowledge-based (KB) respectively. Human erroneous action in SB is called a slip or lapse, the ones in RB and KB are mistakes, and processing time in each of the three levels is apparently different as reported by Rasmussen and Jensen (1974). As shown in Table 1, processing time is largely different in accordance with the level.

Table 1. Perception-Behavior level, error type, processing level and time

Perception-Behavior level	Error type	Processing level	Processing time
SB response	Slip, lapse	Signal-Response	100m.sec
RB behavior	mistake	Sign-Behavior	sec-min.
KB action	mistake	Symbol-Action	min.-hr.

Figure 2. Three levels of information presented and human operator's perfor-mance

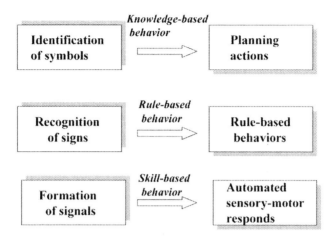

Three Throughputs in Cognition-Action Coupling Process

Logical fallacies are frequently arising in business, particularly in approaching and dealing with problematic situations (Gomez, 1999, Probst and Gomez, 1992) Logic for retrospective analysis and for prospective analysis make a substantial difference in introducing conceptual models. Perspectives to evaluate human action are differ-ent among traditional ways of human action, information processing psychology, or cognitive system engineering. Social problems can not be solved, nor resolved, simply by dealing with single loop learning or a particular way in a particular dis-cipline. Complexity of social problems requires all three throughputs of learning processes, single loop learning, double loop learning and triple loop learning in solving social problems. Innovative organization developed by knowledge genera-tion and knowledge generalization is made in the recursive information processing of three levels supported by technology, which leads to organizational flexibility or resilience Relevance of knowledge management to organizational learning and to technology is as discussed in Chapter 2.

As shown in Figure 3, the purpose of single loop learning in the recursive process of action-learning cycle is to improve work efficiency by the how-type of learning by means of a sort of deficient supply technology, and is based on input-output systematic thinking. The purpose of double loop learning is to enhance business effectiveness by what-type of learning by the support of another action-inducing technology, and is based on input-outcomes systemic thinking. Triple loop learn-

Figure 3. Action-learning cycles in three throughputs

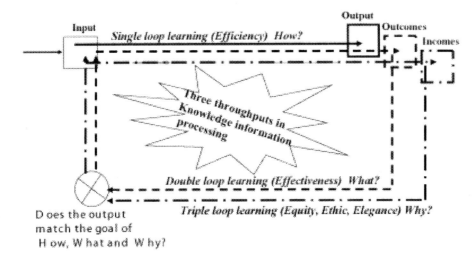

ing is for calling attention to the participants to share corporate vision, mission and responsibility, to pay attention to ethicality, equity and elegance of organizational atmosphere by why-type of learning with the support of advanced technology, and is based on input-incomes systemic thinking long term.

Feedback and Feed Forward Process of Information Processing

It is important to deliver a good quality of service for harnessing knowledge management in the feed-forward process, or inside-out knowledge flow, rather than a feedback process, or outside-in knowledge flow of information. Once people get information from the external society, they start and have to make final decisions for their action through inside-out knowledge flow. Prospective approaches considering the values for clients or patients are required in addition to retrospective consideration and analysis. Three important purposes in making a final decision for their action are actor's performance reliability, organizational behavior validity and human action viability in the feed-forward process through which service quality and security are enhanced for both service-providers and recipients, as shown in Figure 4. Service or care providers are required to take action through the recursive processes of organizational learning for providing better quality of service and

Figure 4. Cognition-action coupling processes in the organization by the frameworks of input-output systematic thinking, input-outcomes systemic thinking and input-incomes systemic thinking of which purposes are performance reliability, behavior validity and human action viability

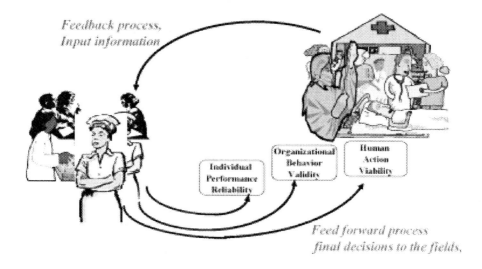

security which fit to the end-clients' needs. There are inseparable cognition-action coupling processes on three levels of information processing, the level of input-output systematic thinking which can be evaluated by individual performance reliability, the level of input-outcomes systemic thinking which can be evaluated by human behavior validity, and the level of input-incomes systemic thinking evaluated by human action viability. Individual performance in SB level, or in single loop learning level, organizational behavior in RB level, or in double loop learning level, and human action in KB level or in triple loop learning level, are enhanced in the recursive process of organizational learning under the organizational constraints, and also under organizational climate which is aligned to fit all the participants.

Holistic Principles for Developing Stakeholders' Actions in Organization

Three principles of human action development in organizations are 1) participative principle 2) continuity principle and 3) holistic principle which form two axes, horizontal coordination and vertical integration. Coordination is to do with the interaction of the units at the same level in horizontal direction and integration among different

Figure 5. Holistic principle for developing the stakeholders' actions in terms of horizontal coordination and vertical integration

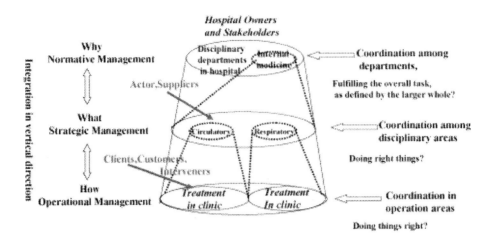

levels in vertical direction (Ackoff, 1998, 1999). Figure 5 illustrates by three levels of coordination in horizontal axes, such as operational management level, strategic management level and normative management level, and integration in vertical axes corresponding with horizontal axes. All the stakeholders, such as hospital owners, suppliers, clients/customers, academic disciplines, clinicians, administrators, are required to be mindful of their roles and responsibilities relevant to hospital visions and missions for the year. Without providing three principles of human action development, specifically holistic principles defined by Ackoff (1998), high quality of service and security are hardly expected to meet social demands.

INFORMATION INTERPRETATION IN INTERNAL WORLD

There are two ways of information processing, i.e. information transmission processing and information hermeneutic processing. The purpose of information transmission process is to increase transmission speed of information signals and signs and to improve transmission efficiency, while the purpose of information hermeneutic process is to enhance effectiveness in interpreting information symbols which have different meanings depending upon the information in the receivers' mindsets. The information hermeneutic process in which people think of the meaning of the information presented to them is much more important in evaluating human action rather than just in measuring the time sent or in counting error resulting in the information transmission process. The symbols of knowledge-information are able to be interpreted into various meanings by the receivers. You have to make a judgment and to select the final decision; otherwise, you would not be satisfied. Appreciation of reality or real world in the field is a set of rhetoric, Σ rhetoric ☐ reality. Appreciation is limitless, and varies in anyway, anytime in the future upon the change of individual mindscape and also the change of social culture. A variety of meaning exists in appreciation.

Appreciation of Stone Garden

When I visited the rock/stone garden in Kyoto (Figure 6) designed as a Zen Garden and registered as a world culture heritage in 1994 with my foreign friends we sat in front of the garden. The atmosphere of this garden took me to the time that the garden was designed in 1450, and the balance of small and large stones moved me to visualize the images of children and a mother, sometimes later on it changes, it changes into a wife and a husband or combination of wild birds and fish in the river. The change of my mindscape depends upon my internal world. The time and situation I visit the garden make my images change; yet the landscape of this stone garden for someone with a foreign culture seems just as it is, a garden with scattered stones without any meanings. My friend is used to seeing the gardens designed symmetrically or colorfully as in European gardens. Heterogeneous or dissimilar elements make asymmetrical balance, and appreciation on beauty is

Figure 6. Rock/stone garden in Ryoan Temple in Kyoto

emerged by enhancing individuality of each elements and avoidance of repetitive elements (Maruyama, 1980, 1994). There exist different mindscapes which derive various interpretations of the information presented, depending upon the difference of social and cultural backgrounds.

Reality is a Set of Rhetoric

The narrative process in interpreting information depends upon the circumstances you have interfaced and upon your interest. You need to develop your capability to interpret information presented. In addition to academic knowledge and skills which are given verbally, you need to enhance a sense of the field through your experience, and to enhance perception, judgment in terms of the fact and values, envisagement of desired relationship (Vickers, 1965, 1983, Blunden, 1994). In assessing human action, researchers are required to adopt multiple methodologies which comprise broad areas of physiological, psychological and social sciences. Snap-shot measurement in cross sectional study by a particular academic discipline is inadequate in assessing human action. The participants of the organization are required to become aware of their working surroundings to appreciate or understand their work roles, and the goals in individuals and business. They are also required to maintain a higher and more intense appreciation of the events which they may encounter in the workplace. The participants' appreciation on organizational and technological environments is a set of rhetoric on reality, and in fact, the ways of individual appreciation are unlimited in the flux of ideas and events in society, as shown in Figure 7. The tools and methodologies for implementing organizational culture transformation, for enhancing organizational development (Cooperrider, Sorensen, Whitney, and Yeager, 2000, Cooperrider, and Whitney, 2005, Barrett, 2006, Thatchenkery, and Chowdhry, 2007, Reed, 2007) were derived from Appreciative Systems Theory originally proposed by Vickers (1965, 1983)

JUXTAPOSING SCIENTIFIC AND INTERPRETIVE PERSPECTIVES FOR ORGANIZATIONAL LEARNING DEVELOPMENT (OLD) AND ORGANIZATIONAL RESILIENCE DEVELOPMENT (ORD)

Continuous changing of organization is required to enhance organizational flexibility or resilience to cope with the turbulence in society and to develop business competency by managing knowledge. Flexibility or resilience of the organization is one of the very important characteristics in making business successful by aligning complex organizational environments. Participative and coherent attitudes in

Figure 7. Appreciation of reality, such as consciousness of society, environment or workplace, is a set of rhetoric

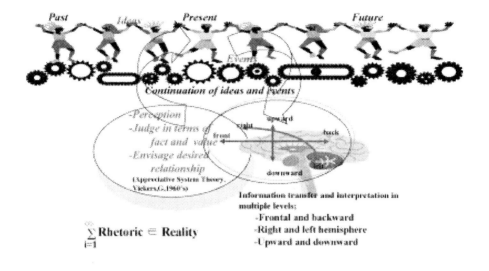

multi-disciplinary team members is crucial in changing organizational atmosphere into a resilient or adaptive onr. Enforcement of operations management and enhancement of cultural resilience are important in decreasing organizational entropy by activating collaboration among multi-disciplinary team members, and in overcoming organizational vulnerability, small disruptions or particular threats which may happen in the course of day-to-day operation. Adaptability of organization to the changes in society can be feasible in developing organizational learning process and organizational resilience in terms of juxtaposition of scientific and interpretive perspectives.

Organization is developed into a learning organization through recursive learning process in enhancing resilience or flexibility of the organization. A learning organization is the organization where people continuously expand their capacity to generate ideas and generalize ideas, where they willingly exchange their ideas. By so doing, they develop their careers and skills they require, and they can align organizational values among different disciplinary staff and also the clients. All the stakeholders can share organizational culture which gives great power for them to act in order to develop the organizational climate and to achieve the organizational goals and to have access to the enterprise's visions at all levels, such as individual, group, organization and business as a whole. Multilevel methodology necessitates measuring and evaluating the alignment of any misfits among people, as well as between man and technology (von Bertalanffy, 1968, Simon, 1969, Kozlowski and

Farr, 1988, Klein and Kozlowski, 2000). The relevance of human capital management to value creation has not yet been adequately studied and explained. The models of ORD and the models related with ORD, such as in interpersonal relationship development, business strategy development or ecological policy development, need to be explored respectively in local workplaces of the future.

The ORD will be created through the participation of excellent human capital that has ability and capability to share and amplify the values, not just simply by performing the work given, but also by having confidence to take necessary action in a challenging work environment. Possessing the valuable and rare resources of clever and talented workers provides the basis for value creation, but merely possessing such human resources hardly guarantee the ORD and the development of competitive advantages. The OLD is needed for enhancing the ORD which is driven by clever and talented workers inspiring each other and amplifying together. Talented workers' absorbing capacities are enhanced during the course of organizational learning (Tsai, 2001, Todorova and Durisin, 2007) The efforts of developing resilience and security can generate significant 'collateral benefits', helping avoid logical fallacies and pitfalls, tightening processes and increasing flexibility (Sheffi, 2007). Resilience of the organization plays complementary roles in facilitating individual absorbing capacity and organizational learning process. Collaborative and risk-sharing relationships among multiple disciplines are the sources of energy and power of the organization which allow the organization to overcome particular disruptions or unanticipated occurrences. It is imperative to prepare the methodology for aligning the cognitive misfit of organizational values among multiple disciplinary staff, and for converging and aligning the relevance gap between different paradigms among all the stakeholders which was also discussed in Chapter 5.

The ORD is just a way of making lemonade from lemon (Sheffi, 2007). I think action development in the fields can be said in the similar expression. In making lemonade from lemon, inner sense has the power to be able to control external information frequently presented in society. The ORD is enhanced in the course of the OLD in which knowledge management plays an important role for the participants to be aware and pay attention to any events of occurrences in their organizational environment. The participants are required to have responsibility in information processing to be reflective or a hyper-cyclic both in feedback and feed-forward processes so as to fit to social needs. Foresight rather than hindsight and pro-action rather than reaction make the participants take action for enhancing resilience of the organization. Resilience engineering is established to provide redesigning tools of organization for the participants to create foresight, recognize and tide over disruptions (Hollnagel, Woods and Leveson,N, 2006, Sheffi, 2007). During the processing of information on how, what and why the participants learn, the meaning of organizational purposes is understood so that they can take purposeful actions through continuous efforts supported and supplemented by appropriate information systems and technologies. According to systemic management or organizational fitness and control developed by European researchers (Beer,1990, Flood and Romm, 1996, Flood and Romm, 1997, Jackson,2000, Schwaninger,1996, Schwaninger,2000, Schwaninger,2006, Espejo, Schumann, Schwaninger and Bilello, 1996), three logical levels, such as operational, strategic and normative rationalities in systemic or holistic management are provided for controlling interdependent and complex organizational environment, and for achieving comprehensive fitness. Conceptual process models of organizational learning were also described in Chapter 2.

CONCLUSION

It frequently happens that conceptual frameworks provided by a particular discipline are misinterpreted and misunderstood in applying these TO different disciplines, especially in the procedural courses of data and information in the field, which leads to accidental events even if the person in charge insists that his/her procedures adopted are correct in dealing with the information acquired. He/she may insist that he/she took an appropriate action as trained. We need to pay attention to conceptual complexity and abstruseness of knowledge when working with multi-disciplinary professionals in the field.

Fostering a sense of the field is important in structuring and interpreting knowledge information acquired in the field. It is required to focus on how acquired knowledge is conceptually structured, compiled or chunked through three levels in cognition-action coupling processing. Sense of the field plays a crucial role in determining a final decision and for developing organization resilience or flexibility by building on common grounds for productive dialogue between and within disciplinary fields.

REFERENCES

Ackoff, R. L. (1998). A systemic view of transformational leadership. *Systemic Practice and Action Research, 11*(1), 23–36. doi:10.1023/A:1022960804854

Ackoff, R. L. (1999). *Recreating corporation: A design of organization for the 21st century.* Oxford University Press.

Ackoff, R. L. (1999). *Ackoff's best: His classic writings on management.* John Wiley and Sons.

Barrett, R. (2006). *Building a values-driven organization: A whole system approach to cultural transformation.* Butter-worth Heinemann, Elsevier.

Bass, B. M. (1999). Two decades of research and development in transformational leadership. *European Journal of Work and Organizational Psychology, 8*(1), 9–32. doi:10.1080/135943299398410

Beer, S. (1990). *The heart of enterprise.* John Wiley and Sons, Ltd.

Blunden, M. (1994). Vickers and post liberalism. *The American Behavioral Scientist, 38*(1), 11–25. doi:10.1177/0002764294038001003

Checkland, P., & Holwell, S. (1998). *Information, systems, and information systems: Making sense of the field.* John Wiley and Sons, Inc.

Cooperrider, D. L., Sorensen, P. F., Whitney, D., & Yeager, T. F. (2000). *Appreciative inquiry: Rethinking human organization toward a positive theory of change.* Stipes Publishing.

Cooperrider, D. L., & Whitney, D. (2005). *Appreciative inquiry: A positive revolution in change.* Barrett-Koehler.

Espejo, R., Schumann, W., Schwaninger, M., & Bilello, U. (1996). *Organizational transformation and learning: A cybernetic approach to management.* John Wiley and Sons, Ltd.

Flood, R., & Romm, N. R. A. (1996). *Diversity management: Triple loop learning.* John Wiley and Sons, Ltd.

Flood, R., & Romm, N. R. A. (1997). *Critical systems thinking: Current research and practice.* John Wiley and Sons, Ltd.

Gomez, P. (1999). *Integrated value management.* International Thomson Business Press.

Hollnagel, E., Woods, D. D., & Leveson, N. (2006). *Resilience engineering: Concepts and Precepts.* Ashgate Publishing.

Jackson, M. (2000). *Systems approaches to management.* Kluwer Academic/Plenum Publishers.

Klein, K. J., & Kozlowski, S. W. J. (2000). *Multilevel theory, research, and methods in organizations: Foundations, extensions, and new directions.* Jossey-Bass Inc.

Kozlowski, S. W. J., & Farr, J. L. (1988). An integrative model of updating and performance. *Human Performance, 1*, 5–29. doi:10.1207/s15327043hup0101_1

Maruyama, M. (1980). Mindscapes and science theories. *Current Anthropology*, *21*, 589–599. doi:10.1086/202539

Maruyama, M. (1994). *Mindscapes in management: Use of individual differences in multicultural management*. Dartmouth Publishing Company.

Probst, G., & Gomez, P. (1992). Thinking in networks to avoid pitfalls of managerial thinking. In M. Maruyama (Ed.), *Context and complexity: Cultivating contextual understanding*. Springer-Verlag.

Rasmussen, J. (1986). *Information processing and human-machine interaction: An approach to cognitive engineering*. Amsterdam, North-Holland.

Rasmussen, J., & Jensen, A. (1974). Mental procedures in real life tasks: A case study of electronic troubleshooting. *Ergonomics*, *7*, 193–207.

Rasmussen, J., & Pejitersen, A. M. (1995). Virtual ecology of work. In J. Flach, LP. Hancock, J. Caird & K. Vicente (Eds.), *Global perspectives on the ecology of human-machine systems* (pp. 121-156).

Rasmussen, J., Pejtersen, A. M., & Goodstein, L. P. (1994). *Cognitive systems engineering*. John Wiley and Sons.

Reed, J. (2007). *Appreciative inquiry: Research for change*. Sage publications.

Saito, M., Ikeda, M., & Seki, H. (2000). A study on adaptive action development: Interference of mood states with perceived performance and perceived efficacy. In *Proceedings of the 14th International Congress of Ergonomics*, San Diego (Vol. 5, pp. 48-51).

Saito, M., Inoue, T., & Seki, H. (2005). Organizational control mode, cognitive activity, and performance reliability. In N. Wickramasinghe, J. N. D. Gupta & S. K. Sharma (Eds.), *Creating knowledge-based healthcare organization* (pp. 179-192). Hershey, PA: Idea Group Publishing.

Saito, M., Murakami, G., & Karashima, M. (2007). Effect of communication and emotional types on team reciprocity in healthcare organization. *International Journal of Healthcare Technology and Management*, *8*(3/4), 196–208. doi:10.1504/IJHTM.2007.013160

Schwaninger, M. (1996). Enabling systemic management. In R. Espejo, W. Schumann, M. Shwaninger & U. Bilello (Eds.), *In organizational transformation and learning: A cybernetic approach to management* (pp. 227-270). John Wiley and Sons.

Schwaninger, M. (2000). Managing complexity: The path toward intelligent organization. *Systemic Practice and Action Research, 13*(2), 207–241. doi:10.1023/A:1009546721353

Schwaninger, M. (2006). *Intelligent organizations: Powerful models for systemic management.* Springer.

Sheffi, Y. (2007). *The resilient enterprise: Overcoming vulnerability for competitive advantage.* MIT Press.

Simon, H. A. (1969). *The sciences of the artificial.* Cambridge, MA: MIT Press.

Thatchenkery, T., & Chowdhry, D. (2007). *Appreciative inquiry and knowledge management: A social constructionist perspective.* Edward Elgar.

Todorova, G., & Durisin, B. (2007). Absorbing capacity: Valuing a reconceptualization. *Academy of Management Review, 32*(3), 774–786.

Tsai, W. (2001). Knowledge transfer in intraorganizational networks: Effects of network position and absorptive capacity on business unit innovation and performance. *Academy of Management Journal, 44*(5), 996–1004. doi:10.2307/3069443

Vickers, G. (1965). *The art of judgment.* New York: Basic Books.

Vickers, G. (1983). *Human systems are different.* London: Harper & Row.

von Bertalanffy, L. (1968). *General systems theory.* New York: Braziller.

Chapter 7
The Intelligence Continuum and Emergency and Disaster Scenarios

Nilmini Wickramasinghe
Illinois Institute of Technology, USA

ABSTRACT

Application of germane knowledge and pertinent information is always important; however, it is imperative in emergency and disaster situations where a few seconds lost reading irrelevant data can translate into loss of life. To address the issue, this chapter discusses the intelligence continuum, which ensures the systematic and appropriate application of the critical tools, techniques, technologies, and tactics of knowledge management (KM) to ensure that only relevant knowledge is used at all times.

INTRODUCTION

Recently, the world has witnessed several large scale natural disasters, the Tsunami that devastated many of the countries around the rim of the Indian Ocean in December 2004, extensive flooding in many parts of Europe in August 2005 and hurricane Katrina in September 2005 and the earthquakes in Pakistan. These emergency and disaster situations (E&DS) serve to underscore the utter chaos that ensues in the aftermath of such disasters, the many casualties and loss of life not

DOI: 10.4018/978-1-60566-284-8.ch007

to mention the devastation and destruction that is left behind. One recurring theme that is apparent in all these situations is that irrespective of warnings of the eminent threats, countries have not been prepared and ready to exhibit effective and efficient crisis management. This chapter examines the application of the tools, techniques and technologies of the knowledge economy to develop a prescriptive model that will support superior decision making in E&DS and thereby enable effective and efficient crisis management. A critical and common theme for effecting any and all appropriate crisis management is to quickly extract pertinent and useful data which is by nature multi-spectral and residing in various and often disparate locations, analyze these data in aggregate to develop a complete picture in order to support superior decisions. To do this effectively and efficiently it is imperative to embrace the tools, techniques and processes of the knowledge economy in general (Wickramasinghe, 2006; Wickramasinghe and Schaffer, 2006; Liebowittz, 1999; Shapiro and Verian, 1999; Zack, 1999; Wilcox, 1997; Wigg, 1993) and more specifically the intelligence continuum.

DESCRIPTION OF MODEL

The Intelligence Continuum consists of a collection of key tools, techniques and processes of the knowledge economy; i.e. including data mining, business intelligence/analytics and knowledge management which are applied to a generic system of people, process and technology in a systematic and ordered fashion (Wickramasinghe and Schaffer, 2006). Taken together, they represent a powerful instrument for refining the raw data material stored in data marts and/or data warehouses and thereby maximizing the value and utility of these data assets. As depicted in Figure 1 the intelligence continuum is applied to the output of the generic information system. Once applied, the results become part of the data set that are reintroduced into the system and combined with the other inputs of people, processes, and technology to develop an improvement continuum. Thus, the intelligence continuum includes the generation of data, the analysis of these data to provide a "diagnosis" and the reintroduction into the cycle as a "prescriptive" solution.

The key capabilities and power of the model are in analyzing large volumes of disparate, multi-spectral data so that superior decision making can ensue. This is achieved through the incorporation of the various intelligence tools and techniques which taken together make it possible to analyze all data elements in aggregate. Currently, most analysis of data is applied to single data sets and uses at most two of these techniques (Wickramasinghe, 2006; Wickramasinghe and Schaffer, 2006; Newell et al., 2002; Schultze and Leidner, 2002; Nonaka and Nishiguchi, 2001; Nonaka, 1994). Thus, there are neither the power nor the capabilities to analyze

Figure 1. Intelligence Continum (adapted from Wickramasinghe & Schaffer, 2006)

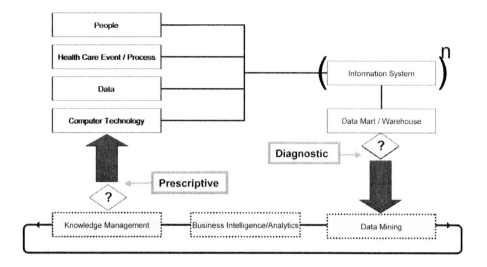

large volumes of multi-spectral data [ibid]. Moreover the interaction with domain experts is typically non-existent, in current methods. Applying these capabilities then to E&DS scenarios the benefits of the intelligence continuum model are profound indeed. E&DS scenarios are concomitant with complex, unstable and unpredictable environments where the unknown or position of information inferiority prevails. Hence, these scenarios are chaotic, and typically sub-optimal decision making results. In contrast, the tools and techniques of the intelligence continuum can serve to transform the situation of information inferiority to one of information superiority in real time through the effective and efficient processing of disparate, diverse and seemingly unrelated data. This will then enable decision makers to make superior decisions and chaos will be lessened and order restored.

DATA MINING

Due to the immense size of the data sets, computerized techniques are essential to help decision makers understand relationships and associations between data elements. Data mining is closely associated with databases and shares some common ground with statistics since both strive toward discovering structure in data. However, while statistical analysis starts with some kind of hypothesis about the data, data mining does not. Furthermore, data mining is much more suited to deal with heterogeneous databases, data sets and data fields, which are typical of data in E&DS that contain numerous types of text and graphical data sets. Data mining also draws heavily from many other disciplines, most notably machine learning, artificial intelligence, and database technology.

From a micro perspective, data mining is a vital step in the broader context of the knowledge discovery in databases (KDD) that transforms data into knowledge by identifying valid, novel, potentially useful, and ultimately understandable patterns in data (Bendoly, 2003; Cabena et al., 1998; Adriaans and Zantinge, 1996; Fayyad et al., 1996) KDD plays an important role in data-driven decision support systems that include query tools, report generators, statistical analysis tools, data warehousing, and on-line analytic processing (OLAP). Data mining algorithms are used on data sets for model building, or for finding patterns and relationships in data. How to manage such newly discovered knowledge, as well as other organizational knowledge assets, is the realm of knowledge management.

STEPS IN DATA MINING

The following steps are typically undertaken in data mining (Choi and Lee, 2003; Holsapple and Joshi, 2002; Becerra-Fernandez and Sabherwal, 2001; Fayyad et al., 1996). These steps are iterative, with the process moving backward whenever it is required to do so.

1. Develop an understanding of the application, of the relevant prior knowledge, and of the end user's goals.
2. Create a target data set to be used for discovery.
3. Clean and preprocess the data (including handling missing data fields, noise in the data, accounting for time series, and known changes).
4. Reduce the number of variables and find invariant representations of the data if possible.
5. Choose the data-mining task (classification, regression, clustering, etc.).
6. Choose the data-mining algorithm.
7. Search for patterns of interest (this is the actual data mining).
8. Interpret the patterns mined. If necessary, iterate through any of steps 1 through 7.
9. Consolidate the knowledge discovered, prepare reports and then use/re-use the newly created knowledge.

A data mining project usually starts with data collection or data selection, covering almost all steps (described above) in the KDD process. In this respect, the first three steps of the KDD process (i.e., selection, preprocessing and transformation) are considered exploratory data mining, whereas the last two steps (i.e., data mining and interpretation/evaluation) in the KDD process are considered predictive data mining. The primary objectives of data mining in practice tend to be description (performed by exploratory data mining) and prediction (performed by predictive data mining). Description focuses on finding human-interpretable patterns describing the data while prediction involves using some observations and attributes to predict unknown or future values of other attributes of interest. The relative importance of description and prediction for particular data mining applications can vary considerably. The descriptive and predictive tasks are carried out by applying different machine learning, artificial intelligence, and statistical algorithms.

A major goal of exploratory data mining is data cleaning, unification and understanding. Some of the data operations undertaken during exploratory data mining include: sampling, partitioning, charting, graphing, associating, clustering, transforming, filtering, and imputing. Predictive data mining deals with future values of variables and utilizes many algorithms; including regression, decision trees, and neural networks. Predictive data mining also involves an assessment step, which compares the effectiveness of different models according to many performance metrics.

Data mining then, is the non-trivial process of identifying valid, novel, potentially useful, and ultimately understandable patterns from data (Fayyad et al., 1996). It is essential to emphasize here the importance of the interaction with experts who always play a crucial and indispensable role in any knowledge discovery process in facilitating prediction of key patterns and also identification of new patterns and trends.

BUSINESS INTELLIGENCE/ANALYTICS

Another technology-driven technique, like data mining connected to knowledge creation is the area of business intelligence and the now newer term of business analytics. The business intelligence (BI) term has become synonymous with an umbrella description for a wide range of decision-support tools, some of which target specific user audiences (Wickramasinghe, 2006; Wickramasinghe and Schaffer, 2006). At the bottom of the BI hierarchy are extraction and formatting tools which are also known as data-extraction tools (refer to Figure 2). These tools collect data from existing databases for inclusion in data warehouses and data marts. Thus the next level of the BI hierarchy is known as warehouses and marts. Because the data come from so many different, often incompatible systems in various file formats, the next step in the BI hierarchy is formatting tools, these tools and techniques are used to "cleanse" the data and convert it to formats that can easily be understood in the data warehouse or data mart. Next, tools are needed to support the reporting and analytical techniques. These are known as enterprise reporting and analytical tools. OLAP (on-line analytic process) engines and analytical application-development tools are for professionals who analyze data and do, for example business forecasting, modeling, and trend analysis. Human intelligence tools form the next level in the hierarchy and involve human expertise, opinions, and observations to be recorded to create a knowledge repository. These tools are at the very top of the BI hierarchy and serve to amalgamate analytical and BI capabilities along with human expertise. Business analytics (BA) is a newer term that tends to be viewed as a sub-set of the broader business intelligence umbrella and concentrates on the analytic aspects within BI by focusing on the simultaneous analysis of patterns and trends in a given context (Wickramasinghe and Schaffer, 2006).

KNOWLEDGE MANAGEMENT

Knowledge management is an emerging management approach that is aimed at solving the current business challenges to increase efficiency and efficacy of core business processes while simultaneously incorporating continuous innovation. Specifically, knowledge management through the use of various tools, processes and techniques combines germane organizational data, information and knowledge to create business value and enable an organization to capitalize on its intangible and human assets so that it can effectively achieve its primary business goals as well as maximize its core business competencies (Wickramasinghe, 2006; Liebowitz, 1999; Shapiro and Verian, 1999; Zack, 1999; Wilcox, 1997; Wigg, 1993). Broadly speaking, knowledge management involves four key steps of creating/generating knowledge, representing/storing knowledge, accessing/using/re-using knowledge, and disseminating/transferring knowledge (Wickramasinghe, 2006).

From Figure 3 it is important to notice that these steps are all interrelated, continuous and impact each other and the knowledge itself throughout the organization.

Knowledge Management (KM), as has already been addressed in more detail in preceeding chapters, as a discipline is said not to have a commonly accepted or de facto definition. However, some common ground has been established which covers the following points. KM is a multi-disciplinary paradigm (Gupta, Iyer and Aronson, 2000) which often uses technology to support the acquisition, generation, codification and transfer of knowledge in the context of specific organisational processes. Knowledge can either be tacit or explicit (explicit knowledge typically takes the form of company documents and is easily available, whilst tacit knowledge is subjective and cognitive). As tacit knowledge is often stored in the minds of healthcare

Figure 2. Key business intelligence techniques (source: Wickramasinghe & von Lubitz, 2007)

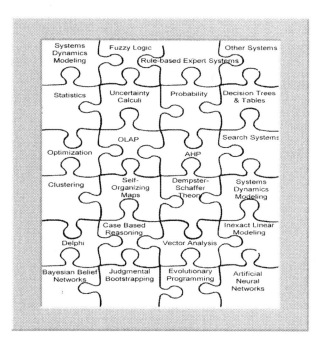

Figure 3. The four key steps of knowledge management (source: Wickramasinghe, 2005)

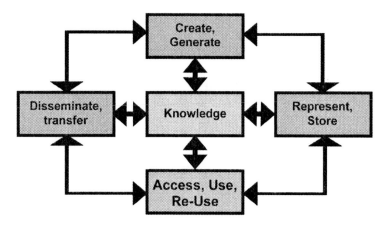

professionals, the ultimate objective of KM is to transform tacit knowledge into explicit knowledge to allow effective dissemination (Bali, 2005). In addition, KM initiatives should be incorporated in conjunction with the technological revolution that is occurring within healthcare organizations. A balance is required between organizational and technological aspects of the healthcare process (Dwivedi et al, 2001a). Moreover, KM can enable the healthcare sector (including professions allied to disaster management) to successfully overcome the information and knowledge explosion by way of appropriate frameworks customized for healthcare institutions (Dwivedi et al, 2001b; Dwivedi et al, 2002a). This becomes particularly pertinent in E&DS scenarios.

Mechanisms have been suggested (Levi et al, 2002) to retain the knowledge invested in the preparedness of Mass Casualty Situations (MCS). Effective disaster management needs to link data collection and analysis to the decision-making process. Knowledge of the epidemiology of deaths, injuries, and illnesses is essential to determine effective responses and to provide clear public education. Additionally, the temporal patterns for the medical care required must be established so that the needs in future disasters can be anticipated (Noji, 2000), thereby ensuring a better state of preparedness and readiness.

It is useful to distinguish preparedness; the availability of all resources, both human and physical, necessary for the management of, or the consequences of, a specific event, from readiness; which is defined as instantaneous ability to respond to a suddenly arising crisis or event in the external environment (Wickramasinghe and von Lubitz, 2007). Hence, preparedness is based on the anticipation of the occurrence of an event, in contrast to readiness, which is based solely on the immediate capability to contain the crisis through the initiation of correct response to the event. In relation to KM, both a heightened state of preparedness and readiness require KM and more especially benefit from enacting the IC.

USING THE IC TO SUPPORT PREPAREDNESS AND READINESS

Hierarchically, gathering of information precedes transformation of information into useable knowledge (Massey et al., 2002; Alavi and Leidner, 1999). Hence, the rate of information collection and the quality of the collected information will have a major impact on the quality (usefulness) of the generated knowledge (Award and Ghaziri, 2004).

As stated, being prepared means having the necessary resources in anticipation of a particular event. The IC model in Figure 1 facilitates this because it enables us to analyze prior occurrences and utilize the extant knowledge base as illustrated

Figure 4. Iterative power of IC model

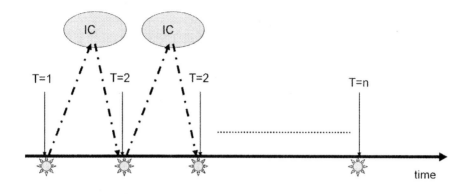

in Figure 4. Thus after the event at T=1 it is necessary to gather and analyse the multi-spectral data, by applying the various BI/BA techniques, data mining techniques and KM techniques in turn and as required. From this it will be possible to prescribe the key resources ie appropriate human and non-human inputs to content with the event occurring at time T=2 (Figure 4). In this way the extant knowledge base of the current state is built upon to contend with the event in the future state, or next time period which will always ensure that the future state is more prepared and capitalizing on knowledge and lessons learnt from the previous time period as depicted in Figure 5.

In contrast to preparedness, readiness requires the application of the lessons learnt from the previous time period to be used to facilitate better and faster orientation during the unexpected/crisis event so that more effective and efficient utilization of resources occurs. Once again the IC model is the key in facilitating the identification of the key lessons learnt.

CRITICAL ISSUES IN E&DS

To understand the power of using the IC model in E&DS it is useful to analyse critical issues when hurricanes Katrina and Rita hit the US. At the time even though there was significant warning of the imminent danger and consequent problems New Orleans was neither prepared nor ready. Why was this? In terms of preparedness: a large part of this is due to the fact that data and information about the impending event were scattered across multiple sources and were at times conflicting. Hence, it was difficult to decipher fact from irrelevant and erroneous data and information and therefore it was not possible to plan a satisfactory state of preparedness. How

Figure 5. Continuous application of IC

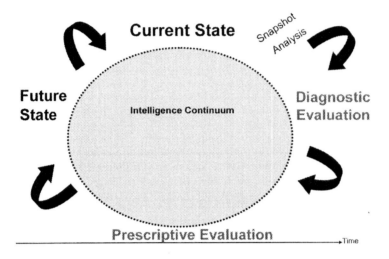

might the IC model help? The utilization of the IC model in such a scenario would facilitate the timely and rigorous analysis of multi-spectral data and information. This would enable pertinent information and germane knowledge to be extracted and thereby be used to facilitate effective decision making in the development of an appropriate state of preparedness. If such a state was achieved before hurricane Katrina hit, when hurricane Rita hit shortly after it would have been a relatively simple task to update the strategies and protocols for effecting appropriate consequence management at this time.

In terms or readiness: once again the IC model would have been tremendously beneficial. By analyzing data from past E&DS scenarios using the tools and techniques of the IC model it would then be possible to develop appropriate training strategies for key people including hospital staff and police. In this way, the casualties after the striking of the hurricane could have been lessened considerably and much of the chaos that arose calmed. After the experience of hurricane Katrina critical lessons learnt during the effecting of consequence management would then also be available to facilitate superior consequence management when hurricane Rita hit. In this way as depicted in Figure 5 the future state builds on the extant knowledge base of the current state.

Most importantly in E&DS scenarios time is critical. The timely execution of effective decision making saves many lives, reduces chaos and panic and facilitates effective consequence management. The IC by enabling the systematic and powerful application of sophisticated techniques to large amounts of normally disparate data and information serves to support the extraction of critical knowledge that is vital for decision making most especially in E&DS scenarios.

CONCLUSION

Sound emergency management requires the ability to (Alexander, 2004; 2002; Marincioni, 2001):-

1. Focus on solvable problems
2. Prioritise the elements of a problem in terms of how much progress can be achieved with each element in a small amount of time
3. delegate responsibility
4. Manage the "span of control"
5. Communicate clearly and rationally
6. Keep a level head in a crisis
7. Make sound decisions

However, when we analyze the recent natural disasters a common recurring and unfortunate situation is that countries and regions are never as prepared and ready for the imminent disaster as they could perhaps have been. It is too late once the disaster strikes to have an organized and systematic fashion for contending with the aftermath. We believe that the intelligence continuum model can be applied to existing and disparate data elements from past disasters to build a predictive model that can facilitate the development of sound procedures and protocols which in turn would then facilitate preparedness and readiness a priori so that ex ante operations can in fact be more effective and efficient, decision making superior and order would replace much of the chaos.

REFERENCES

Adriaans, P., & Zantinge, D. (1996). *Data mining.* Addison-Wesley.

Alavi, M., & Leidner, D. (1999). Knowledge management systems: Issues, challenges, and benefits. *Communications of the Association for Information Systems, 1,* paper no. 5.

Alberts, D. S., Garstka, J. J., & Stein, F. P. (2000). N*etwork centric wardare: Developing and leveraging information superiority* (pp. 1-284). CCRP Publication Series. Washington, D.C: Department of Defense. Retrieved from http://www.dodccrp.org/publications/pdf/Alberts_NCW.pdf

Alexander, D. (2002). *Principles of emergency planning and management.* London: Terra Publishings.

Alexander, D. (2004). Cognitive mapping as an emergency management training exercise. *Journal of Contingencies and Crisis Management, 12,* 150–159. doi:10.1111/j.0966-0879.2004.00445.x

Award, E., & Ghaziri, H. (2004). *Knowledge management.* Upper Saddle River, NJ: Prentice Hall.

Bali, R. K. (Ed.). (2005). *Clinical knowledge management: Opportunities and challenges.* USA: IGP.

Becerra-Fernandez, I., & Sabherwal, R. (2001). Organizational knowledge management: A contingency perspective. *Journal of Management Information Systems, 18*(1), 23–55.

Bendoly, E. (2003). Theory and support for process frameworks of knowledge discovery and data mining from ERP systems. *Information & Management, 40,* 639–647. doi:10.1016/S0378-7206(02)00093-9

Boyd, J. R. (1976). Destruction and creation. In R. Coram (Ed.), *Boyd.* New York: Little, Brown & Co.

Boyd, J. R. (1987). In *Patterns of conflict.* Unpublished briefing (accessible as "Essence of Winning and Losing," http://www.d-n-i.net).

Brown, J. S., & Duguid, P. (2002). *The social life of information* (pp. IX-328). Boston: Harvard Business School Press.

Cabena, P., Hadjinian, P., Stadler, R., Verhees, J., & Zanasi, A. (1998). *Discovering data mining from concept to implementation.* Prentice Hall.

Cebrowski, A. K., & Garstka, J. J. (1998). Network-centric warfare: Its origin and future. *U.S. Nav. Inst. Proc., 1,* 28–35.

Choi, B., & Lee, H. (2003). An empirical investigation of KM styles and their effect on corporate performance. *Information & Management, 40,* 403–417. doi:10.1016/S0378-7206(02)00060-5

Chung, M., & Gray, P. (1996). Special section: Data mining. *Journal of Management Information Systems, 16*(1), 11–16.

Courtney, J. (2001). Decision making and knowledge management in inquiring organizations: Toward a new decision-making paradigm for DSS. *Decision Support Systems, Special Issue on Knowledge Management, 31*, 17–38.

Drucker, P. (1993). *Post-capitalist society.* New York: Harper Collins.

Dwivedi, A., Bali, R. K., James, A. E., & Naguib, R. N. G. (2001a). Telehealth systems, considering knowledge management and ICT issues. In *Proc of the IEEE-EMBC 23ʳᵈ Annual International Conference of the IEEE Engineering in Medicine and Biology Society (EMBS)*, [CD-ROM], Istanbul, Turkey.

Dwivedi, A., Bali, R. K., James, A. E., & Naguib, R. N. G. (2001b). Workflow management systems, the healthcare technology of the future? [*Annual International Conference of the IEEE Engineering in Medicine and Biology Society*]/[*EMBS*], [CD-ROM] [Istanbul, Turkey.]. *Proceedings of the IEEE, EMBC-2001*, 23.

Dwivedi, A., Bali, R. K., James, A. E., & Naguib, R. N. G. (2002a). The efficacy of using object oriented technologies to build collaborative applications. In *Healthcare and Medical Information Systems, Proc of the IEEE Canadian Conference on Electrical and Computer Engineering (CCECE) 2002*, Winnipeg, Canada (Vol. 2, pp. 1188-1193).

Fayyad, U., Piatetsky-Shapiro, G., & Smyth, P. (1996). From data mining to knowledge discovery: An overview. In U. Fayyad, G. Piatetsky-Shapiro, P. Smyth & R. Uthurusamy (Eds.), *Advances in knowledge discovery and data mining.* Menlo Park, CA: AAAI Press/The MIT Press.

Gupta, B., Iyer, L. S., & Aronson, J. E. (2000). Knowledge management: Practices and Challenges. *Industrial Management & Data Systems, 100*(1), 17–21. doi:10.1108/02635570010273018

Holsapple, C., & Joshi, K. (2002). Knowledge manipulation activities: Results of a Delphi study. *Information & Management, 39*, 477–479. doi:10.1016/S0378-7206(01)00109-4

Levi, L., Michaelson, M., Admi, H., Bregman, D., & Bar-Nahor, R. (2002). National strategy for mass casualty situations and its effects on the hospital. *Prehospital and Disaster Medicine, 17*(1), 12–16.

Liebowittz, J. (1999). *Knowledge management handbook.* London: CRC Press.

Maier, R., & Lehner, F. (2000). Perspectives on knowledge management systems theoretical framework and design of an empirical study. In *Proceedings of 8ᵗʰ European Conference on Information Systems (ECIS)*.

Marincioni, F. (2001). A cross-culture analysis of natural disaster response: The northwest Italy floods of 1994 compared to the U.S. midwest floods 1993. *International Journal of Mass Emergencies and Disasters, 19*(2), 209–236.

Massey, A., Montoya-Weiss, M., & O'Driscoll, T. (2002). Knowledge management in pursuit of performance: Insights from Nortel Networks. *MIS Quarterly, 26*(3), 269–289. doi:10.2307/4132333

Newell, S., Robertson, M., Scarbrough, H., & Swan, J. (2002). *Managing knowledge work.* New York: Palgrave.

Noji, E. K. (2000). The public health consequences of disasters. *Prehospital and Disaster Medicine, 15*(4), 147–157.

Nonaka, I. (1994). A dynamic theory of organizational knowledge creation. *Organization Science, 5*, 14–37. doi:10.1287/orsc.5.1.14

Nonaka, I., & Nishiguchi, T. (2001). *Knowledge emergence.* Oxford: Oxford University Press.

Schultze, U., & Leidner, D. (2002). Studying knowledge management in information systems research: Discourses and theoretical assumptions. *MIS Quarterly, 26*(3), 213–242. doi:10.2307/4132331

Shapiro, C., & Verian, H. (1999). *Information rules.* Boston: Harvard Business School Press.

Shin, M. (2004). A framework for evaluating economies of knowledge management systems. *Information & Management, 42*(1), 179–196.

von Lubitz, D., Carrasco, B., Fausone, C., Gabbrielli, F., Kirk, J., Lary, M., & Levine, H. (2005). Bioterrorism, medical readiness, and distributed simulation training of first responders. In J. Johnson, M. Cwiek & G. Ludlow (Eds.), *Community and response to terrorism (vol. II): A community of organizations: Responsibilities and collaboration among all sectors of society* (pp. 267-312). Westport, CT: Praeger (Greenwood Publ. Group).

von Lubitz, D., & Wickramasinghe, N. (2006a). Healthcare and technology: The doctrine of network-centric healthcare. *International Journal of Electronic Healthcare, 4*, 322–344.

von Lubitz, D., & Wickramasinghe, N. (2006b). Dynamic leadership in unstable and unpredictable environments. *Intl. J. Innovation Learning, 4*, 339–350.

Wickramasinghe, N. (2005). A holistic approach to knowledge management. In D. Schwarz (Ed.), *Encyclopaedia of knowledge management.* Hershey, PA: Idea Group.

Wickramasinghe, N. (2006). Knowledge creation: A metaframework. *International J. Innovation and Learning, 3*(5), 558–573.

Wickramasinghe, N., & von Lubitz, D. (2007). *Knowledge-based organizations: Theories and fundamentals.* Hershey, PA: IGI Global.

Wickramasinghe, N., & Schaffer, J. (2006). Creating knowledge driven healthcare processes with the intelligence continuum. [IJEH]. *International Journal of Electronic Healthcare, 2*(2), 164–174.

Wigg, K. (1993). *Knowledge management foundations.* Arlington: Schema Press.

Wilcox, L. (1997). Knowledge-based systems as an integrating process. In J. Liebowitz & L. Wilcox (Eds.), *Knowledge management and its integrative elements.* New York: CRC Press.

Zack, M. (1999). *Knowledge and strategy.* Boston: Butterworth Heinemann.

Chapter 8

Evaluation of Human Action
Foucault's Power/ Knowledge Corollary

Nilmini Wickramasinghe
Illinois Institute of Technology, USA

ABSTRACT

The people dynamic is especially significant when trying to understand knowledge management. One aspect of interactions between groups of people is the impact of knowledge, be it a gain or a lack of knowledge. The work of Michael Foucault addresses this in his thesis on power/knowledge. By analyzing traditional theories and introducing Foucault's power/knowledge ideas, the following provides some insights into the actions and interactions of people within organizational settings.

INTRODUCTION

In today's knowledge economy, innovating organizations are challenged to maximize a critically important asset -- their human capital. The interaction of knowledge workers with information and communication technologies (ICTs) has presented a particularly interesting dynamic to researchers who study changes in related behavioral phenomena. One such phenomenon is self-monitoring. The following serves to outline the economics of self-monitoring and the integral role of ICTs in enabling knowledge workers to self-monitor. By merging Foucault's power/knowledge ideas

DOI: 10.4018/978-1-60566-284-8.ch008

with classical agency theory, it becomes possible to gain a richer understanding of human capital dynamics in a knowledge economy.

DYNAMICS OF SELF-MONITORING

Self-monitoring activities have been examined from psycho-cognitive perspectives (Mehra et al., 2001; Kilduff and Day, 1994; Caldwell and O'Reilly, 1982) and from structuralist power/knowledge perspectives (Foucault, 1980; Poster, 1990; Coombs et al, 1992). Although these writings appear to take radically different views of self-monitoring phenomena, we find that they each address different but complementary issues that together shape a more holistic explanation of the self-monitoring activities we have observed.

ORGANIZATIONAL BEHAVIORS AND INCENTIVES

What is self-monitoring, and why do people do it? According to psychological theorists, the propensity to self-monitor is a personality trait that ranges from high to low. High self-monitors actively try to shape their social worlds by constructing public selves that they believe will affect the perceptions of others in socially-enhancing ways (Snyder and Gangestad, 1986). There is some evidence that they are correct in this belief. Researchers have linked self-monitoring activities to a range of workplace-related outcomes, including performance, leadership, information management and boundary spanning (Kilduff and Day, 1994; Zaccaro et al., 1991; Caldwell and O'Reilly, 1982). For high self-monitors the incentives are the rewards associated with career advancement, such as monetary compensation, higher organizational rank, and enhanced reputation within the organization, the industry and the wider social space. Therefore, to understand self-monitoring as a personality trait means that we must study how those traits form and how those traits influence identity-shaping behavior (Erikson, 1974; Winter et al., 1998).

However, structuralists and interactionists argue that social networks mediate the effects of self-monitoring (White, 1992; Goffman, 1959). Researchers have found that the effects of self-monitoring activities do depend on the social actor's position in the network, but that high-self monitors tend to occupy the central positions (Mehra et al., 2001). In earlier studies, high self-monitors were found to be particularly effective as boundary spanners, who benefit from self-monitoring by acting as go-betweens who are able to obtain information about resources and opportunities from a number of disconnected sources (Caldwell and O'Reilly, 1982).

While these studies have begun to examine the social networks of self-monitors, they have not systematically linked the use of ICTs to self-monitoring and network exchanges that affect career outcomes. Yet, within organizations, an increasing number of communications and interactions are aided by ICTs, which are generally provided and supported by the organization expressly for such purposes. One might hypothesize that high-self monitors would also use ICTs to greater effect. Extensive research work by Wickramaisnghe and Lamb (Wickramasinghe, 1999; Wickramasinghe and Lamb, 2002) suggests that effective self-monitoring *does* also depend on ICT availability and use; and that there *is* an economic effect of ICT-aided self-monitoring – not only to the individual, but also to the organization. In other words, ICTs facilitate self-monitoring behaviors that result in beneficial effects. Moreover, some ICT systems also allow the organization, department or group to self-monitor and profile itself, in ways that aggregate or reflect on individual activities (Lamb and Poster, 2003.)

Observations in healthcare organizations (Wickramasinghe, 1999; Wickramasinghe and Lamb, 2002; Wickramasinghe, 2007) and other recent studies (Bloomfield et al., 1997; Doolin, 2004), however, caution against an easy correlation between ICT-aided self-monitoring and desired outcomes. Among medical professionals, it is actually rather difficult to extract self-monitoring behaviors from organizational monitoring activities. As we will describe in detail in later sections, physicians act as managers, principals and practitioners within their healthcare organizations, and they actively participate in developing the monitoring controls that guide their own activities in complex ways. In healthcare settings, psycho-cognitive self-monitoring theories that center on the individual have limited explanatory capability. They can describe and predict small group behavior in terms of individual interactions, but they do not address the institutional and organizational questions that arise when self-monitoring and monitoring issues are confounded.

TECHNIQUES AND TECHNOLOGIES

Foucault (1977) offers another way to understand self-monitoring behavior: as surveillance. He claims that self-monitoring activities primarily serve the controlling principals of society, and only secondarily serve the self-monitoring individuals themselves. Techniques and technologies align individual goals with organizational goals, as prescribed in management control literature (Kelly, 1990; Keen, 1991).

Within regimes of disciplinary control (e.g. total institutions, such as the prison), Foucault describes how 'architectures' (like Bentham's Panopticon) can be designed to induce people, regardless of their personality traits, to monitor their own behavior in conformance to specific guidelines or norms. Central to this understanding is the idea that power/knowledge is a unit of operation that can be exercised to exert control over others through dividing practices, scientific classifications, and subjectification. "Power is not something that is acquired, seized or shared, something one holds onto or allows to slip away…" (Foucault, 1981 p. 94). Power is relational "…it becomes apparent when it is exercised … [and] is not associated with a particular institution, but with practices, techniques, and procedures" (Townley, 1993, p. 520). Similarly, knowledge does not exist in isolation as independent and detached; "[k]nowledge is the operation of discipline. It delineates an analytical space and … provides the basis for action and intervention" (Townley, 1993, p. 520). "It is not possible for power to be exercised without knowledge, it is impossible for knowledge not to engender power" (Foucault, 1980, p.52).

While Foucault's analyses draw examples from 18th and 19th century historical contexts to shape integrated concepts of power, knowledge and control (cf. Rabinow, 1984); contemporary historians, sociologists and philosophers have linked those concepts to current processes of organization (Poster, 1990; Deleuze, 1992; Bourdieu, 1992). Hierarchical organization is the classic example of a "dividing practice"; and when used in conjunction with "classification" schemes based on education, function, etc. these can structure organizational "architectures" (aka "technologies of normalization" or "technologies of domination") that enforce subjectification and control. From this view, organizational rules and professional norms are seen as social constraints that define the appropriate form of behavior in a specific context. Studies have shown that an individual will follow these guidelines even if it is not in his or her self-interest to do so (Bourdieu, 1992). Although plausible explanations of this behavior do not necessarily demand a Foucauldian perspective, these findings have been interpreted as evidence of "subjectification". The idea of subjectivity and the role of the individual are recurrent themes throughout Foucault's work. "From a Foucauldian perspective, the human subject is not "given" but produced …constituted through correlative elements of power and knowledge" (Townley, 1993, p. 522).

More importantly for this discussion, in the face of these processes of control, the individual is continually seeking techniques and strategies to increase or regain power/knowledge (Townley, 1993; Knights and Willmott, 1985). In terms of individual activity, subjectification involves three related practices with which individuals seek to shape their social worlds: self-understanding, self-observation (also understood as a form of surveillance that often involves computerized monitoring), and self-description (including many forms of computerized recording, profiling and tracking) (Knorr Cetina, 1999). By engaging in these activities, individuals are, ironically, complicit in their own control. Poster (1990, 1995, 2001) has further described the ways in which databases, intranets and other ICTs serve to augment this participatory surveillance and the associated discourses of power/knowledge. Taken altogether, these empirically based extensions of Foucault's theoretical work into contemporary settings have spawned assertions that ideas about an information society are better understood as concepts about "societies of control" (Deleuze, 1992).

Foucault believed that the economy of discourse in the exchange of knowledge constituted the manifestation of power in social settings. He also argued that the knowledge thus exchanged does not have to be the "truth", but be known as true by the people exchanging such discourse. Foucault also argued that there is no implicit need for "meaning" of what is exchanged. Power is exercised in social settings by discourse, namely, by intensive interaction among individuals in which there are exchanges of statements as knowledge, hence power. This can be extended to the notion of knowledge workers and their growing influence on current social settings.

Foucault had argued that people who have obtained power and are exercising it have what he believed to be "specialized knowledge". The strong link between power and knowledge is such that one in essence defines and creates the other. In this framework, knowledge workers are by definition harbingers of power—even if they don't necessarily know it. In Foucault's model there is a necessary implication for human action that suggests that what we know about a given topic is not only linked to action but also bound by it, in a form of "bounded rationality". For example, what we know about healthcare is predicated upon and bound by our actions within hospitals, and what we know about strategy is predicated upon and bound by the exercise of strategic power such as military power. This is also in line with John Kenneth Galbraith's assertion that global national strategy is predicated upon the range of military aircraft, so that if we know that a city of military base in a given country is within range of our military aircraft from our own bases, then our strategy extends to that country and so is our strategic power.

Human action is influenced, almost one might say dictated to by the knowledge one has, upon which the knowledge is predicated. Such knowledge, according to Foucault, does not have to be meaningful nor does it have to be true, as long as the one who received such knowledge receives it via discourse as true knowledge.

The extension of such a model also applies to healthcare delivery and healthcare policy. Many terms which apply in healthcare policy and which provide policy makers with a modicum of power in their social/economic setting are knowledge but not necessarily true or meaningful knowledge. Thus, there are certain terms which become "slogans" and which help in the discourse about healthcare delivery and healthcare policy. Terms such as "uninsured", "access and availability", and "quality healthcare delivery" or "best available medical technology" are such terms which in effect set the tone for the discourse.

Foucault has been criticized by many scholars, and for a variety of reasons. One was the issue of discourse and its use as the mainstay of knowledge exchange. Linguists such as Noam Chomsky had precise criticisms, whereas other philosophers argued that Foucault's model leads to rejection of the values of freedom and justice and may lead to exercise of power as a controlling device via the discourse of knowledge. Foucault himself defended his ideas by claiming that he is a strong supporter of the "human spirit" and of his freedoms.

KNOWLEDGE WORKERS

Within our changing society and its shifting organizational forms, a new type of employee has emerged: the knowledge worker. Unlike industrial age employees, these workers own their means of production; i.e., their knowledge; they possess specialized skills and training which they have acquired by investing significant personal resources in their education; and they are empowered to make decisions that have far reaching consequences for the organizations in which they work (Kelly, 1990; Drucker, 1999; Nonaka and Takeuchi, 1995).

Who are these people, and what do they do? In the business trade literature, "knowledge workers" are so broadly defined as to include almost anyone who deals with information or uses a computer during the course of a normal workday. In the context of innovating organisations, and for much of the academic literature we have cited, knowledge workers as healthcare practitioners, accountants, engineers, lawyers, scientists and other highly trained individuals.

Reich (1992) and Drucker (1999) have suggested that a different type of management style is required to adequately support the information use and knowledge production activities of these organization members. They emphasize that managed employees are changing 'from subordinates into fellow executives, and from employees, however well paid, into partners' (Drucker, 1999; p. 57). In fact, many of these workers are "professionals" who, in earlier times, might have been expected to conduct their business through an independent practice. However, as Heinz et al. (1998) have observed among law firms, professional practice has been increasingly rationalized and aligned with corporate efforts to control costs and time, and to standardize output.

Florida (2002) finds evidence that among knowledge workers there is a "creative" class whose innovative efforts demand even more flexible working conditions in the form of "soft control" and "self-management." From an organizational perspective, this means that management needs to find ways to encourage these workers to self-monitor. High self-monitors perform better for themselves and for the organization, but there are costs for such activity, which can be better appreciated when centrality in social networks is understood as a necessary part of effective self-monitoring (Mehra et al. 2001). ICTs can reduce interaction costs by eliminating (automating) some and by managing others in ways that expand the span of control (Blau et al., 1976); and ICT systems have been put forward in solutions to this problem of resource management in healthcare. "At one extreme, then, is the possibility of recasting the identity of doctors as quasi-managers, with budgets, responsibilities, and delegated powers over their professional colleagues. However, there is also the possibility of an alternative pattern in which the new management information generated by ICT systems is diffused into the peer-based professional discourse of doctors, in the belief that their practices will gradually evolve in directions consistent with the values of the architects of Resource Management. This could be seen as the encouragement of 'self-control' or 'auto-regulation'" (Coombs et al., 1992: 67).

AGENCY THEORY EXPLANATIONS

Despite the dystopian tendencies of Foucauldian explanations, they resonate with empirically supported characterizations of today's empowered knowledge worker; and they highlight the need to revisit these ideas with a socio-economic focus on the role for ICTs in self-monitoring. In an effort to synthesize the complementary aspects of psycho-cognitive and structural perspectives of self-monitoring, and to leverage the explanatory power of classic theory in current contexts, it is vital to explicitly include knowledge workers within agency theory's domain of agents.

Much of what is known about the economics of human resource management in industrial age organizations is distilled in the concepts of agency theory. Agency theory (Alchian & Demsetz, 1972; Jensen & Meckling, 1976; Ross, 1973; Wilson, 1968) is primarily concerned with the relationship between the principal (employer or purchaser of services) and the agent (employee or contractor) and the achievement of goal-aligned behavior. The principal requires certain specific tasks to be performed and hires agents to perform these tasks on his/her behalf. In doing so however, the principal needs to guard against sub-optimal behavior (or low goal-aligned behavior), namely, the divergence between the agent pursuing activities, which facilitate his/her own goals being achieved, in preference to the achievement of the principal's goals. In practice, the difficulties revolve around trying to get people to do exactly what they have been hired to do, and to do even more, but only when that activity furthers the goals of the principal, as well as their personal goals.

By engaging an agent to perform certain specific activities on his/her behalf, the principal must incur some costs, known as *agency costs*, which are made up of:

a. monitoring costs[1],
b. residual loss,
c. and decision information costs (Jensen and Meckling, 1976; 1992).

Monitoring costs result from the principal having to perform activities to check that the agent is performing his/her tasks appropriately (e.g. surveillance, activity tracking, and record keeping). Residual loss represents the cost to the principal of misaligned goals (e.g. doing the wrong thing right, or doing the right thing wrong.) Decision information costs are associated with the location of decision rights (e.g. longer chains of command and wider spans of control, incur greater communication costs).

Integral to agency theory as discussed by Wickramasinghe (1999; 2007) is the relationship between these *agency costs* and the achievement of a high level of *goal alignment*. Specifically, the theory says that as the monitoring costs (M) increase so does the level of goal alignment (GA) and hence the residual loss (RL) decreases. This concept reflects the understanding that agents who are watched more carefully, are more likely to do what the principal has hired them to do. This "watching" is costly (M↑), but it ensures higher goal alignment (GA↑) between the principal and his/her agents, which in turn is reflected by a lower residual loss (RL↓).

Figure 1 illustrates these relationships. Figure 2 shows the graphical representation of the impact of increasing a monitoring cost from M1 to M2; which is an increase in goal alignment from GA1 to GA2. Figure 2 shows that such an increase in goal alignment effects a corresponding decrease in residual loss; i.e., a change from RL1 to RL2.

Decision information costs reflect the distribution of power/knowledge among agents and principals. In order to make decisions, the principal requires localized information that the agent has acquired. The transference of this information from agent to principal incurs a cost. Specifically, agency theory states that the higher the decision information costs (DI), the higher the level of goal alignment (GA); and whenever goal alignment increases, residual losses decrease. Figure 3 illustrates graphically the direct relationship between decision information costs and goal alignment.

Agency theory assumes that all costs (monitoring costs, residual loss and decision information costs) are borne by the principal. Therefore, the principal must be judicious in implementing the right level of monitoring and in designing the most effective organizational structure, in order to achieve maximum goal alignment at minimum cost. But what if the principal could induce his/her agents to bear some of the monitoring costs themselves – that is, to self-monitor? Agency theory is mute on this point.

In fairness to agency theorists, traditional, industrial-age employees did not present much opportunity for principals to consider self-monitoring options. However, contemporary knowledge workers who are prevalent in innovating organizations are indeed very different in two important ways:

Figure 1. Monitoring costs, residual loss and goal alignment (adapted from Wick-ramasinghe, 1999)

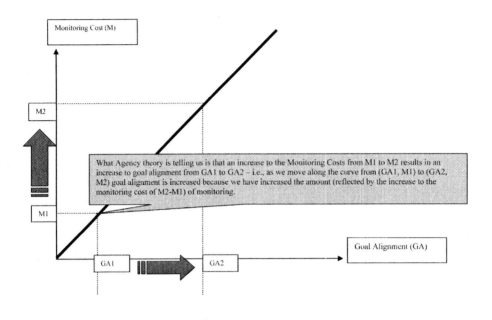

Figure 2. Residual loss (RL) vs. Goal alignment (GA)

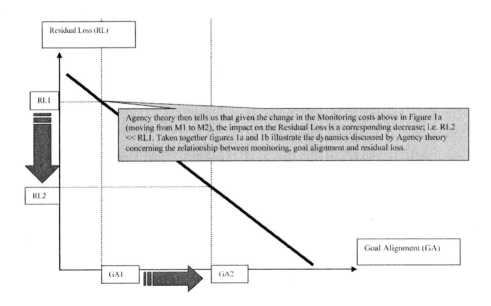

Figure 3. Decision information costs and goal alignment (adapted from source Wickramasinghe, 1999)

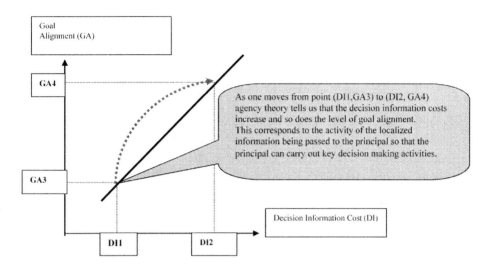

1.   Both critical knowledge and the decision right are co-located with the knowledge worker agent. This means that the principal has less control over agent activities, and therefore the potential for goal-aligned behavior is low.
2.   Most knowledge workers are guided by a specific professional code of behavior and/or ethics. This means that they are likely to align their own goals for career advancement with the goals of their profession, and to monitor their own behavior to maintain that goal alignment.

We know that high self-monitors perform better for themselves and for the organization, and that self-monitoring could have implications for principals if only researchers could determine what motivates high and low self-monitors (Mehra et al., 2001). Within organizations, however, getting agents to self-monitor may be more dependent on organizational architectures than on personality traits. "Self-monitoring orientation is a stable component of the individual's personality, but a stable personality trait can be expressed through a range of possible behaviors. In sociological research, individuals tend to take on the attributes and ideas of their associates rather than relying on their own inner beliefs and values (e.g. Carley, 1991.)" (Mehra et al., 200: 142).

FOUCAULT'S COROLLARY

To understand the implications of self-monitoring performed by knowledge workers and enabled through ICT use it is useful to consider physicians. The working context of the primary care physician (PCP) in today's US healthcare system bears little resemblance to the romanticized country doctor who operates independently in service to his or her local community. The organizational structures of the healthcare industry have reshaped the action of 21st century professionals in profound ways. Like other professionals in law and academia, physicians' roles have become increasingly rationalized by economic and quality concerns (Heinz et al., 1998). Moreover, given the current state of healthcare delivery in the US, healthcare organizations throughout the nation are embracing various types of ICTs (billing and practice management systems, PACS and/or automated medical record systems) in an attempt to provide cost effective quality healthcare. The PCP in such an environment is a knowledge worker agent, contracted or employed to provide healthcare services for a managed care principal organization. However, these knowledge worker agents differ significantly from the employee agent of classical agency theory – *their ICT-enhanced self-monitoring practices enable them to achieve even higher levels of alignment with a set of organizational goals that they continually refine through boundary spanning activities.*

This change in agency calls for a corresponding corollary to agency theory. Figure 4 (a, b and c) depicts the shift in economic dynamics as self-monitoring, enabled through ICT use, becomes part of agent behavior.

Various longitudinal studies conducted by Wickramasinghe and Lamb (Wickramasinghe, 1999; Wickramasinghe and Lamb, 2002; Wickramasinghe, 2007) clearly demonstrate that ICT-enabled monitoring and self-monitoring resulted in an increase in goal aligned behavior (GA↑). The impetus for this increase resides with the knowledge worker agent who, in addition to the principal, exercises decision rights. For instance, managed care organisations do not make treatment decisions, but sets guidelines to influence PCP decision makers. Because this knowledge worker agent has decision rights, the decision information (DI) costs of the principal are low and constant:

1. Low because little localized information or idiosyncratic knowledge is passed to the MCO pertaining to patient treatments; only information about treatments, costs and outcomes are relayed. The cost of passing this information is not a DI cost, rather a monitoring cost (M↑).
2. Constant because the PCP is continuously making these decisions and fine-tuning the goals of the principal. The PCP is a knowledge worker agent hired specifically to make such decisions.

Figure 4. Interaction of agency costs with goal alignment in the context of the Knowledge Worker Agent (adapted from Wickramasinghe, 1999)

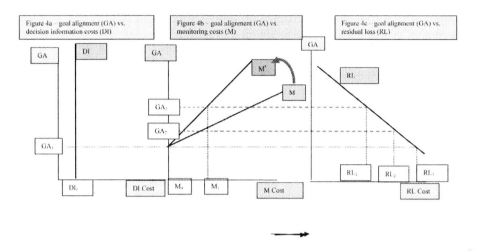

We illustrate this shift in Figure 5, where DI cost is at DI_1 and the DI cost curve is vertical. A vertical DI cost curve with a low DI cost intercept indicates that the knowledge worker agent, the PCP, possesses the decision rights and little localized information or idiosyncratic knowledge is being passed to the principal, the MCO. We can also see from this figure that the level of goal alignment is low at GA.

Once the principal has relinquished decision rights, it faces the problem of low goal alignment. Traditionally, this problem has been resolved through monitoring. ICTs are often designed and implemented to perform effective, efficient monitoring functions; with higher goal alignment as a direct and indirect result. This ICT impact, described in Figure 5, Scenario 3, rotates the monitoring cost curve in Figure 5 from M to M', resulting in higher goal alignment (GA↑), which in Figure 5 is reflected by lower residual loss (RL↓). In other words, the ICT-related increment in monitoring costs buys a larger increase in goal alignment *when it enables self-monitoring in the knowledge worker agent*. This effect is not by virtue of the enterprise-wide ICT in and of itself, but of the power/knowledge dynamic that it activates in the presence of knowledge worker agents.

Like other theories that appear to break down when applied to current scenarios, agency theory seems to meet its Waterloo in the case of healthcare knowledge workers with ICTs that have been implemented to facilitate better practice management. It does not adequately account for self-monitoring. By integrating Foucault's power/knowledge dynamic with classical agency theory, however, it becomes possible to explain not only the dynamics of self-monitoring, but also the benefits that accrue

Figure 5.

In the context of a knowledge worker agent the DI cost is fixed and low, DI1 (as in Figure 4a); thus agency theory tells us that the corresponding level of goal alignment will also be low, GA1. We then have the following possible scenarios depicted in figures 4b and 4c:

<u>Scenario 1</u>: no monitoring (i.e. base case) – Total cost (TC_1) = DI_1 +RL_1 +M_0 = TC_1 and GA_1

<u>Scenario 2</u>: monitoring w/o ICTs (i.e. the practices without the respective billing practice management systems)

$$Total\ cost\ (TC_2) = DI_1 + M_1 + RL_2 = TC_2\ and\ GA2 > GA1$$

<u>Scenario 3</u>: enterprise-wide ICTs (i.e. the practices with the respective billing/practice management systems)

$$Total\ cost\ (TC_3) = DI_1 + M_1 + RL_3 = TC_3\ and\ GA_3 \gg GA_2$$

Thus the impact of enterprise-wide ICTs enabling self monitoring is that $GA_3 \gg GA_2, GA_1$; $TC_3 \ll TC_2$, TC_1

Furthermore, the shift in the curve M to M' represents the role of self monitoring in effecting a higher level of goal alignment (GA_3). We can represent this mathematically by a change in the gradients between the two functions (M and M':
Gradient of curve $M = (GA_2 - GA_1)\ /\ (M_1 - M_0)$
Gradient of curve $M' = (GA_3 - GA_1)\ /\ (M_1 - M_0)$
$\rightarrow$Gradient (M') - Gradient (M) = *self monitoring cost* which is primarily borne by the knowledge worker agent

to principals and knowledge worker agents who effectively leverage self-monitoring activities.

We find some evidence that ICT-enhanced self-monitoring is a widely-practiced professional (and semi-professional) activity in a survey study conducted by Kirsch et al. (2002). Their research addressed control and management of information systems (IS) development projects, and the interactions between IS developers and their client organizations. The study described the ICT-enhanced self-monitoring behavior of IS developers, and results suggested that informal control is particularly salient for IS-client relationships. In particular, Kirsch et al. found that when IS developers could use ICTs to profile their own performance, they were more likely to self-monitor. Kirsch et al. identify this dynamic as the relationship between "outcome measurability" and "self control." A clear confirmation of the corollary to agency theory here can be seen, as well as strong quantitative support for our qualitative descriptions of self-monitoring activities: knowledge worker agents (i.e. IS developers) used available performance monitoring ICTs (M↑) to self-monitor; effecting a corresponding increase in goal alignment (GA↑). Interestingly, their results suggest that as behavior observability decreases, the use of self control increases; and as outcome measurability increases, the use of self control increases. In other words, "self-control will be exercised when behavior observability is low, or when outcome measurability is high" (Kirsch et al., 2002, p. 493.) This is further evidence of a power/knowledge dynamic in which the individual is continually seeking techniques and strategies to increase or regain power/knowledge, and of the effectiveness of ICT-enhanced self-monitoring to benefit not only the principal, but also the autonomy-seeking knowledge worker agent.

These findings, and recent publications (Doolin, 2004; Kohli and Kettinger, 2004), strongly indicate that ICT-enhanced self-monitoring can establish a win-win scenario for principals and knowledge worker agents, but only when boundary-spanners are able to negotiate the new order by adjusting organizational goals, ICT implementations, and/or outcome measures. For example, Doolin's (2004) study of a performance tracking casemix ICT system in a New Zealand hospital found that, while several senior doctors served as clinician managers, the system seemed to be gaining acceptance. When subsequent hospital reorganization eliminated the new boundary-spanning role of clinician manager, physician resistance relegated the casemix system to the relatively minor function of only measuring performance against contracts. In an action research study, Kohli and Kettinger (2004) took another tack. They studied two ICT system interventions at a midwest US hospital – both intended to increase physicians behavioral alignment with hospital cost and quality goals. Their first intervention was a decision support monitoring system, which *did* make physician behaviors more observable, but which *did not* gain acceptance among the physicians. In their second intervention, they engaged a physician leader as a boundary-spanner to help introduce a new interface to the physician profiling system and to lead physician discussions about the profile data. Two years later, improvements in cost and quality control attributed to system use indicated that the second intervention was a success, even though not all of the hospital physicians used it.

CONCLUSION

Given the growing dominance of knowledge workers in all organizations, and the importance of effective and efficient operations in today's highly competitive globalizing environments, the need for theories that provide better strategies for human capital management is increasing. We believe that a power/knowledge enrichment of classical agency theory addresses this need in a way that may prove beneficial to knowledge worker agents and organizational principals alike.

This synthesis of power/knowledge dynamics and agency theory economics invites a wide array of research approaches to further study – from special case studies to surveys to simulations – and points to some interesting topics for theoretic extension. An application of such a synthesis to case studies of ambient organizations that operate through networks of outsourced services would help to specify the micro-dynamics of agency in a knowledge economy. More detailed observation of the transitions that self-monitoring boundary-spanners are able to effect in their organizational settings would be similarly helpful – particularly if these are tied to surveys that link boundary-spanning and self-monitoring behaviors to structural support for ICT use and goal alignment outcomes (i.e. a combination of the approaches used by Kilduff and Day, 1994; and Kirsch et al., 2002.) What is particularly germane in the context of innovating organizations in a knowledge economy is that the behaviours of self-monitoring and boundary spanning are significant to the on going success and competitiveness of such organizations; hence, it is incumbent to foster and nurture such behavior.

REFERENCES

Alchian, A., & Demsetz, H. (1972). Production, information costs, and economic organisations. *American Economic Journal Review, 62*(5), 777–795.

Blau, P. M., & Flabe, C. M. (1976). Technology and organization in manufacturing. *Administrative Science Quarterly, 21*(1). doi:10.2307/2391876

Bloomfield, B. P., Coombs, R., Owen, J., & Taylor, P. (1997). Doctors as managers: Constructing systems and users in the national health service. In Bloomfield, et al. (Eds.), *Information technology and organizations: Strategies, networks, and integration* (pp. 112-134). Oxford: Oxford University Press.

Bourdieu, P. (1992). *The logic of practice*. Trans. Richard Nice, Stanford University Press.

Boyatzis, R. (1998). *Transforming qualitative information thematic analysis and code development*. Thousand Oaks, CA: Sage Publications.

Caldwell, D. F., & O'Reilly, C. A. (1982). Boundary spanning and individual performance: The impact of self-monitoring. *The Journal of Applied Psychology, 67*, 124–127. doi:10.1037/0021-9010.67.1.124

Carley, K. (1991). A theory of group stability. *American Sociological Review, 56*, 331–354. doi:10.2307/2096108

Carley, K. (2002). Computational organization science: A new frontier. In A. M. Sackler (Ed.), *Colloquium serices on adaptive agents, intelligence, and emergent human organization: Capturing complexity through agent-based modeling*, October 4-6, 2001, Irvine, CA (Vol. 99, suppl. 3, pp. 7257-7262). National Academy of Sciences Press.

Coombs, R., Knights, D., & Wilmott, H. C. (1992). Culture, control, and competition: Towards a conceptual framework for the study of information technology in organizations. *Organization Studies, 13*(1), 51–72. doi:10.1177/017084069201300106

Deleuze, G. (1992). Postscript on the societies of control. *October, (59)*, 3-7.

Doolin, B. (2004). Power and resistance in the implementation of a medical management information system. *Information Systems Journal, 14*, 343–362. doi:10.1111/j.1365-2575.2004.00176.x

Drucker, P. (1999). Beyond the information revolution. *Atlantic Monthly, 284*(4), 47–57.

Eisenhardt, K. (1989). Building theories from case study research. *Academy of Management Review, 14*, 532–550. doi:10.2307/258557

Erikson, E. H. (1974). *Dimensions of a new identity*. New York: Norton.

Florida, R. (2002). *The rise of the creative class: And how it's transforming work, leisure, community, and everyday life*. Basic Books.

Foucault, M. (1977). *Discipline and punish: The birth of the prison*. Penguin.

Foucault, M. (1980). *Power/knowledge: Selected interviews and other writings by Michael Foucault, (1972-77)*. G Brighton (Ed.). England: Harvester.

Foucault, M. (1981). *The history of sexuality: Vol. 1, the will to knowledge*. London: Penguin.

Goffman, E. (1959). *The presentation of self in everyday life*. New York: Doubleday.

Heinz, J. P., Laumann, E. O., Nelson, R. L., & Michelson, E. (1998). The changing character of lawyers' work: Chicago in 1975 and 1995. *Law & Society Review, 32*(4), 751–776. doi:10.2307/827738

Jensen, M., & Meckling, W. (1976). Theory of the firm: Managerial behaviour, agency costs, and ownership structure. *Journal of Financial Economics, 3*, 305–360. doi:10.1016/0304-405X(76)90026-X

Jensen, M., & Meckling, W. (1992). Specific and general knowledge, and organizational structure. In L. Werin & H. Wijkander (Eds.), *Contract economics* (pp. 251-291). Blackwell.

Keen, P. (1991). *Shaping the future business design through information technology.* Boston: Harvard Business School Press.

Kelly, R. (1990). Managing the new workforce. *Machine Design, 62*(9), 109–113.

Kilduff, M., & Day, D. (1994). Do chameleons get ahead? The effects of self-monitoring on managerial careers. *Academy of Management Journal, 37*, 1047–1060. doi:10.2307/256612

Kirsch, L. J., Sambamurthy, V., Ko, D.-G., & Purvis, R. L. (2002). Controlling information systems development projects: The view from the client. *Management Science, (48:4)*, 484–498.

Knorr-Cetina, K. (1999). *Epistemic cultures: How the sciences make knowledge.* Cambridge, MA: Harvard University Press.

Kohli, R., & Kettinger, W. J. (2004). Informating the clan: Controlling physicians' costs and outcomes. *MIS Quarterly, 28*(3), 363–394.

Lamb, R., & Poster, M. (2003). Transitioning toward an Internet culture: An interorganizational analysis of identity construction from online services to intranets. In E. H. Wynn, E. A. Whitley, M. D. Myers & J. I. DeGross (Eds.), *Global and organizational discourse about information and technology.* Boston: Kluwer Academic Publishers.

Mehra, A., Kilduff, M., & Bass, D. J. (2001). The social networks of high and low self-monitors: Implications for workplace performance. *Administrative Science Quarterly, 46*, 121–146. doi:10.2307/2667127

Miles, M. B., & Huberman, A. M. (1994). *An expanded sourcebook: Qualitative data analysis, second ed.* Thousand Oaks, CA: Sage Publications.

Nonaka, S., & Takeuchi, N. (1995). *The knowledge creating company.* New York: Oxford University Press.

Poster, M. (1990). *The mode of information: Poststructuralism and social context.* Chicago.

Poster, M. (1995). *The second media age.* Cambridge, MA: Polity Press.

Poster, M. (2001). *What's the matter with the Internet?* Minneapolis: University of Minnesota Press.

Rabinow, P. (Ed.). (1984). *The Foucault reader*. New York: Pantheon Books.

Reich, R. B. (1992). *The work of nations: Preparing ourselves for 21ˢᵗ century capitalism*. Random House.

Ross, S. (1973). The economic theory of agency: The principal's problem. *American Journal of Economic Review, 2*, 134–139.

Simons, R. (1995). *Levers of control*. Boston: Harvard Business School Press.

Snyder, M., & Gangestad, S. (1986). On the nature of self-monitoring: Matters of assessment, matters of validity. *Journal of Personality and Social Psychology, 51*, 125–139. doi:10.1037/0022-3514.51.1.125

Strauss, A., & Corbin, J. (1990). *Basics of qualitative research: Grounded theory procedures and techniques*. Newbury Park, CA: Sage Publications.

Townley, B. (1993). Foucault, power/knowledge, and its relevance for human resource management. *Academy of Management Review, 18*(3), 518–545. doi:10.2307/258907

White, H. C. (1992). *Identity and control*. Princeton, NJ: Princeton University Press.

Wickramasinghe, N. (1999). *IS/IT as a tool to achieve goal alignment in the context of the knowledge worker in the healthcare industry*. Unpublished doctoral dissertation, Case Western Reserve University.

Wickramasinghe, N. (2007). Achieving goal alignment with healthcare knowledge workers through ICT use. Melbourne: Heidelberg Press.

Wickramasinghe, N., & Lamb, R. (2002). Enterprisewide systems enabling physicians to manage care. *International Journal of Healthcare Technology and Management, 4*(3/4). doi:10.1504/IJHTM.2002.001144

Wickramasinghe, N., & Lamb, R. (2002). Managing managed care: The enabling role of IS/IT. *Journal of Management in Medicine, 16*(2/3). doi:10.1108/02689230210434961

Wilson, R. (1968). The theory of syndicates. *Econometerica, 36*, 119–132. doi:10.2307/1909607

Winter, D. G., John, O. P., Stewart, A. J., Klohnen, E. C., & Duncan, L. E. (1998). Traits and motives: Toward an integration of two traditions in personality research. *Psychological Review, 105*(2), 230–250. doi:10.1037/0033-295X.105.2.230

Zaccaro, S. J., Foti, R. J., & Kenny, D. A. (1991). Self-monitoring and trait-based variance in leadership: An investigation of leader flexibility across multiple group situations. *The Journal of Applied Psychology, 76*, 308–315. doi:10.1037/0021-9010.76.2.308

ENDNOTE

[1] Jensen and Meckling (1976) also identify a bonding term (and corresponding bonding cost). Bonding is connected to activities, which involve agents aligning themselves to outside investors or the organization itself in terms of stock options and other means. Our study focuses on US physicians and healthcare organisations, and the regulated nature of this industry doesn't generally permit such behaviours. The regulations pertaining to healthcare foundations do allow for some bonding activities, like some ownership interests, and even partnerships; but traditional stock option arrangements are prohibited. Bonding arrangements don't occur in our study data, and thus the bonding component does not enter into our current empirical discussion, but it will be a focus in our continued research.

Chapter 9

Key Considerations for the Adoption and Implementation of Knowledge Management in Healthcare Operations[1]

Nilmini Wickramasinghe
Illinois Institute of Technology, USA

Elie Geisler
Illinois Institute of Technology, USA

ABSTRACT

The importance of knowledge management (KM) to organizations in today's competitive environment is being recognized as paramount and significant. This is particularly evident for healthcare both globally and in the U.S. The U.S. healthcare system is facing numerous challenges in trying to deliver cost effective, high quality treatments and is turning to KM techniques and technologies for solutions in an attempt to achieve this goal. While the challenges facing the U.S. healthcare are not dissimilar to those facing healthcare systems in other nations, the U.S. healthcare system leads the field with healthcare costs more than 15% of GDP and rising exponentially. What is becoming of particular interest when trying to find a solution is the adoption and implementation of KM and associated KM technologies in the healthcare setting, an arena that has to date been notoriously slow to adopt technologies and new approaches for the practice management side of healthcare. We examine this issue by studying the barriers encountered in the adoption and

DOI: 10.4018/978-1-60566-284-8.ch009

implementation of specific KM technologies in healthcare settings. We then develop a model based on empirical data and using this model draw some conclusions and implications for orthopaedics.

INTRODUCTION

The industrial economy has given way to the electronic economy creating an entirely new set of rules, opportunities, threats, and challenges (Accenture). The growth of electronic commerce (e-commerce) is vast, complex, and rapidly expanding. The evolution of the 'Information Age' in medicine is mirrored in the exponential growth of medical web pages, increasing number of online databases, and expanding services and publications available on the Internet. In order to make sense of the mass of data and information that is now being generated, organizations are turning to knowledge management techniques and technologies.

The healthcare sector is no exception to this. What we believe is not only interesting but also critical to understand is the adoption and implementation of knowledge management techniques and technologies in the healthcare sector–an industry that has to date been very slow to embrace new information technologies to benefit the administrative, as opposed to the clinical, aspect of medical practice (Battista and Hodge, 1999). To date, little has been written about knowledge management (KM) in healthcare, and even less on the phenomenon of the adoption and implementation of KM technologies and systems (Shakeshaft and Frankish, 2003).

In this chapter we address the void in the literature by presenting some results from a study of KM adoption in a select healthcare setting. This is a case of KM in an orthopedics practice in the United States. We analyze this case with a model that identifies the barriers to the process of adoption and implementation of KM in healthcare organizations. We believe that this type of research may lead to a better understanding of what it is about KM that is so crucial for healthcare today, and a better understanding of the processes and mechanisms that would help in its implementation (Eger et al., 2003).

The Healthcare Industry

Healthcare is not only a growing industry but it is also the biggest service business across the globe. Between 1960-1997 the percentage of Gross Domestic Product (GDP) spent on healthcare by 29 members of the Organizations for Economic Cooperation and Development (OECD) nearly doubled from 3.9 to 7.6% with the US spending the most–13.6% in 1997 (OECD Health Data 98). Hence, healthcare expenditures are increasing exponentially and reducing them; i.e., offering effective and efficient quality healthcare treatment, is becoming a priority globally. Technology and automation have the potential to help reduce these costs (Institute of Medicine, 2001; Wickramasinghe, 2000).

In their continuing effort to increase the role of technology in their operations, healthcare providers are exploring many opportunities that incorporate IT and tele-communications with e-commerce strategies to improve service and cost effectiveness to its key stakeholders. Many such e-initiatives, including the e-medical record, are currently being implemented in various countries; however, these alone have been found to be inadequate for achieving the desired performance and economic goals without also concurrently incorporating KM techniques and technologies into clinical and administrative practices (Wickramasinghe and Mills, 2001).

KEY FACTORS INFLUENCING THE US HEALTHCARE SECTOR

In the US, two key factors are leading the various stakeholders throughout the healthcare industry to adopt various new technologies with the aim to enable these organizations to practice better management. These factors are: (i) managed care and (ii) the Health Insurance Portability and Accountability Act (HIPAA, Public Law 104-191).

Managed care was introduced over a decade ago as an attempt to stem the escalating costs of healthcare in the US. It is aimed at creating value through competition, with the intended result of providing adequate quality healthcare and yet to minimize, or at least to hold, the line on costs (Wickramasinghe & Silvers, 2003) The principal participants involved in any managed care arrangement include the following five categories of stakeholders: the Managed Care Organization (MCO), the purchaser, the member, the healthcare professional, and, if applicable, an administrative organization (Knight, 1998).

The Health Insurance Portability and Accountability Act was signed by President Clinton on 21 August 1996. This Act is definitely providing a strong impetus for the US healthcare sector to embrace various e-technologies because it aims to improve the productivity of the American healthcare system by encouraging the development of information systems based on the exchange of standard management and financial data and by using EDI (Electronic Data Interchange). In addition, the Act also requires organizations exchanging transactions for healthcare to follow national implementation guidelines for EDI established for this purpose. This poses many significant challenges to healthcare institutions. A key challenge is the need to make significant investments in technology to facilitate and enable these functions to take place and to also develop the appropriate standards and protocols required. In 2005-

2006 the Bush Administration has also announced several initiatives to encourage the use of information technology in healthcare delivery.

THE FUTURE FOR HEALTHCARE

Healthcare has been shaped by each nation's own set of cultures, traditions, payment mechanisms, and patient expectations. Given the common problem facing healthcare globally, i.e., exponentially increasing costs, no matter which particular health system one examines, the future of the healthcare industry will be shaped by commonalities based on this key unifying problem and the common solution; namely, the embracing of new technologies to stem escalating costs and improve quality healthcare delivery.

Currently, the key trends in the future that will perhaps significantly impact healthcare include: (i) empowered consumers, (ii) e-health adaptability; and (iii) a shift to focus on healthcare prevention. Key implications of these future trends include (i) health insurance changes, (ii) workforce changes as well as changes in the roles of stakeholders within the health system, (iii) organizational changes and standardization, and (iv) the need for healthcare delivery organizations and administrators to make difficult choices regarding practice management (Wickramasinghe, 2000). In order to be well positioned to meet and manage these challenges within the US and elsewhere in the world, healthcare organizations are turning to KM techniques and technologies. Thus, as the role of KM in healthcare increases in importance, it becomes crucial to understand the process of adoption and implementation of KM systems.

THE NATURE OF KNOWLEDGE MANAGEMENT

Knowledge is a critical resource in any organization and is also crucial in the provision of healthcare. Access to the latest medical research knowledge is often the difference between life and death, between accurate or erroneous diagnosis, and between early intervention or a prolonged and costly hospital stay. Knowledge management deals with the process of creating value from an organization's intangible assets(Wickramasinghe and Mills, 2001; Edwards et al., 2005). It is an amalgamation of concepts borrowed from the artificial intelligence/knowledge based systems, software engineering, BPR (business process re-engineering), human resources management, and organizational behavior (Purvis et al. 2001). Knowledge management deals with conceptualization, review, consolidation, and action phases of creating, securing, storing, combing, coordinating, and retrieving knowledge. In essence, then, knowledge management is a process by which organizations collect, preserve, and utilize what their employees and members know about their jobs and about activities and procedures in their organization (Xu and Quaddus, 2005).

THE NEED FOR KNOWLEDGE MANAGEMENT

Sustainable competitive advantage is dependent on building and exploiting core competencies. In order to sustain competitive advantage, resources which are idiosyncratic (thus scarce) and difficult to transfer or replicate are required. A knowledge-based view of the firm identifies knowledge as the organizational asset that enables sustainable competitive advantage especially in hyper competitive environments or in environments experiencing radical discontinuous change.

Thus, it makes sense that the organization that knows more about its customers, products, technologies, markets, and their linkages should perform better Gafni and Birch, 1993). Many organizations are drowning in information overload yet starving for knowledge. Knowledge management is believed to be the current savior of organizations, but its successful use entails much more than developing Lotus Notes' lessons learnt databases. Rather it involves the thoughtful design of various technologies to support the knowledge architecture of a specific organization (Wickramasinghe and Mills, 2001).

THE VALUE OF KNOWLEDGE MANAGEMENT TO HEALTHCARE ORGANIZATIONS

Knowledge management is a still relatively new phenomenon and a somewhat nebulous topic that needs to be explored. However, organizations in all industries, both large and small, are racing to integrate this new management tool into their infrastructure. Knowledge management caters to the critical issues of organizational adaptation, survival, and competence in the face of increasingly discontinuous environmental change (Rubenstein and Geisler 2003). Essentially, it embodies organizational processes that seek synergistic combination of data and information processing capacity of information technologies, and the creative and innovative capacity of human beings.

Knowledge management realizes the importance of safeguarding and using the collective knowledge and information of an organization. Through surveys, interviews, and analysis, knowledge management seeks to excavate, measure, assess, and evaluate the knowledge and information held within an organization with the intention of making the organization more efficient and profitable. Essentially,

Figure 1. Aspects of a generic knowledge management system and their importance in the organization

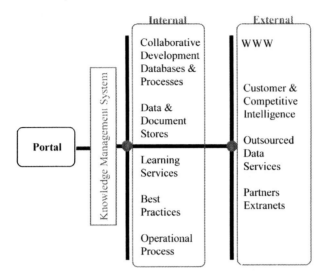

knowledge management sifts through the collective knowledge of an organization, codifies it into an information base, and then spreads it throughout the organization so it can be easily accessed (Wickramasinghe and Mills, 2001; Geisler, 2006).

The knowledge management system is extremely helpful in the internal and external sectors of an organization. Internally, knowledge management is designed to enhance the maintenance and organization of the data bases. Externally, it aims to make a better impact on the customer and external partners. Figure 1 depicts the importance of knowledge management in an organization.

THE ROLE OF KNOWLEDGE MANAGEMENT IN HEALTHCARE ORGANIZATIONS

The healthcare sector is characterized by its diversity and the distributiveness of its component organizations. There is a continuous process of generation of knowledge within each of these components (such as providers, patients, suppliers, payers, and regulators), as well as an immense volume of knowledge created at the interfaces among these organizations (Jadad et al., 2000; Pavia, 2001).

Healthcare provider organizations are a special type of organizations in that they are for the most part motivated by topics such as quality and service, but without the profit drivers that animate private industry. At the same time they are highly professional institutions, populated by people with specialized knowledge that needs to be constantly updated, shared, and leveraged (van Beveren, 2003). This phenomenon creates even more pressure on healthcare providers and others in the sector to manage the knowledge that flows through the sector.

Although there has been little empirical investigation of how knowledge management benefits healthcare organizations, it is safe to assume that its contributions would be at least as positive as they are being shown to be in other sectors of the economy (Eid, 2005).

The role of knowledge management in healthcare organizations would be important in both clinical and administrative practices. Clinical care would be much more effective with increased sharing of medical knowledge and "evidence-based" experience within and among healthcare delivery organizations (Nykanen and Karimaa, 2006).

Administrative practices in healthcare organizations will benefit from the systemic interfaces of knowledge about technology, costs, "best-practices," efficiencies, and the value of cooperation. Such effects of knowledge creation and sharing would make it easier and more effective to manage the healthcare organization.

Finally, the role of knowledge management is especially crucial in the *interface* between the clinical and administrative functions. By and large these two categories of activities are separated by differentiations such as professional specializations, role in the organization, and goals and standards of practice. Hence, there is a tendency to avoid sharing knowledge and exchanging experience-based lessons so as not to upset the existing balance of power of the organization.

Tools and Techniques of KM

KM tools and techniques are defined by their social and community role in the organization in 1) the facilitation of knowledge sharing and socialization of knowledge (production of organizational knowledge); 2) the conversion of information into knowledge through easy access, opportunities of internalization and learning (supported by the right work environment and culture); 3) the conversion of tacit knowledge into "explicit knowledge" or information, for purposes of efficient and systematic storage, retrieval, wider sharing and application. The most useful KM tools and techniques can be grouped as those that capture and codify knowledge and those that share and distribute knowledge (Duffy, 2000; 2001; Maier, 2001).

Capture and Codify Knowledge

There are various tools that can be used to capture and codify knowledge. These include databases, various types of artificial intelligence systems including expert systems, neural networks, fuzzy logic, genetic algorithms and intelligent or software agents.

i.   **Databases:** Databases store structured information and assist in the storing and sharing of knowledge. Knowledge can be acquired from the relationships that exist among different tables in a database. For example; the relationship that might exist between a customer table and a product table could show those products that are producing adequate margins, providing decision-makers with strategic marketing knowledge. Many different relations can exist and are only limited by the human imagination. These relational databases help users to make knowledgeable decisions, which is a goal of knowledge management. Discrete, structured information is still managed best by a database management system. However, the quest for a universal user interface has led to the requirement for access to existing database information through a web browser.

ii.   **Case-Based Reasoning Applications:** Case-Based Reasoning (CBR) applications combine narratives and knowledge codification to assist in problem solving. Descriptions and facts about processes and solutions to problems are recorded and categorized. When a problem is encountered, queries or searches point to the solution. CBR applications store limited knowledge from individuals who have encountered a problem and found the solution and are useful in transferring this knowledge to others.

iii. **Expert Systems:** Expert systems represent the knowledge of experts and typically query and guide users during a decision making process. They focus on specific processes and typically lead the user, step by step, toward a solution. The level of knowledge required to operate these applications is usually not as high as for CBR applications. Expert systems have not been as successful as CBR in commercial applications but can still be used to teach knowledge management.

iv.   **Using I-net Agents - creating individual views from unstructured content:** The world of human communication and information has long been too voluminous and complex for any one individual to monitor and track. Agents and I-net standards are the building blocks that make individual customization of information possible in the unstructured environment of I-nets. Agents will begin to specialize and become much more than today's general purpose search engines and "push" technologies. Two complementary technologies have emerged that allow us to coordinate, communicate and even organize information, without rigid, one-size-fits-all structures. The first is the Internet/Web technologies that are referred as I-net technology and the second is the evolution of software agents. Together, these technologies are the new-age building blocks for robust information architectures, designed to help information

consumers find what they are looking for in the way that they require. The web and software agents make it possible to build sophisticated, well performing information brokers designed to deliver content, from multiple sources, to each individual, in the individual's specific context and under the individual's own control. The software agents supported with I-net infrastructure can be highly effective tools for individualizing the organization and management of distributed information.

Systems to Share and Distribute Knowledge

Computer networks provide an effective medium for the communication and development of knowledge management. The Internet and organizational intranets are used as a basic infrastructure for knowledge management. Intranets are rapidly becoming the primary information infrastructure for enterprises. An intranet is basically a platform based on internet principles accessible only to members of an organization/community. The intranet can provide the platform for a safe and secured information management system within the organization, help people to collaborate as virtual teams, crossing boundaries of geography and time. While the internet is an open-access platform, the intranet, however, is restricted to members of a community/organization through multi-layered security controls. The same platform, can be extended to an outer ring (e.g. dealer networks, registered customers, online members, etc.), with limited accessibility, as an extranet. The extranet can be a meaningful platform for knowledge generation and sharing, in building relationships, and in enhancing the quality and effectiveness of service/support. The systems that are used to share and distribute knowledge could include; Group collaboration systems; Groupware, intranets, extranets and internet, office systems; word processing, desktop publishing, or web publishing.

HOW TO BECOME A KNOWLEDGE-BASED ENTERPRISE

Simply implementing a knowledge management system does not make an organization a knowledge based business. For an organization to become a knowledge-based business several aspects must be considered. An organization that values knowledge must integrate knowledge into its business strategy and sell it as a key part of its products and services. To do this requires a strong commitment to knowledge management directed from the top of the organization. Furthermore, it is necessary for specific people, process and technology issues to be considered. First, the knowledge architecture should be designed that is suitable given the context of a particular organization in its industry as well as the activities, products or services it may provide. From the knowledge architecture it is important to focus on the organization's structure and culture and key people issues. Do the structure and culture support a knowledge-sharing environment or perhaps a more team focussed, sharing culture needs to be fostered. In addition, strategies need to be adopted for continuous training and fostering of knowledge workers. Then, it is necessary to consider the processes of generating, representing, accessing and transferring knowledge throughout the organization. This also requires an evaluation of the technologies required. Finally, a knowledge based business should also enable organizational learning to take place so that the knowledge that is captured is always updated and current, and the organization is continually improving and refining its product or service as well as enhancing its extant knowledge base.

BARRIERS AND FACILITATORS TO THE ADOPTION AND IMPLEMENTATION OF KNOWLEDGE MANAGEMENT IN HEALTHCARE ORGANIZATIONS

There are four categories of barriers to the adoption and implementation of knowledge systems in healthcare organizations. The first is technology factors. These barriers are: (1) the attributes inherent in the technology, such as compatibility with other systems, complexity, and trialability; (2) applicability to the task for which the technology is being adopted; (3) ease of maintenance; (4) quality (in terms of errors, breakdowns, and non-responsiveness); and (5) ease of updating or replacement. Relative ease of use will impact the degree of implementation of the technology. Technologies that are very complex, not compatible with existing systems, or hard to maintain and to update or replace will be more difficult to adopt (Fichman and Kemerer, 1999; Kaplan, 1987).

The second category of barriers is the set of organizational barriers. These include the traditional barriers to technology adoption, such as political rivalries, lack of senior management support for such technology and innovation, and prior experience of the organization with similar types of technologies and their implementation. Unsuccessful past events tend to hinder any current attempts to adopt and implement technology.

In healthcare organizations there is also the added burden of the differences among organizational units in their assessment of needs for the technology and the hindering effects of the high specialization of clinical departments. The reality in such organizations is a considerable differentiation in how needs are assessed and what they mean to other units across the organization. Difficulties in establishing systemic value for a technology will hinder its adoption and implementation. Unless the technology under consideration has a wide appeal to a variety of clinical specialties (e.g., a diagnostic innovation), there will be resistance from other units and specialties to the adoption of a technology whose perceived value is restricted to a single clinical specialty (Scott et al., 2006).

A third category is human factors. These include cultural barriers, a complex learning curve needed to implement the technology, and unfavorable perception of the role of the technology, its value to the organization, and its chances of successfully contributing to tasks and goals of the organization (Brender et al., 2006; Martens & Goodrum, 2006).

In the healthcare environment there is also the impact of barriers inherent in the technological aptitudes of the clinical personnel, and their attitudes towards technological innovations in the practice of medicine (Laupacis, 1992). The usual formula for adoption of technologies by medical professionals is to follow other industries where such technologies have been implemented and successfully diffused. Only then would healthcare organizations assume the risk of adoption and their clinical personnel would be willing to adopt and implement.

The fourth and final set of barriers is the economic factors of the cost and cost-benefits of the technology. In the healthcare delivery environment capital expenditures for costly technological innovations are evaluated with extra care. An excellent case must be made for the value to be derived from the adoption of the technology before the purchase is authorized. It is less arduous for healthcare organizations to approve and adopt less costly technologies with widespread use in the organization.

FACILITATORS TO ADOPTION AND IMPLEMENTATION

The factors that seem to facilitate the adoption and implementation of healthcare technology are not necessarily the inverse or lack of barriers. They are affirmative factors that act to make the adoption and the implementation processes more feasible.

Two categories of these facilitating factors can be described. The first is the pressures that the external environment imposes on healthcare delivery organizations(Wickramasinghe and Reddy, 2006). This includes such factors as the requirements imposed by payers and regulators for billing and reporting purposes. These requirements may be based on administrative and clinical procedures and methodologies that must be made possible with the adoption and implementation of innovative technologies. Thus, healthcare delivery organizations would feel compelled to act and to facilitate the adoption of these technologies.

The second category includes factors inherent in the processes of healthcare delivery and in the perceived need to make them more productive and more efficient. For example, medical errors are embedded in the processes of healthcare delivery. This problem may trigger and facilitate the adoption and implementation of technologies, whose purpose is to alleviate the problem (Institute of Medicine, 2001).

Another example includes the need to make procedures more efficient, due to such economic realities as "capitation," DRGs (Diagnosis Related Groups), and "managed care." When payors set limits to reimbursements for diagnoses and treatments, hospitals will explore ways to be more efficient and to reduce the cost of practice of medicine. Technology becomes one of the solutions, hence the impact of this situation as a facilitator of the adoption and implementation of healthcare technologies (Shakeshaft and Frankish, 2003; Nykanen and Karimaa, 2006; Kaplan, 1987).

CLINICAL EXAMPLE: OPERATING ROOM

We discuss the major barriers and facilitators in the context of the clinical operating room because this is a case example that serves as a perfect microcosm for illustrating all the major challenges and potential benefits of a well structured KM initiative. Moreover in today's context the operating room must also exhibit the characteristics of an innovating organization. The orthopaedic operating room represents an ideal environment for the application of a continuous improvement cycle that is dependant on the application of the tools and techniques of KM. For those patients with advanced degeneration of their hips and knees, arthroplasty of the knee and hip represent an opportunity to regain their function. Before the operation ever begins in the operating room, there are a large number of interdependent individual processes that must be completed. Each process requires data input and produces a data output such as patient history, diagnostic test and consultations. From the surgeon's and hospital's perspective, they are on a continuous cycle of addressing central issues regarding access, quality and value at the micro level, or individual patient level, as well as at the macro level, or monthly/yearly target level. The interaction between these data elements is not always maximized in terms of operating room scheduling and completion of the procedure. Moreover, as the population ages and patient's functional expectations continue to increase with their advanced knowledge of medical issues; reconstructive Orthopaedic surgeons are being presented with an increasing patient population requiring hip and knee arthroplasty. Simultaneously, the implants are becoming more sophisticated and thus more expensive. In turn, the surgeons are experiencing little change in system capacity, but are being told to improve efficiency and output, improve procedure time and eliminate redundancy. However, the system legacy is for insufficient room designs that have not been updated with the introduction of new equipment, poor integration of the equipment, inefficient scheduling and time consuming procedure preparation. Although there are many barriers to Re-Engineering the Operating Room

Figure 2. The key steps of knowledge management

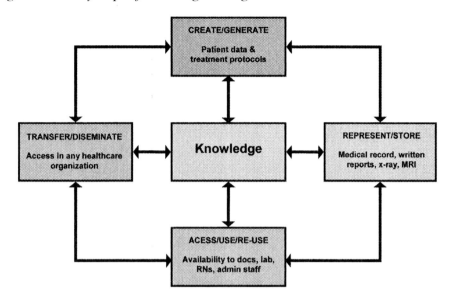

such as the complex choreography of the perioperative processes, a dearth of data and the difficulty of aligning incentives, it is indeed possible to effect significant improvements through the application of the KM. Figure 2 outlines critical KM steps that become important in such a setting

The entire process of getting a patient to the operating room for a surgical procedure can be represented by three distinct phases: preoperative, intraopertive and postoperative. In turn, each of these phases can be further subdivided into the individual yet interdependent processes that represent each step on the surgical trajectory. As each of the individual processes are often dependant on a previous event, the capture of event and process data in a data warehouse is necessary. The diagnostic evaluation of this data, and the re-engineering of each of the deficient processes will then lead to increased efficiency. For example, many patients are allergic to the penicillin family of antibiotics that are often administered preoperative in order to minimize the risk of infection. For those patients who are allergic, a substitute drug requires a 45 minute monitored administration time as opposed to the much shortened administration time of the default agent. Since the antibiotic is only effective when administered prior to starting the procedure, this often means that a delay is experienced. When identified in the preoperative phase, these patients should be prepared earlier on the day of surgery and the medication administered in sufficient time so that the schedule is not delayed. This prescriptive reengineering has directly resulted from mining of the data in the information system in conjunction with an examination of the business processes and their flows. By scrutinizing the delivery of care and each individual process, increased efficiency and improved quality should be realized while maximizing value. For knee and hip arthroplasty, there are over 432 discrete processes that can be evaluated and reengineered as necessary through the application of a spectrum of KM tools and techniques (Wick-ramasinghe and Schaffer, 2006).

In terms of the four major categories of barriers identified earlier the case vignette of the operating orthopaedic OR exhibits instances of all of these. In each stage from pre-operative, intraopertive and finally postoperative various clinical and administrative technologies are necessary. However, for effective and efficient process flow it is essential that these technologies are compatible and support seamless information flow (Wickramasinghe and Schaffer, 2006) By adopting the spectrum of KM tools and techniques what we find is that it becomes easier to monitor and evaluate these various technologies in action which in turn results in more effective use of the technology and efficient surgeries with heightened results. The continuous improvement also facilitates enhanced co-ordination between the various people, form surgeons, to nursing staff and even the patient, involved throughout the pre-operative, intraopertive and postoperative stages; once again with the result of superior operations and the achievement of the six quality aims outlined by the American Institute of Medicine(Institute of Medicine, 2001) and hence addresses many of the human and organizational barriers.

In a similar fashion, the spectrum of KM tools and techniques also help to alleviate many of the organizational and human barriers. This is primarily due to the fact that critical data is now being captured and transformed into pertinent information and germane knowledge (Wickramasinghe, 2006). This in turn support and enables effective decision making (ibid) Finally, in terms of economic factors, more efficient and effective performance is not only achieved but sustainable. This facilitates faster throughput, higher quality and superior results which combine to decrease costs which are to a large extent due to the cumulative additive effect of various inefficiencies (Wickramasinghe and Schaffer, 2006).

CONCLUSION

The preceding discussion has served to highlight the significance and key role for knowledge management in healthcare today. Specifically, this was done by discussing some of the major challenges facing healthcare today in terms of demographics, technology and finance and how KM tools and techniques might help to ameliorate this situation. In addition major barriers, including technology, organizational, human and economic and facilitators both external and internal to the organisation were identified that must be considered when trying to implement an appropriate

KM solution in healthcare. Finally, an example of how beneficial the incorporation of such a perspective is in redesigning the current state of the orthopaedic OR to a future state of the OR was given. Taken together then, this chapter serves to under score the importance of taking a holistic approach to addressing the challenges currently faced by healthcare. Furthermore, by focusing on diagnosing the current state and then finding appropriate solutions so that it is possible to prescribe strategies to make the key inputs into the healthcare information system more effective and efficient it will then be possible to realize the value proposition for healthcare. While medical science has made revolutionary changes and advances, healthcare in contrast has made incremental change at best. The disparity between these two is one of the major reasons why today's healthcare industry is faced with its current challenges. We believe that by embracing the tools and techniques of KM it will be possible for healthcare to make evolutionary changes and thereby meet patients' greater expectations.

REFERENCES

Battista, R., & Hodge, M. (1999). The evolving paradigm of health technology assessment: Reflections for the millenium. *Canadian Medical Association Journal, 160*(10), 1464–1468.

Brender, J., Ammenwerth, E., Nykonen, P., & Talmon, J. (2006). Factors influencing success and failure of health informatics systems--a pilot Delphi study. *Methods of Information in Medicine, 45*(1), 125–136.

Duffy, J. (2001). The tools and technologies needed for knowledge management. *Information Management Journal, 35*(1), 64–67.

Edwards, J., Shaw, D., & Collier, P. (2005). Knowledge management systems: Finding a way with technology. *Journal of Knowledge Management, 9*(1), 113–125. doi:10.1108/13673270510583009

Eger, M., Godkin, R. L., & Valentine, S. (2001). Physician's adoption of information technology: A consumer behavior approach. *Health Marketing Quarterly, 19*(2), 3–6. doi:10.1300/J026v19n02_02

Eid, R. (2005). International Internet marketing: A triangulation study of drivers and barriers in the business-to-business context in the United Kingdom. *Marketing Intelligence & Planning, 23*(3), 266–280. doi:10.1108/02634500510597300

Fichman, R., & Kemerer, C. (1999). The illusory diffusion of innovation: An examination of assimilation gaps. *Information Systems Research, 10*(3), 255–261. doi:10.1287/isre.10.3.255

Gafni, A., & Birch, S. (1993). Guidelines for the adoption of new technologies: A prescription for uncontrolled growth in expenditures and how to avoid the problem. *Canadian Medical Association Journal, 148*(6), 913–922.

Geisler, E. (2006). (in press). A typology of knowledge management transactions: Strategic groups and role behavior in organizations. *Journal of Knowledge Management, 11*(1).

Institute of Medicine. (2001). *Crossing the chasm-a new health system for the 21st century*. Washington, D.C.: National Academy Press, Committee on Quality of Healthcare in America.

Jadad, A., Haynes, R., Hunt, D., & Brondman, G. (2000). The Internet and evidence-based decision making: A needed synergy for efficient knowledge management in healthcare. *Canadian Medical Association Journal, 162*(3), 362–367.

Kaplan, B. (1987). The medical computing lag: Perceptions of barriers to the application of computers to medicine. *International Journal of Technology Assessment in Health Care, 3*(1), 123–136. doi:10.1017/S026646230001179X

Knight, W. (1998). *Managed care: What it is and how it works*. MD: Aspen Publication.

Laupacis, A. (1992). How attractive does a new technology have to be to warrant adoption and utilization? Tentative guidelines for using clinical and economic evaluations. *Canadian Medical Association Journal, 146*(4), 473–486.

Maier, R. (2001). *Knowledge management systems*. Berlin: Springer.

Martens, B., & Goodrum, A. (2006). The diffusion of theories: A functional approach. *Journal of the American Society for Information Science and Technology, 57*(3), 330–341. doi:10.1002/asi.20285

Nykanen, P., & Karimaa, E. (2006). Success and failure factors in the regional health information system design process--results from a constructive evaluation study. *Methods of Information in Medicine, 45*(1), 89–124.

Pavia, L. (2001). The era of knowledge in healthcare. *Health Care Strategic Management, 19*(2), 12–13.

Purvis, R., Samamburthy, V., & Zmud, R. (2001). The assimilation of knowledge platforms in organizations: An empirical investigation. *Organization Science, 12*(2), 117–132. doi:10.1287/orsc.12.2.117.10115

Rubenstein, A., & Geisler, E. (2003). *Installing and managing workable knowledge management systems.* Westport, CT: Praeger Publishers.

Scott, T., Rundall, T., Vogt, T., & Hsu, J. (2006). Kaiser permanente's experience of implementing an electronic medical record: A qualitative study. *British Medical Journal, 331*(3), 1313–1316.

Shakeshaft, A., & Frankish, C. (2003). Using patient-driven computers to provide cost-effective prevention in primary care: A conceptual framework. *Health Promotion International, 18*(1), 67–77. doi:10.1093/heapro/18.1.67

van Beveren, J. (2003). Does healthcare for knowledge management? *Journal of Knowledge Management, 7*(1), 90–97. doi:10.1108/13673270310463644

Wickramasinghe, N. (2000). IS/IT as a tool to achieve goal alignment: A theoretical framework. *International J. HealthCare Technology Management, 2*(1/2/3/4), 163-180.

Wickramasinghe, N. (2006). Knowledge creation: A metaframework. *International J. [IJIL]. Innovation and Learning, 3*(5), 558–573.

Wickramasinghe, N., & Mills, G. (2001). MARS: The electronic medical record system. The core of the Kaiser galaxy. *International Journal of Healthcare Technology and Management, 3*(5/6), 406–423. doi:10.1504/IJHTM.2001.001119

Wickramasinghe, N., & Reddy, H. (2006). *Knowledge management and evidence-based medicine.* Working paper.

Wickramasinghe, N., & Schaffer, J. (2006). Creating knowledge driven healthcare processes with the intelligence continuum. *International Journal of Electronic Healthcare, 2*(2), 164–174.

Wickramasinghe, N., & Silvers, J. B. (2003). IS/IT the prescription to enable medical group practices to manage managed care. *Health Care Management Science, 6*(2), 75–86. doi:10.1023/A:1023376801767

Xu, J., & Quaddus, M. (2005). A six-stage model for the effective diffusion of knowledge management systems. *Journal of Management Development, 24*(4), 362–374. doi:10.1108/02621710510591352

ENDNOTE

[1]   This material was presented at the May 2007 IRMA conference Vancouver.

Chapter 10
Realising the Healthcare Value Proposition
The Need for KM and Technology

Nilmini Wickramasinghe
Illinois Institute of Technology, USA

ABSTRACT

Succinctly stated, the healthcare value proposition revolves around access, quality, and value. Healthcare organizations globally are struggling to realize this value proposition with the U.S. being the country noted for having the most expensive rather than the highest value healthcare system. The following discusses how KM and technology can facilitate the attainment of the healthcare value proposition.

INTRODUCTION

Healthcare is a growing industry. Between 1960-1997 the percentage of Gross Domestic Product(GDP) spent on healthcare by 29 members of the Organizations for Economic Cooperation and Development (OECD) nearly doubled from 3.9-7.6% with the US spending the most -13.6% in 1997[1] and today the US spends nearly 20% (Wickramasinghe et al., 2008). Hence, healthcare expenditure is increasing exponentially and reducing this expenditure; i.e. offering effective and efficient quality healthcare treatment is becoming a priority globally. Technology and automation have the potential to reduce these costs (America Institute of Medicine, 2001;

DOI: 10.4018/978-1-60566-284-8.ch010

Wickramasinghe, 2000; Wickramasinghe and Schaffer, 2006); thus, the adopting and adapting of technologies and new techniques throughout the healthcare industry, appears to be the way to stem these escalating costs currently facing the healthcare industry worldwide. The adoption of data mining coupled with knowledge management techniques and strategies appears to be a prudent option for healthcare organizations. This is demonstrated by firstly highlighting the current challenges facing healthcare and presenting the key quality areas that need to be addressed as underscored by the Committee on the Quality of Healthcare in America. Then a brief description of knowledge management, the major types of knowledge and the knowledge spiral is given. Next the role of data and information in healthcare is presented before describing data mining and its role in the knowledge discovery process as well as how it can enable the knowledge spiral to be realized is outlined. Following this, the power of data mining is illustrated by applying the techniques of data mining to a healthcare data set. This serves to highlight the benefits of data mining and knowledge management to healthcare by showing that through realizing the knowledge management spiral with data mining not only is it possible to adhere to the healthcare quality aims stated by the Committee on the Quality of Healthcare in America but it is also possible to support and enable superior clinical practice and administrative management throughout healthcare; thereby, making data mining and knowledge management strategic imperatives for this industry. Finally conclusions are drawn.

CHALLENGES CURRENTLY FACING HEALTHCARE

Healthcare is an important industry that touches most, if not all of us. Healthcare is noted for using leading edge technologies and embracing new scientific discoveries to enable better cures for diseases and better means to enable early detection of most life threatening diseases. However, the healthcare industry globally, and in the US specifically, has been extremely slow to adopt technologies that focus on better practice management and administrative needs (Wickramasinghe and Mills, 2001; Wickramasinghe and Schaffer, 2006).

In the final report compiled by the Committee on the Quality of Healthcare in America (America Institute of Medicine, 2001), it was noted that improving patient care is integrally linked to providing high quality healthcare. Furthermore, in order to achieve a high quality of healthcare the committee identified 6 key aims; namely, 1) healthcare should be safe – avoiding injuries to patients from the care that is intended to help them, 2) effective - providing services based on scientific knowledge to all who could benefit and refraining from providing services to those who will not benefit (i.e. avoiding under use and overuse), 3) patient-centered – providing care that is respectful of and responsive to individual patient preferences, needs, and values and ensuring that patient values guide all clinical decisions, 4) timely – reducing waiting and sometimes harmful delays for both those receiving care and those who give care, 5) efficient - avoiding waste and 6) equitable – providing care that doesn't vary in quality based on personal characteristics.

Most of the poor quality connected with healthcare is related to a highly fragmented delivery system that lacks even rudimentary clinical information capabilities resulting in poorly designed care processes characterized by unnecessary duplication of services and long waiting times and delays (ibid). The development and application of sophisticated information systems is essential to address these quality issues and improve efficiency, yet healthcare delivery has been relatively untouched by the revolution of information technology and new management business models such as knowledge management that is transforming so many areas of business today (America Institute of Medicine, 2001; Wickramasinghe, 2000; Wickramasinghe and Mills, 2001; Stegwee and Spil, 2001; Wickramasinghe and Silvers, 2002) .

KNOWLEDGE MANAGEMENT

Knowledge management is a key approach to solve current problems such as competitiveness and the need to innovate which is faced by businesses today. The premise for the need for knowledge management is based on a paradigm shift in the business environment where knowledge is central to organizational performance (Drucker 1993). This macro-level paradigm shift also has significant implications upon the micro-level processes of assimilation and implementation of knowledge management concepts and techniques (Swan et al., 1999) i.e., the Knowledge Management Systems(KMS) that are in place. In essence then, knowledge management not only involves the production of information but also the capture of data at the source, the transmission and analysis of this data as well as the communication of information based on or derived from the data to those who can act on it(Davenport and Prusak, 1998).

In today's context of escalating costs in healthcare, managed care, regulations such as the Healthcare Information Portability and Accountability Act (HIPAA) and a technology savvy patient, the healthcare industry can no longer be complacent regarding embracing technologies and techniques to enable better, more effective and efficient practice management. We believe such an environment is appropriate for the adoption of a knowledge management perspective and key tools and technologies such as data mining.

THE KNOWLEDGE SPIRAL

Knowledge is not static; rather it changes and evolves during the life of an organization. What is more, it is possible to change the form of knowledge; i.e., turn tacit knowledge into explicit and explicit knowledge into tacit or to turn the subjective form of knowledge into the objective form of knowledge (Wickramasinghe, 2002). This process of changing the form of knowledge is known as the knowledge spiral (Nonaka, 1994). According to Nonaka (ibid): 1) Tacit to tacit knowledge transfer usually occurs through apprenticeship type relations where the teacher or master passes on the skill to the apprentice. 2) Explicit to explicit knowledge transfer usually occurs via formal learning of facts. 3) Tacit to explicit knowledge transfer usually occurs when there is an articulation of nuances; for example, if a famous surgeon is questioned as to why he does a particular procedure in a certain manner, by his articulation of the steps the tacit knowledge becomes explicit. and 4) Explicit to tacit knowledge transfer usually occurs as new explicit knowledge is internalized it can then be used to broaden, reframe and extend one's tacit knowledge. Integral to this changing of knowledge through the knowledge spiral is that new knowledge is created (ibid) and this can bring many benefits to organizations. In the case of transferring tacit knowledge to explicit knowledge for example, an organization is able to capture the expertise of particular individuals; hence, this adds not only to the organizational memory but also enables single loop and double loop organizational learning to take place(Huber, 1984). In healthcare, this may translate, for example, to the developing of better protocols and codes or even further refinement to existing DRGs (diagnosis related groupings).

KEY ROLE OF DATA AND INFORMATION IN HEALTHCARE

The proliferation of databases in every quadrant of healthcare practice and research is evident in the large number of claims databases, registries, electronic medical record data warehouses, disease surveillance systems, and ad hoc research database systems. Not only does the number of databases grow daily, but even more importantly, so does the amount of data within them. Pattern-identification tasks such as detecting associations between certain risk factors and outcomes, ascertaining trends in healthcare utilization, or discovering new models of disease in populations of individuals rapidly become daunting even to the most experienced healthcare researcher or manager (Holmes et al., 2002). Add to all of this, the daily volumes of data generated and then accumulated from a healthcare organization administrative system, clearly then, the gap between data collection and data comprehension and analysis becomes even more problematic. IT tools coupled with new business

models such as knowledge management should be embraced in an attempt to address such healthcare woes (Berinato, 2002; McGee, 1997).

Computerized techniques are essential to helping physicians as well as administrators address this problem. Of particular relevance are the relatively young and growing fields of data mining, knowledge discovery, and knowledge management. Data mining is closely associated with databases and shares some ground with statistics – both strive toward discovering some structure in data. However, while statistical analysis starts with some kind of hypothesis about the data, data mining does not. Furthermore, data mining is much more suited to deal with heterogeneous data fields which are typical of medical databases. Data mining also draws heavily from many other disciplines, most notably machine learning, artificial intelligence, and database technology.

DATA MINING AS AN ENABLER FOR REALIZING THE KNOWLEDGE SPIRAL

One of the key strengths of data mining as a tool for facilitating knowledge discovery; and thereby, its benefit to healthcare is concerned with its ability to enable the realization of the knowledge spiral. Furthermore, data mining supports both the subjective and objective components of knowledge. In this way, data mining supports the sense making activities as well as the Lokean/Leibnitzian functions and thus the information processing activities.

To get a better appreciation of the capabilities of data mining in this context, let us consider each of the types of knowledge transfer described above. This is illustrated in Figure 1. From this drill down of the knowledge component we can see the types of knowledge and the knowledge spiral. In addition, we note that the extant knowledge base is transformed into a new superior knowledge base.

Table 1 demonstrates the key to the power of data mining, namely; that with the one technology we have the potential to address all four aspects of the knowledge spiral; and hence supporting all possible transferring of knowledge on both the clinical practice and administrative sides of healthcare. The implications for this technology are tremendous especially when we factor in the high level of data and information intensiveness in the healthcare environment.

METHODOLOGY

We are trying to represent a phenomenon; namely the knowledge spiral and construct a model that will enable us to use data mining to realize this knowledge spiral. As argued by Geisler (1999),in such instances when one is trying to model or represent a phenomenon in management or organizations more traditional methodologies such as contingency theory are less useful and we need "…a different form of representation of organizational phenomenon [that] would better offer a better view of the world"; namely, we need to turn to the approach of dynamic morphology (Geisler, 1999 p37). Integral to the dynamic morphology approach is that a) we look at events as dynamic and b) the emphasis is on transformations rather than

Figure 1. Drill down of the knowledge component. Through data mining and the interaction of people with the knowledge that is gained from data mining both extant tacit and explicit knowledge are changed into new explicit and tacit knowledge respectively via the knowledge spiral so that the New K-Base >> Extant K-base

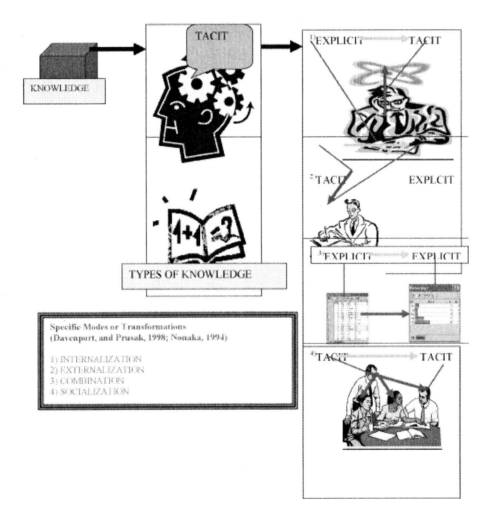

Table 1. Data mining as an enabler of the knowledge spiral

	EXPLICIT[2]	TACIT
EXPLICIT	Performing exploratory data mining, such as summarization and visualization, it is possible to upgrade, expand, and/or revise current facts and protocols.	By assimilating and internalizing knowledge discovered through data mining, physicians can turn this explicit knowledge into tacit knowledge which they can apply to treating new patients
TACIT	Interpretation of findings from data mining helps the revealing of tacit knowledge, which can then be articulated and stored as explicit cases in the case repository.	Interpreting treatment patterns for example for hip disease discovered through data mining enables interaction among physicians – hence making it possible to stimulate and grow their own tacit knowledge.

co-variation; unlike with contingency theory where the emphasis tends to be on co-variation and causality. When looking at the knowledge spiral and the role for data mining in realizing the knowledge spiral the dynamic nature of the events and the transformations that take place i.e., the transforming of explicit to tacit and tacit to explicit knowledge are central and thus the need for an appropriate methodology to capture these important aspects is critical; hence the use of dynamic morphology is an appropriate methodology for our purposes.

Figure 2 shows the generic framework of Dynamic Morphologies. In Figure 3 these are then applied to the knowledge spiral. This application is geared towards showing how Data Mining can be applied in a rational and systematic manner to the uncovering of knowledge.

The antecedent event is the existence of information/data which serves as the basis

Figure 2. Simplified schematic of a dynamic morphology – adapted from [2]

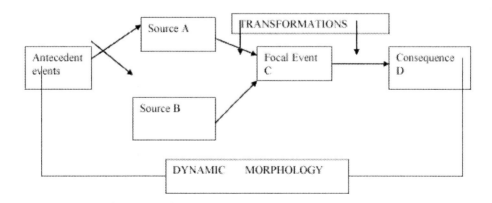

Figure 3. Application of the dynamic morphological methodology to the explicit to explicit transformation in the knowledge spiral. The KDD process is the antecedent event that results in knowledge whose constituent parts are source A (tacit K) and Source B (explicit K). Through the Combination Transformation (one of the 4 possible transformations of the K Spiral) we can see the focal event of capturing explicit K being transformed to the consequence of creating new explicit K. Thereby, highlighting the explanatory power of dynamic morphology to the knowledge transformations that occur in the knowledge spiral enabled by data mining

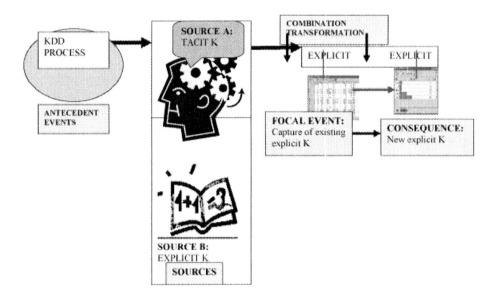

for data mining. For example, the patient information database is such an antecedent event, where patients undergo procedures and tests and these are deposited in their database. The medical history of patients thus forms the antecedent event or the basis for further conduct of data mining. The sources are both tacit and explicit—as can be seen in Figure 3. The tacit knowledge is that of the healthcare providers and the explicit are databases in the hospital or clinic, such as information about procedures (e.g., how to perform appendectomies), about equipment and medical technologies (what do we have available in the operating rooms) and about the medical staff. In addition, there are administrative databases such as financial information and information about regulatory requirements and constraints.

Tacit knowledge is that which the medical and administrative staffs possess. Explicit is the knowledge which resides in the databases described above. So, according to the Dynamic Morphology framework, the focal event becomes a patient who is entering the healthcare delivery facility (Event C in Figure 2). The transformations

Table 2. Data mining and knowledge management supporting the key quality aims

Aim	KM/DM Potential Sample Applications
Safety	Auto-alerting when drugs of inappropriate reactions are prescribed together.
Effectiveness	Age/weight- appropriate dose recommendation.
Patient-Centered	Enabling patients' self-service capabilities in appointment scheduling and secure personal information access.
Timeliness	Prediction of disease occurrence and hence timely and proactive treatment.
Efficiency	Accounting and billing analytics to identify and correct inefficiencies.
Equity	Automatic auditing and control capabilities.

that take place include data mining of the antecedent event and the sources. What do we know that is in the databases that we can access and utilize in order to care for the patient? What do we know about the patient's own medical information? How does such information match up against the data of a similar population we have in our databases that we are mining? For example, if the patient is female, African-American, age 55, the data mined from the existing data bases point to a strong possibility of such illnesses as Diabetes and Hypertension. What do we know about the facilities at our disposal and procedures to treat this patient?

The focal event is the treatment of this patient. The consequence is the result or outcome from this treatment, which now becomes new explicit knowledge and can be fed back into the existing data bases for subsequent data mining for future patients.

The more we standardize this process, the less we depend on tacit knowledge and the more we can now have direct feeding of the data mined into our focal event of treating patients. This will in turn facilitate a more robust process of quality healthcare delivery (Table 2)

BENEFITS OF KNOWLEDGE MANAGEMENT AND DATA MINING TO HEALTHCARE

Data mining can be applied at the clinical as well as the hospital administration levels. At the clinical level, for example, data mining could help in early detection of diseases from historical databases of symptoms and diagnosis – thus providing an early warning system that leads to a much more effective healthcare system. At the hospital administration level, for example, data mining could help in tracking certain kinds of anomalies or frauds, which may reveal areas of potential improvement and may help realignment of resources (e.g., equipment, personnel, etc.). Other benefits of data mining include expanding individual as well as organizational knowledge, and therefore enabling the healthcare system to do more with its given resources – i.e., achieve more efficiencies. This is especially useful in addressing situations of shortages of resources such as the shortage of nurses (a key problem currently in the US) by being able to do more with the limited nursing staff the organization has. The possibilities of using data mining in healthcare are virtually limitless. The strategic significance of data mining and knowledge management technologies to healthcare is hardly disputable in our opinion. Thus, we believe competitive and forward-looking healthcare organizations need to initiate pilot applications and proof of concept projects to start reaping the benefits of these technologies.

Data mining is now increasingly being used in a variety of healthcare database environments, including insurance claims, electronic medical records, epidemiologic surveillance, and drug utilization. Companies are also using data mining to help improve patient services. For example, United Healthcare, a $10.5 billion health-care services company in Minneapolis, USA with an IT budget of about $320 million and an IS staff of 2500, is using data-mining applications to learn more about treatment and preventative care for patients(Krzysztof, 2001). Data mining will enable clinicians and managers to find valuable new patterns in their databases, leading to potential improvement of resource utilization and patient health. As these patterns are based on clinical or administrative practice, they represent the ultimate in evidence-based medicine and healthcare. In particular, healthcare data can be analyzed for trends and/or changes, and the appropriate healthcare professionals can be alerted should major shifts in trends or changes be discovered.

The role that knowledge management and data mining play in achieving the aims of healthcare as stated by the Committee on the Quality of Healthcare in America (American Institute of Medicine, 2001) identified earlier, are summarised in Table 2. This serves to highlight the ubiquitous benefits of data mining to all areas of quality healthcare treatment and hence, demonstrating how data mining adds significant value to healthcare delivery.

CONCLUSION

Any successful knowledge discovery effort should start with a thorough under-standing of the problem as well as the data. Exploratory data mining enhances such understanding and possibly enables participants to formulate some hypotheses. The next phase in the discovery process involves a development of some model - clas-sification, clustering, or prediction. The model needs to be evaluated – data-tested and professionally-verified. Where to start in the knowledge discovery process is a matter of where an organization is positioned along a knowledge discovery continuum. At the early stages, one usually starts with a pilot project of a limited scope which serves as a proof of concept for the feasibility and utility of the data mining technology within the given organizational context. Such a pilot requires an organizational championship and a significant amount of data, as the knowledge discovery process is data-driven and data-intensive by nature. The outcome of the pilot should provide sufficient metrics for evaluating the usefulness of the data mining technology.

Our chapter has served to identify the key role for data mining and knowledge management in healthcare. We did this by discussing some of the major challenges facing healthcare today. Next, we discussed knowledge management and in particular highlighted the role of the knowledge spiral. Our discussion of data mining served to demonstrate how data mining enables the realization of the knowledge spiral. In order to do this we introduced the methodological approach of dynamic morphology and applied it to the transformations effected by the knowledge spiral. The power of data mining lies in the fact that it can realize the four major transformations of knowledge in the knowledge spiral.

Data mining and knowledge management then can be seen to offer many advantages to enabling cost effective, high quality healthcare to ensue as we discuss in this paper; but of even greater appeal is that these techniques are relevant to both the clinical practice and administrative management concerns of healthcare. Thereby, making them a most powerful and apropos remedy to the numerous maladies and challenges currently facing healthcare. Therefore, we believe data mining and knowledge management are critical necessities for any forward thinking healthcare organization.

REFERENCES

American Institute of Medicine. (2001). *Crossing the quality chasm-a new health system for the 21ˢᵗ century*. Washington, D.C.: National Academy Press.

Berinato, S. (2002, June 15). CIOs at the heart of healthcare change. *CIO Magazine*.

Boland, R., & Tenkasi, R. (1995). Perspective making perspective taking. *Organization Science*, *6*, 350–372. doi:10.1287/orsc.6.4.350

Davenport, T., & Prusak, L. (1998). *Working knowledge*. Boston: Harvard Business School Press.

Drucker, P. (1993). *Post-capitalist society*. New York: Harper Collins.

Fayyad, Piatetsky-Shapiro, & Smyth. (1996). From data mining to knowledge discovery: An overview. In Fayyad, Piatetsky-Shapiro, Smyth & Uthurusamy (Eds.), *Advances in knowledge discovery and data mining.* Menlo Park, CA: AAAI Press/ The MIT Press.

Geisler, E. (1999). *Methodology, theory, and knowledge in the managerial and organizational sciences.* London: Quorum Books.

Holmes, J., Abbott, P., Cullen, P., Moody, L., Phillips, K., & Zupan, B. (2002, November 9-13). Clinical data mining: Who does it, and what do they do? *AMIA 2002 Symposium.*

Huber, G. (1984). The nature and design of postindustrial organizations. *Management Science, 30*(8), 928–951. doi:10.1287/mnsc.30.8.928

Krzysztof, J., & Cios (Eds.) (2001). Medical data mining and knowledge discovery. Physica-Verlag.

Malhotra, Y. (2000). Knowledge management and new organizational form. In Malhotra (Ed.), *Knowledge management and virtual organizations.* Hershey, PA: Idea Group Publishing.

McGee, M. K. (1997, September 22). High-tech healing. *Information Week.*

Nonaka, I. (1994). A dynamic theory of organizational knowledge creation. *Organization Science, 5*, 14–37. doi:10.1287/orsc.5.1.14

Polyani, M. (1958). *Personal knowledge: Towards a post-critical philosophy.* Chicago: University Press Chicago.

Polyani, M. (1966). *The tacit dimension London.* Routledge & Kegan Paul.

Schultz, U. (1998, December). Investigating the contradictions in knowledge management. *Presentation at IFIP.*

Stegwee, R., & Spil, T. (2001). *Strategies for healthcare information systems.* Hershey, PA: Idea Group Publishing.

Swan, J., Scarbrough, H., & Preston, J. (1999). Knowledge management–the next fad to forget people? In *Proceedings of the 7th European Conference in Information Systems.*

Wickramasinghe, N. (2000). IS/IT as a tool to achieve goal alignment: A theoretical framework. *International Journal of Healthcare Technology and Management, 2*(1/2/3/4), 163–180. doi:10.1504/IJHTM.2000.001089

Wickramasinghe, N., Bali, R., & Schaffer, J. (2008). The healthcare intelligence continuum: Key model for enabling KM initiatives and realising the full potential of SMT in healthcare delivery. *Intl. J. Biomedical Engineering and Technology, 1*(4), 415–427. doi:10.1504/IJBET.2008.020070

Wickramasinghe, N., & Mills, G. (2001). MARS: The electronic medical record system the core of the Kaiser galaxy. *International Journal of Healthcare Technology and Management, 3*(5/6), 406–423. doi:10.1504/IJHTM.2001.001119

Wickramasinghe, N., & Schaffer, J. (2006). Creating knowledge driven healthcare processes with the intelligence continuum. [IJEH]. *International Journal of Electronic Healthcare, 2*(2), 164–174.

Wickramasinghe, N., & Silvers, J. B. (2002). IS/IT the prescription to enable medical group practices attain their goals. Forthcoming in *Healthcare Management Science.*

ENDNOTES

[1] OECD Health Data 98

[2] Each entry explains how data mining enables the knowledge transfer from the type of knowledge in the cell row to the type of knowledge in the cell column.

Section 3
Case Studies Illustrating Key Workplace Issues

This section presents four chapters all by Saito as follows: "Perceived Organizational Environment and Perceived Reliability in the Case of Hospital Nurses," Chapter 11, "Roles of Interpersonal Relationship in Improving Organizational Performance in the Case of Hospital Nurses," Chapter 12, "Interference of Mood States at Work with Perceived Performance, Perceived Efficacy, and Perceived Health," Chapter 13, and finally, "Causal Relationship Among Perceived Organizational Environment, Leadership, and Organizational Learning in Industrial Workers," Chapter 14.

The chapters in this section focus on critical current workplace issues in hospitals (in Chapter 11 and 12) and also in industry (Chapters 13 and 14). Effective application of knowledge management tools are made when the participants can understand the current situations of their workplace and share the reality. The participants need appreciation process for sharing the reality. Case studies or field studies are very important for the purpose of identifying the realty in workplace. Without the evidence obtained by case studies or investigations, redesigning innovative workplace operations is unlikely to result in successful outcomes.

The relationship between job cognition and incident behaviors of hospital nurses is presented in Chapter 11. In Chapter 12 nurses' behaviors at a subsystem level without any strategies is described. Significant interference of mood state at work with perceived self-efficacy, perceived performance, and perceived health forms the

focus of Chapter 13. Finally, in Chapter 14 crucial roles of organizational learning and leadership as a leverage for the development of organizational performance in industry provides a good example of how to identify the reality and then start appreciative steps by means of knowledge management tools. The results of these four chapters suggests that understanding and sharing the current workplace information is critical in order to make workplace operations superior through the appropriate application of knowledge management methodologies.

On the completion of this section, readers will be equipped to identify key current workplace issues and to adopt appropriate methodologies of knowledge management in order to effect appropriate organizational redesign to enable effective and superior operations whether in the healthcare sector or manufacturing.

Chapter 11
Perceived Organizational Environment and Performance Reliability in the Case of Hospital Nurses

Murako Saito
Waseda University, Japan

ABSTRACT

Most hospital organizational environments in Japan are required to redesign the current organization into a new type of organization, namely a knowledge-based or an intelligent organization. Team care formation, for instance, which forms a hierarchy with medical doctors having an initiative, and simply gathering some disciplinary staff in plural areas, is not adequate. Redesigning an innovative organization is not possible without appropriate transformation into a flexible and resilient organization that can cope with the contingency of complex social environment. Professional staff in hospitals need to develop their work organization to be more flexible and adaptive to the changes in society. The accidental events which happen in hospitals are rarely controlled only by technical countermeasures or by traditional human resource management, but can be purposefully aligned by the appropriate application of knowledge management methodologies. Accuracy of human action is not merely acquired by avoiding erroneous behavior, rather it is ensured by continuously redesigning work organizational climate for the participants to take an autonomic action with the sense of organizational citizenship and social responsibility. The focus in this chapter is placed on the current situations of work

DOI: 10.4018/978-1-60566-284-8.ch011

organization of hospitals in Japan and on the comparison of perceived nursing work, incidence rates during 24 hours of nursing care work, and reduced reliability among four control modes of organizational environment, such as strategic, tactical, opportunistic, and scrambled. This study suggests that cognitive reliability on work conditions and on perceived work environment plays a critical role in improving performance reliability and in reducing human errors in order to provide a high quality of nursing care.

INTRODUCTION

Traditional technical countermeasures are not sufficient in controlling the incidents that happen in work organizations and in managing complex situations of the accidents occurring in society. Occurrence of accidental events in society are due to human actions which are roughly estimated at over 80% and have been increasing (Reason, 1990, 1997, Hollnagel, 1993, 1998). Systemic management of organizational environment, in addition with a particular human behavior, therefore, is required to cope with complex workplace issues stemming from inappropriate management of the organizational environment, and to take action at least at three levels of management, 1) operational or day-to-day control in terms of efficiency, 2) strategic control or creation of new values in terms of effectiveness, and 3) normative control or fulfilling the overall responsibility in terms of legitimacy; as in systemic management (Schwaninger, 1990, Flood, 1998). In comparison with the effort simply based on a particular discipline, systemic management based on organizational cybernetics is effective in coping with social changes and plays a great role in creating ideas or values for transforming the organization into an innovative one. According to the notable contributions on systemic management (Beer, 1979, Schwaninger, 1990, Flood, 1991, 1996, Espejo, 1993, 1996), holistic or collaborative approaches are required to manage the work environment and to create a viable organizational climate where people are positively related to help each other to recognize and make them share responsibility when accidents may happen in the future. Although the conceptual models and methodologies of systemic management are known, empirical studies by applying systemic management methodologies have been very few. Field studies are required for identifying the occurrence of erroneous behaviors and inappropriate human actions in the workplace, especially in the healthcare sector where it is necessary to raise the level of security and quality of care.

The focus in this Chapter is placed on cognitive reliability which plays a crucial role in determining the accuracy of work performance, and on the relationship of the control status of the organizational environment with work performance in the case of hospital nurses. Evidence on the relationship between perceived organizational environment and performance reliability, and evidence on the comparison of the occurrence pattern of incident during 24 hours by organizational control mode were provided for predicting the occurrence of incident. Improvement of perceived organizational environment plays an important role to develop professional discretion and autonomy which leads to transformation of atmosphere or climate of organizational environment for overcoming specific threats or risks.

PERFORMANCE RELIABILITY

Performance reliability is influenced by the levels of perception and cognition of the work organizational environment. Performance reliability, precisely cognitive reliability, is predicted by evaluating the interaction between the intrinsic control of cognitive function at work and the extrinsic control of the work environment (Hollnagel 1993, 1998). Human error is predicted by measuring the interaction between cognitive functions and work organizational control by using the theoretical model of contextual control mode of cognition (COCOM; Hollagel, 1993). According to the theory of CREAM (Cognitive Reliability and Error Analysis Method) (Hollnagel, 1998), human erroneous actions are evaluated by the level of cognition on the work organizational environment including the technical environment. The level of cognition is measured by nine question items of the common performance condition (CPCs) (Hollagel, 1998), asking how do you cognize working conditions around you, such as 1) how do you cognize the adequacy of the organization, 2) working conditions 3) adequacy of the Man-Machine Interface and operational support, 4) availability of procedures/plans, 5) number of simultaneous goals, 6) available time, 7) time of day/circadian rhythm, 8) adequacy of training and preparation, 9) crew collaboration quality. The subjects are expected to select one of four answers, very efficient/efficient/inefficient/deficient. In this model, organizational control modes are divided into four, such as strategic, tactical, opportunistic and scrambled by the scores counted on two axes of improved reliability and reduced reliability assessed by the CPC. Human error can be predicted by classifying into organizational control mode. Weighing factors in estimating human error are $2.3E+01$ in scrambled, $7.5E+00$ in opportunistic, $1.9E+00$ in tactical, and $9.4E-01$ in strategic. The highest reliability is in the strategic control mode, while the lowest is in the scrambled control mode.

Perceived organizational environment plays a critical role in enhancing cognitive congruence and trust atmosphere among different disciplinary staff. Keeping good interpersonal relationship builds and enhances organizational resilience as well as organizational security, which leads to the reduction of incidental occurrence and the improvement of performance reliability. Occurrence of human error relates with organizational climate or culture as well as a particular mismatch in a man-machine system, or a particular individual behavior.

CURRENT STATUS OF PERCEIVED ORGANIZATIONAL ENVIRONMENT ASSESSED BY THE CPCS

Most health care teams are organized by heterogeneous professional staff, e.g. medical physicians, clinical nurses, nurses' specialists and other clinical specialists. Without a mutual understanding and trust among heterogeneous professional staff, team coherence cannot be maintained and empowered. Innovative actions can only be created in the work organization constituted by multi-disciplinary staff with autonomy and shared responsibility rather than by a homogeneous discipline. Each professional group has group objectives and strategic directions in performing their roles and work in a discretionary manner. Nurses in the mode of strategic control in Japan, however, are very few (0.8% in the averages of six hospitals) in accordance with our investigations as shown in Figure 1 (Saito, Ikeda and Seki, 2000, Saito, Inoue, Seki, 2005, Murakami, 2003, Murakami, Inoue and Saito, 2007). The majority of nurses are in the mode of tactical (57.9%), which signifies 57.9% of the nurses are engaging in a given rule-based work and they do not have adequate latitude of their professional action. It may be very difficult for any professional staffs to take an autonomous action without the mode of strategic control. Nurse groups were not professional as far as we have surveyed in Japan

The roles of nurses in the hospital are crucial for providing the optimum care to the patients and are expected to be professional. Nevertheless, few nurses engage in the higher level hospitals with advanced technology in a strategic control mode. Most of them are placed in one of the subsystems in a hierarchical system. In spite of the assumption that they are decision-making professional staff, most of their work is subsidiary work ordered by some other professional who is in charge of medical diagnosis and treatment. Disturbances and incongruence still exist among heterogeneous professional workers in hospital settings, although they make every effort to develop their careers and to share responsibility. Innovative hospital organization cannot be expected without appropriate transformation of the work organizational environment.

Figure 1. Distribution of nurses' perception on work organizational environment by the mode of organizational control

Control modes — Hospitals tested	Strategic (%)	Tactical (%)	Opportunistic (%)	Scrambled (%)	Total (%)
Hospital A	4(1.1)	215(59.6)	134(37.0)	8(2.2)	361(100.0)
Hospital B	1(0.3)	181(65.3)	164(44.6)	15(4.2)	361(100.0)
Hospital C	4(3.0)	59(44.0)	60(44.8)	11(8.2)	134(100.0)
Hospital D	1(0.6)	112(64.0)	58(33.1)	4(2.3)	175(100.0)
Medical Center-1	0	139(65.9)	67(31.8)	5(2.4)	211(100.0)
Center-2	1(0.5)	132(64.1)	65(31.6)	8(3.9)	206(100.0)
Total (%)	11 (0.8)	838(57.9)	548(37.8)	51(3.5)	1448(100.0)

COMPARISON OF PERCEIVED NURSING WORK BY ORGANIZATIONAL CONTROL MODE

Comparison was made in the regional healthcare sector in Japan by asking questions to 459 female registered nurses, 211 nurses engaging in the hospital affiliated to the university and 248 nurses engaging in the regional healthcare facilities. Their average ages are 25.8 ± 4.8 and 27.8 ± 5.8 in each hospital. Four factors extracted by Factor Analysis, i.e. the goal of organization, member resources, team resources and discretion of professional job were compared among three modes of organizational control, because the nurses in strategic control mode were not observed in the fields surveyed. Significant differences of factor loading among three modes of organizational control were observed in each factor, as shown in Figure 2. As we predicted, nurses' professional roles and their works were significantly different among three modes of organizational control. The lowest factor loading was observed in the mode of scrambled, while the highest was in the mode of tactical.

Figure 2. Comparison of perceived nursing job by organizational control mode

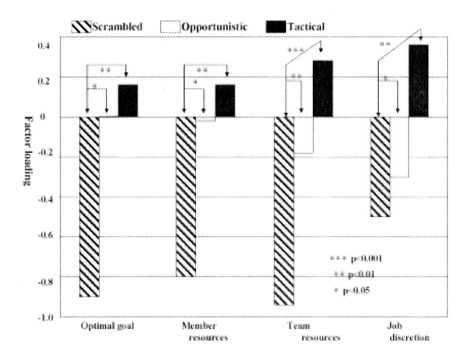

COMPARISON OF INCIDENT RATES DURING 24 HOURS OF HEALTH AND NURSING CARE WORKS

The number of nurses who participated in this survey was 211. Reporting incidence was made for three weeks. Numbers of incident experience were 286 during three weeks, so that some had plural incident experiences and some were without any incident experiences. The highest rate of incident experience was observed in the morning period, between 9 to 11 AM in the mode of scrambled as shown in Figure 3. The reasons why higher occurrence happens in this period include: 1) the patients get out from their beds after taking breakfast to walk to the rest room, 2) nurses are changing work shifts. Each nurse is strictly required to exchange jobs without any delay or mistakes. 3) Surgical operation usually starts in this period. Nurses are required to send the patient to the operation room. An increasing trend of the rate was also observed in the modes of opportunistic and tactical, but in the mode of opportunistic, the trend was rather sporadic during 24 hours of working day. The incident rate in the mode of tactical was kept lower during 24 hours. Three characteristic occurrence patterns of incident experience were observed by cognitive

Figure 3. Average occurrence of incident rate during 24 hours by organizational control mode

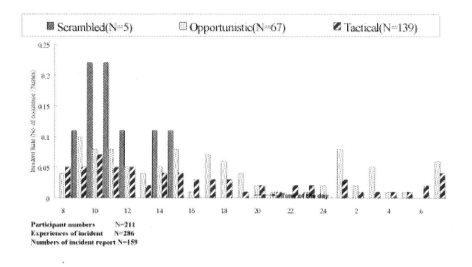

mode of organizational environment.

In the hospitals providing healthcare services for 24 hours, it has been reported that incident experience or accidental cases might happen in some specific periods during 24 hours, such as in the exchange periods of nurses by work shift in the morning, and at midnight when the nurses in charge are very few to take care of all the patients in the ward. Higher rates of incident occurrence may be induced by stressful work conditions in the specific period during 24 hours. According to the surveys we made in the past, nurses' perception on work organizational environment measured by the CPC's gave significant effects on the occurrence of incident experience in addition with the reasons reported in the studies on industrial fatigue, such as work fatigue cumulated by night shift, by the continuation of difficult work, or by conflict among employees without any autonomy and so forth. Enhancement of work perception, job cognition in care-providing areas like healthcare sector, is of importance to keep a high quality of care. The relation between work stress and industrial accident has been studied and clarified by many researchers (Hashimoto,1984, Wickens, 1992, Hollnagel 1998, Endsley and Garland, 2000). Some characteristic occurrence patterns induced by work stress and work conditions were reported in railway, airway operations and manufacturing plants, or sales and some service works

COMPARISON OF REDUCED RELIABILITY BY ORGANIZATIONAL CONTROL MODE

It is really a surprise to find out the fact that very few nurses who perceived organizational environment under which they are working to be strategic, although the group of nurses is the largest among hospital professional staff groups and nurses are expected to be responsible in taking care of patients. Nurses have been placed still to be as one of the subgroups in the hospital organization. It is hard to say whether or not they are autonomous and professional groups with strategic goals for providing care to the patients. Comparison in this study was made among three modes of organizational control without the mode of strategic, i.e. among three modes of organizational control, scrambled, opportunistic and tactical. Significant differences (p<0.001) in reduced reliability of performance were observed among three modes as shown in Figure 4. To keep up higher reliability of performance, organizational environment is to be redesigned for nurses to enable them to perform their jobs in a tactical mode in this study, but hopefully in a strategic mode. The higher mode of organizational control is in the work environment, the lower numbers of the occurrence of erroneous action are assured.

Figure 4. Comparison of reduced reliability in work performance amoung four modes of organizational control perceived

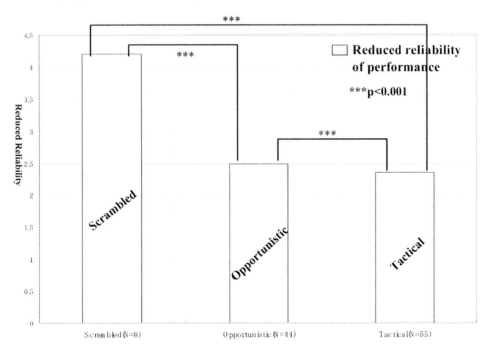

DISCUSSIONS AND IMPLICATION

Cognitive Reliability and Organizational Competence for Overcoming Incidental Situations

Cognitive reliability of work organization plays critical roles in determining organizational performance efficiency and effectiveness. It was predicted by our investigations on comparison of incident experience with reduced performance reliability that incident rates and performance reliability were influenced by cognition modes, such as three modes of perceived organizational environment, tactical, opportunistic and scrambled. To keep the perceptual level of organizational environment to be higher it is important to improve performance reliability and to reduce incident experience. In addition, with rule-based management which has been a major traditional management style, insight into current organizational environment and foresight in the future by strategic plan required in systemic management are inevitable to reduce incident experiences during work and to develop professional expertise and skills for nurses to provide the optimal care to the clients (Rouse, 1993, Tsuokas & Shepherd, 2004). The evidence provided in this Chapter suggests that work performance is improved as the level of nurses' perception on organizational control becomes higher. Quality of care work by nurses increases as the level of perceived organizational control increases, namely a positive relationship exists between quality of nursing care and perceived level of organizational environment. Risk sharing and improvement of work performance could be made by raising perceptual level of work environment in addition with compliance of nurses' job duties. Cognitive reliability on hospital organizational environment is a key concept for hospital management by professional staff.

Characteristic distribution patterns of incident experience shown in Figure 3 suggest that redesigning the work shift system in the morning was urgently required in order to reduce the occurrence of incident experience. In reducing incident experience in every work shift, keeping the higher level of perception on organizational environment is necessary in addition with technical support for redesigning the system of work shift, especially night shift. Redesigning of total organizational climate is also necessary to increase organizational competence for overcoming incidental situations.

Lack of Strategic Mode of Organizational Control

Most healthcare teams are organized by heterogeneous professional staff, e.g. medical physicians, clinical nurses, clinical specialists in nurses and physicians. Without mutual understanding and trust among heterogeneous professional staff, team reciprocity is rarely maintained and empowered. The values could be generated and generalized in the work organization where each disciplinary staff acts in a discretionary manner. Nurses in the mode of strategic control, in reality, are very few in the hospitals we have surveyed, and the majority of them are in the mode of tactical control in which most of their work is given as a routine work or rule-based work they have to follow. It may be difficult for any professional staff to take an autonomous action without strategic control. The roles of nurses in the hospital are crucial for providing the optimum care to the patients. Nevertheless, there are few nurses who can take a professional action in a strategic control mode of organization. Most of the nurses who we surveyed are engaging in one of the sub-systems as a means of super-systems. Most of their work is subsidiary work ordered by some other professionals who are in charge of medical diagnosis and treatment. Disturbances and incongruence still exist among heterogeneous professional workers, although they make every effort to develop their careers and to share responsibility. Innovative hospital organization cannot be expected without appropriate transformation of work organizational environment.

THE PROBLEMS LEFT FOR FURTHER STUDY

The above-description was quite limited in terms of the numbers of the hospital nurses we had surveyed. It is necessary in analyzing the larger group of sample including clinicians, technicians and other healthcare staffs to classify the subjects into cognitive modes of the organizational environment before quantification, because, in reality, there are various types of work process and workers' actions under the constraints of the workplace. Action processes might be different in the different professional disciplines in accordance with their roles and responsibilities, and the constraints of the organizational environment, such as organizational resources, the latitude of professional job, the time allowed, and so forth. Further survey in the future is required for the generalization of cognitive mode of organizational environment.

The problematic situations caused by human error may stem from cognitive misfit of work organization between external and internal cognitive world of the participants. It is, therefore, required that the participants are aware of the present situation and future perspectives of the organizational environment and to take action in changing work organization into an innovative and intelligent organization. In doing so, there are many problems left in the processes of service delivery, both at the individual and organizational levels to be continuously surveyed and identified. Transformation of organizational climate may be feasible to overcome specific threats or risks and to increase organizational flexibility or resilience. Work competence in terms of enhancement of interpersonal relationship as well as improvement of technical skill, and work competence in terms of enlightenment of foresight and insight into the continuation of the past, the present and the future which are not simply the accumulation of knowledge in a particular discipline, skills or attitudes, is required in order to improve professional performance. Further studies in various fields are needed to know cognition congruence or misfit in various workplaces and to understand that interpersonal management competence and perception of strategic organizational control mode are enhanced by changing traditional organization into knowledgeable organization, which leads professional staff to be inspired to take a strategic action.

FUTURE DIRECTIONS

Enhancement of Recognition as a Profession with Sense of OCB and CSR

Compliance with the work given is strongly kept in nurses' minds, but the sense of organizational citizenship and social responsibility are quite inadequate for professional staff who are responsible for providing a high quality of care. Most of the nurses scarcely recognize how to behave as an organizational citizen with corporate social responsibility. The perceptual level of organizational environment is very low in the hospital nurses we surveyed, because of their educational background and generally inadequate training in the field. As mentioned in "Lack of strategic mode of organizational control", they do not take a professional action for which they think they are confident Their attention to their work environment is not pertinent due to inadequate recognition to work environment and also due to inappropriate organizational environment, for instance, quite limited communication, specifically vertical communication with top management, or few safety nets which nurses can rely on. It seems that they do their job by just following the instructions given by their managers or superintendents.

By adopting some appropriate tools of knowledge management, traditional types of organizations can change into Ad Hoc types of organization where they can manage things more effectively, and where they can understand what is the OCB and the CSR. A nurse engaging in an healthcare organization is expected to be a professional staff by conducting knowledge management by values as well as management by objectives and management by instructions. Necessary steps for changing current organizations into knowledgeable organizations are required by continuing to redesign the organization to be more effective to all the stakeholders.

Work Shift Systems Change for Reducing Human Errors

As described in the case study in this chapter, the characteristic pattern of incident occurrence during 24 hours was identified, and redesigning work shift systems is required in considering the occurrence of incidence, work flow during 24 hours, and also manpower and management resources. The work shift systems operated in the hospital surveyed can be to change into more flexible and knowledgeable systems. Intensive countermeasures in parallel with applying appropriate knowledge management methodologies are placed on the particular work periods where higher rates of human error are observed for improving work performance as well as quality of service Flexible and continuous change of organizational culture is expected in coping with complex and unanticipated demands in the future.

ACKNOWLEDGMENT

Author appreciates Murakami,G. for collecting and analyzing data in the fields who is a Doctor course student in University of Kyoto after completed Master course in Saito Lab., in Dept. of Industrial and Management Systems Engineering, School of Science and Engineering, Waseda University

REFERENCES

Beer, S. (1979). *The heart of enterprise*. John Wiley and Sons, Inc.

Endsley, M. R., & Garland, D. J. (2000). *Situation awareness and measurement*. LEA.

Espejo, R. (1996). Enabling systemic management. In R. Espejo, W. Schuhmann, M. Schwaninger & U. Bilello (Eds.), *Organizational transformation and learning: A cybernetic approach to management* (pp. 227-270).

Flood, R. (1996). *Beyond TQM* (pp. 106-118). John Wiley and Son, Inc.

Flood, R. (1998). Action research and the management and systems sciences. *Systemic Practice and Action Research, 11*(1), 79–101. doi:10.1023/A:1022917022601

Graen, G. (1976). Role-making processes within complex organizations. In M. D. Dunnette (Ed.), *Handbook of Industrial and Organizational Psychology* (pp. 1201-1245). Rand McNally.

Hashimoto, K. (1984). *Safety ergonomics* (in Japanese). Central Protection Association of Labor Disaster in Japan.

Hollnagel, E. (1993). *Human reliability analysis: Context and control.* London: Academic Press.

Hollnagel, E. (1998). *Cognitive reliability and error analysis method: CREAM.* Elsevier.

Mingers, J., & Gill, A. (1997). *Multimethodology: The theory and practice of combining management science methodologies.* John Wiley and Sons, Inc.

Murakami, G. (2003). *A study on performance reliability of nursing care work and organizational control.* Graduation theses in Waseda University (in Japanese) (pp. 201-202).

Murakami, G., Inoue, T., & Saito, M. (2007). On cognitive reliability of hospital organizational environment and work performance. *Int. J. Healthcare Technology and Management, 8*(3/4), 388–398. doi:10.1504/IJHTM.2007.013170

Reason, J. (1990). *Human error.* Cambridge University Press.

Reason, J. (1997). *Managing the risk of organizational accidents.* Ashgate.

Rouse, W. B. (1993). *Catalysts for change: Concepts and principles for enabling innovation.* John Wiley and Sons Inc.

Saito, M., Ikeda, M., & Seki, H. (2000). A study on adaptive action development: Interference of mood states with perceived performance and perceived efficacy. In *Proceedings of the 14th International Congress of Ergonomics,* San Diego (Vol.5, pp. 48-51).

Saito, M., Inoue, T., & Seki, H. (2005). Organizational control mode, cognitive activity, and performance reliability. In Wickramasinghe, Gupta & Sharma (Eds.), *Creating knowledge-based healthcare organization* (pp. 179-192). Hershey, PA: Idea Group Publishing.

Saito, M., Watanabe, T., Murakami, G., & Karashima, M. (2005). Communication and emotional types and the effectiveness of team care. In *Proceedings of the 4th International Conference on the Management of Healthcare and Medical Technology,* Aalborg Univ. Denmark (pp. 336-345).

Schwaninger, M. (2000). Managing complexity-the path toward intelligent organization. *Systemic Practice and Action Research, 13*(2), 207–241. doi:10.1023/A:1009546721353

Tsuokas, H., & Shepherd, J. (2004). *Managing the future: Foresight in the knowledge economy.* Blackwell.

Wickens, C. D. (1992). *Engineering psychology and human performance.* Harper-Collins Publishers Inc.

Yossi, S. (2007). *The resilience enterprises: Overcoming vulnerability for competitive advantage.* MIT Press.

Chapter 12

Roles of Interpersonal Relationships in Improving Organizational Performances in the Case of Hospital Nurses

Murako Saito
Waseda University, Japan

ABSTRACT

In this chapter, a comparison of organizational performances representing team reciprocity, communication accuracy, and performance reliability was made with participants' competence of emotional regulation, communication type, and also with the appreciation level of professional work based on our empirical studies on healthcare organization. The results in case study 1 suggest that team reciprocity is significantly influenced by the type of communication, face–to–face (FTF) and computer mediating communication (CMC). The results in case study 2 suggest that interpersonal relationship management played important roles in giving critical effects on organizational performance of team reciprocity, communication accuracy, and performance reliability. The results in case study 3 suggest that appreciation degree of team and organization goals gave significant effects on team reciprocity and performance reliability. Causal relationships among structural variables on work environment, communication, and organizational performances in case study 1, and causal relationships among work demand, organizational environment, and fairness in case study 3, were discussed. Quality of healthcare evaluated by organizational performance is influenced by the condition of how interpersonal relationship plays

DOI: 10.4018/978-1-60566-284-8.ch012

a role in managing emotional regulation, communication, and appreciation of the work environment. Most of the organizational issues are related with loss of confidence and trust among the participants of the organization, which stems largely from inappropriate alignment of interpersonal relationships.

INTRODUCTION

Improvement of quality of care (QOC) has been the major goal in healthcare system redesign. The participants of healthcare organizations; care-providers, care-receivers and their families are also the evaluators of the healthcare system at each point. Hence, there are various interpretations of the information presented and of the events interfaced by these participants. Serious misunderstanding of concepts or terms occurs among people. It is very difficult to adjust the occurrence of cognitive misfits among the participants of the organization. The decrement of the QOC is mainly induced by inadequacy of organizational alignment, by misalignment of organizational work condition, inappropriate application of knowledge, skills and attitudes of the participants (Saito, Ikeda, Seki, 2000, Saito, Inoue, Seki, 2004). Interpersonal relationship in the organizational environment of the workplace gives critical effects on human action.

Human performance is an outcome of the controlled use of human competence adapted to the requirement of the situation (Hollnagel, 1993, 1998, Rasmussen, 1994, Reason, 1997). The binary classification as to whether the task will succeed or fail by measuring erroneous action, therefore, is too simple for identifying the occurrence of incidental action influenced by a changing work environment. Most of the inappropriate and erroneous actions causing decrement of organizational performance are, however, due to misalignment of interpersonal relationship. Re-designing organization in parallel with technological development is needed for improving the QOC in a healthcare organization. Organizational transformation needs to be redesigned into the organization in which the atmosphere becomes a vivid and vigorous climate, and interpersonal relationship turns out to be more transparent and trustworthy.

The QOC, both in appropriateness of caring and in security for patients depends on the level of healthcare staff' cognition or appreciation of the work environment. It is of importance, therefore, to align an appropriate organizational environment, its climate or culture, providing a life long learning atmosphere to inspire individual awareness and also to create organizational knowledge. Redesigning of a work organization is required to provide an appropriate and reliable climate in which accurate information on patient care and security can be shared among heterogeneous disciplines. This Chapter is organized into three parts, first, explanations on the parameters used and on methods are given, second, the analytical results as empirical evidence in case study 1, 2 and 3 are provided, and third, discussion and implications of team reciprocity by communication type, communication accuracy and performance reliability by emotional regulation, and team reciprocity and performance reliability by the degree of appreciation are stated.

EXPLANATION ON PARAMETERS USED AS CRITERIA

Team Reciprocity / Team Coherency

Team reciprocity was measured by using the team-member exchange construct (TMX) developed by Seers, 1989, Seers, Petty, and Cashman, 1995, which was designed to asses employees' exchange relationship to the peer group as a team. The TMX assesses the reciprocity among team members with respect to the member's contribution of ideas, feedback and assistance to other members, constituted by 34 questionnaire items with a 5-point scale, as -2, -1, 0, +1, and +2 respectively. Team reciprocity was used for assessing organizational performance in our empirical studies.

Communication Accuracy and Team Member Resources

Regarding communication accuracy, communication accuracy-1 which means that problem-solutions were made immediately and at the place occurred, and communication accuracy-2 which means to take time for confirmation on patient care information, were extracted. Regarding team member resources, specialist's decision-making and job decision-making representing team member resources-1 and -2 respectively were obtained as latent factors extracted from self-administered questionnaires we had prepared for our studies.

Performance Reliability

Performance reliability was measured by using the scores of the CPC's (Common Performance Conditions, developed by Hollnagel,1998), composed by nine conditions, such as (1) adequacy of organization (2)working conditions (3)adequacy of MMI (Man-Machine Interface) and operational support (4)adequacy of procedure (5)number of simultaneous goals (6)available time (7)time of day (8)adequacy of training and experience (9)crew collaboration quality, with a three or four-point scale in each condition. Occurrence of human error can be predicted by the score of the CPC's.

PERFORMANCE COMPARISON

Performance comparison was made by communication type, by emotional regulation and by appreciation degree.

Communication Type

Communication type may be different depending upon academic disciplinary fields and in the process of their work in organization, and also in actual situations they may encounter in their practices. Communication among the participants plays a critical role in improving work efficiency and effectiveness in organizational environment. Different types of communication among various disciplines were found in our empirical studies in the past and two types of communication were identified, such as computer-mediated communication (CMC) and face-to-face communication (FTF).

Emotional Regulation

Emotional regulation plays a decisive role in fostering a dynamic collaboration type of care. Job competence of emotional regulation is a learned capability based on emotional intelligence that results in outstanding performance. Emotional competence is a learned ability which is classified into self-awareness, self-management, social awareness and interpersonal relationship management, according to emotional intelligence (EI) developed by Boyatzis, Goleman and Rhee 2000, Cheniss and Goleman 2001. Our study suggests that the regulations in social awareness and in interpersonal relationship management had strong effects on the performances, such as performance reliability, accuracy of communication, development of team and member resources (Murakami, 2005Saito, Inoue, Seki, 2004, Saito, Watanabe, Murakami, Karashima,2005, Saito, Murakami, Karashima,2007). Emotional regulation is an important modulator for the improvement of the QOC

Appreciation on Work Environment

The theories on the continuous or recursive process of organizational learning in the field we have referred to in our surveys are appreciation system theory (Vickers, 1965, 1983), soft systems methodology (Checkland,,1993, Checkland and

Holwell,1998, Checkland and Scholes,1999), and knowledge creation process (Nonaka, and Takeuchi, 1995, Nonaka and Nishiguchi, 2001) The authors found that the essence of Vickers' theory was quite similar to the 'pure experience' which emerged in the practical field and which was the essence of Nishida's theory on inquiry into the good (Nishida, 1911, 1990). Many models of appreciation processes are reported, such as the seven stages of internal and external thinking process in soft system methodology (Checkland, 1993), four stages of socialization, externalization, combination and internalization in knowledge creation process (Nonaka and Takeuchi,1995) and many other processes have been reported by the researchers in the past (Deming, 1982, Probust and Gomez, 1992, Maruyama, 1992, 1994, Minger and Gill, 1996, Gomez, 1999, Kaplan and Norton, 2006). In this chapter, the degree of appreciation rather than the recursive process of appreciation is focused on in order to assess human performance at the level of individuals and collectives.

METHODS

Subjects Surveyed

Three studies carried out in a local hospital and national hospitals were selected for this paper to explain the effect of interpersonal relationship, communication and emotional types on organizational performances. The subjects surveyed in case study 1 were 360 nurses engaging in national hospital, their verage ages ± SD were 25.7 ± 5.8. The subjects surveyed in case study 2 were 248 national hospital nurses. The subjects surveyed in case study 3 were 175 nurses engaging in local hospital, their average ages ± SD were 32.1± 9.1.

Survey Methods

The self-administered questionnaires were prepared for the surveys on organizational climate made in the past. The questionnaires we made consisted of 38 question items with a 4-point scale. The questionnaires on communication are 40 items with a 4-point scale, nursing care work of 36 items with a 4-point scale, and some questionnaire items for job appreciation on each disciplinary goals, teamwork goals and organizational goals. Team reciprocity consisting of 10 question items developed by Seers (1989), emotional intelligence competence consisting of 21 question items developed by Boyatzis, Goleman, and Rhee (2000) were applied. Performance reliability was measured by using the scores of the CPC's (Common Performance Conditions developed by Hollnagel,1998), composed of nine conditions, such as (1) adequacy of organization (2)working conditions (3)adequacy of

MMI (Man-Machine Interface) and operational support (4)adequacy of procedure (5)number of simultaneous goals (6)available time (7)time of day (8)adequacy of training and experience (9)crew collaboration quality, with a three or four-point scale in each condition.

COMPARISON OF TEAM RECIPROCITY BY COMMUNICATION IN STUDY 1

Communication was classified into two types, the face-to-face type (the FTF, n=104) and the computer-mediated communication (the CMC, n=90). Figure 1 showed significant difference between two communication types of the CMC and the FTF by using two latent factors extracted by Factor Analysis, such as team member cooperation and the effectiveness of multi-disciplinary conferences representing team reciprocity. Both in team member cooperation and effectiveness of multi-disciplinary conferences, the FTF communication was positively perceived more than the CMC. The CMC is generally accepted as an efficient communication tool, and the FTF is more effective to enhance team reciprocity.

The causal relationship (GFI=0.946, AGFI=0.892, RMR=0.032) among organizational climate, communication, team reciprocity in the FTF was shown in Figure 2. The exogenous variable($\xi 1$) of frequency in communication representing communication gave significant effect($\gamma=0.48$, p<0.01) on a good atmosphere for exchanging ideas and the experience representing organizational climate($\eta 1$) and

Figure 1. Team reciprocity by communication type

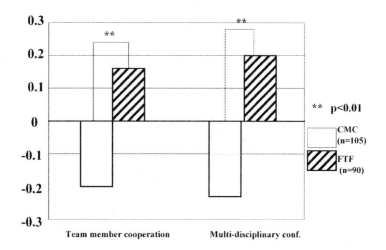

Figure 2. Causal relationship among organizational climate, communication, team reciprocity in FTF type

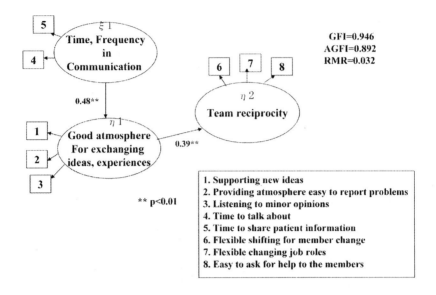

Figure 3. Causal relationship among organizational climate, communication, team reciprocity in CMC type

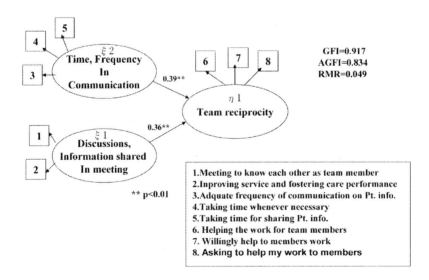

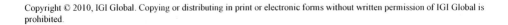

then this endogenous variable integrated as tacit knowledge($\eta 1$) which gave significant effect ($\beta=0.39$, p<0.01) on team cooperation representing team reciprocity as criterion variable($\eta 2$).

The causal relationship (GFI=0.917, AGFI=0.834, RMR= 0.049) among organizational climate, communication, team reciprocity in the CMC was shown in Figure 3. Two exogenous variables($\xi 1,\xi 2$) as explicit knowledge gave each direct effect ($\gamma=0.39$, p<0.01, $\gamma=0.36$, p<0.01) separately, discretely on team cooperation representing team reciprocity as an endogenous variable($\eta 1$).

COMMUNICATION ACCURACY, MEMBER AND TEAM RESOURCES AND PERFORMANCE RELIABILITY BY EMOTIONAL REGULATION IN CASE STUDY 2

The scores of interpersonal relationship management were obtained from the questionnaire inventory of Emotional Intelligence Competence (EIC) developed by Boyatzis, Goleman, Rhee, 2000. According to Cherniss and Goleman, 2001 as the developer of the EIC, the framework of the EIC consists of four conceptual domains, self-awareness, social awareness, self-management and relational management. According to our studies, performance reliability of care-providers was given significant effect by relational management competence through communication accuracy as mediators (Murakami, 2005, Saito, Murakami and Karashima 2007). Comparison of communication accuracy, member and team resources and performance reliability between the higher and the lower score groups of relational management competence was shown in Figure 4, Figure 5 and Figure 6. Significant differences were obtained between the higher and lower score groups. The results suggested that the difference in healthcare service was induced by management competence of interpersonal relationship.

Significant differences between two groups of the higher and the lower score of relation management competence were observed as shown in Figure 4 and Figure 5. Two factors shown in Figure 4 are the timely solution of the problem or problems-solution immediately after occurrence as communication accuracy-1, and confirmation on patient care information as communication accuracy-2. Two factors shown in Figure 5 are specialist's decision-making or decision-making based on each discipline as member resource-1 and job decision as member resources-2.

Two performance reliability scores shown in improved reliability and reduced reliability in care performance which were measured by using the CPC's developed by Hollnagel,1998 were also a significant difference between two groups of the higher and the lower score of relationship management competence as shown in

Figure 4. Comparison of communication accuracy between the higher and the lower groups of interpersonal relationship management (N=124)

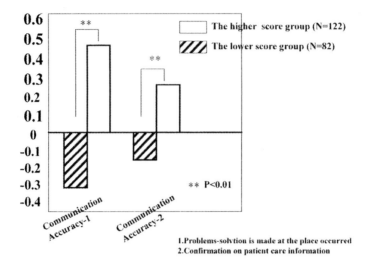

Figure 5. Comparison of team member resources between the higher and the lower groups of interpersonal relationship management (N=124)

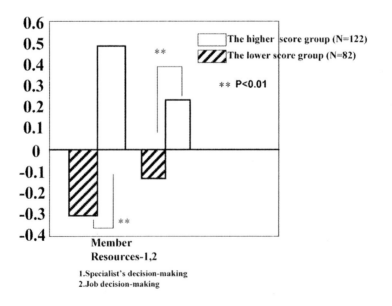

Figure 6. Comparison of performance reliability between the higher and the lower group of interpersonal relationship management

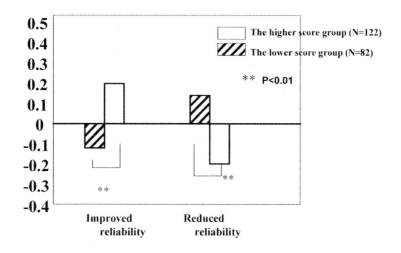

Figure 6. Intangible assets embedded in organization, such as management competence of interpersonal relationship play critical roles in improving care performance reliability.

COMPARISON OF TEAM RECIPROCITY AND PERFORMANCE RELIABILITY BY JOB APPRECIATION IN CASE STUDY 3

Classification of Appreciation on Team and Organizational Goals

Subjects of 175 hospital nurses were classified into two groups, i.e. the higher and the lower groups in the appreciation level of disciplinary goal in the individual, team goals and goal achievement of organization. As shown in Figure 7, significant difference between two groups was observed in terms of the goals in the discipline, team goal and goal achievement in organization (Saito, Murakami, Nishiguchi, Seki, 2006). In the higher group, Group 1, the degree of appreciation in achieving disciplinary goal appeared slightly higher than the appreciative degrees in team goal and organizational goal, while in the lower group, Group 2, the degree of disciplinary goal appeared slightly lower than the degree of appreciation in team goal and organizational goal. These results suggest that development of individual

Figure 7. Clustering nurses by the degree of appreciation on goals

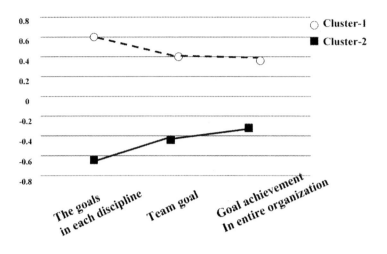

disciplinary knowledge and skills seem important for professional workers like nurses in the higher level of appreciation, while the nurses in the lower level of appreciation seem uninterested and nonchalant to individual development and also in the achievement of team and organizational goals.

Comparison of Team Coherence, Performance Reliability between Two Groups

Organizational performances, such as team coherence or team reciprocity and performance reliability as two important indicators assessing organizational performance, were compared between two groups clustered by appreciation on team and organization goals as shown in Figure 7.

As shown on Figure 8, organizational performances represented by team coherence and performance reliability significantly (P<0.01) differed between two groups of the higher and the lower groups in appreciation, i.e. Group 1 and Group 2. Nurses in Group 1 are expected to provide care with security and safety mind more than the ones in Group 2. Incidence experience and accidental occurrence caused by human error is predicted by performance reliability according to the CREAM (Cognitive Reliability and Error Analysis Method) (Hollnagel, 1998) Average weighing factors of error occurrence for four control modes of organization, such as scrambled, opportunistic, tactical and strategic are 2.3E+01, 7.5E+00, 1.9E+00, and 9.4E-01.

Nurses in Group 1 who marked higher factor loadings in team reciprocity are able to maintain better interpersonal relations among team members than the ones in

Figure 8. Comparison of organizational performance, such as team coherency, performance reliability between the higher and the lower in appreciation of organizational goal

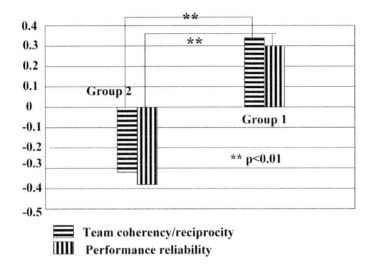

Group 2. Group 1 might be engaging in a recursive process of organizational learning for keeping team coherence and performance reliability to be higher. Individual and organizational performance in Group 1 might be leveraged by communication through organizational learning and might be more effective and cooperative than in Group 2.

Comparison of Multiple Causal Relationship between Two Groups

Causal relationship in the lower group was constructed by the factors representing physical and extrinsic factors, such as work time, frequency of patient visit for caring, while causal relationship in the higher group was constructed by the factors representing intrinsic factors, such as work discretion, mutual understanding, work cooperation. As shown in Figure 9, the meanings of structural variables on work demands, organizational environment and fairness evaluation were different between the two groups. Work cooperation representing work demand($\xi 1$) and team work atmosphere representing organizational environment($\eta 1$) in Group 1 of higher appreciation linked to criterion variable of fairness representing evaluation of individual effort($\eta 2$), while in Group 2 of lower appreciation, working time and time for patient care representing work demand ($\xi 1$) and organizational environment

Figure 9. Causal relationship among environment, work demand, and evaluation fairness in the higher and the lower group in work appreciation

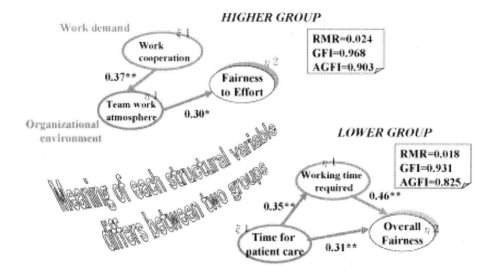

(η1)linked to criterion variable of overall evaluation of hospital(η2). These linkages were testified to by good fit index (GFI=0.968, AGFI=0.903, RMR=0.024 in Group 1, GFI=0.931, AGFI=0.825, RMR=0.018 in Group 2). Direction and strength in causation among three variables, such as work demand, organizational environment and fairness as criterion variable, and also the meaning of the structural variables, were different between the two groups.

In a healthcare organization structured by multi-disciplinary staff, appreciation settings vary and are unlimited in individual rhetoric in the practical field, so that each member is required to be aware of the problematic situation precisely and in time, and also to make the effort in sharing the outcomes responsibility. It is difficult to keep higher consciousness and appreciation of organizational context, attributing meaning to perception in the field without adequate communication and good interpersonal relationship.

Significant difference in organizational performance was observed between two groups, the higher and the lower group of appreciation on work environment. Higher organizational performances of team reciprocity and performance reliability were observed in the group with the higher level of appreciation on organizational context.

DISCUSSIONS AND IMPLICATION

Team Reciprocity by Communication Type

We have identified two types of communication of the FTF and the CMC. Each has specific characteristics and plays an important role in providing care. Team reciprocity which is important to facilitate organizational knowledge and to develop interpersonal relationship management was higher in the FTF than in the CMC. In the FTF type, team reciprocity had a significantly integrated effect through communication among team members in a reliable atmosphere of organizational climate, while in the CMC, each predictor played discrete and independent roles on team reciprocity. This result suggests that transmission of explicit knowledge is independently and efficiently made by the CMC, while in the FTF communication, interpretation or understanding of tacit knowledge as well as explicit knowledge is recursively integrated to create organizational knowledge.

Communication Accuracy, Performance Reliability by Emotional Regulation

Interpersonal relationship management competence which is one of four competencies for evaluating emotional intelligence competence, and which is an important intangible asset, plays a critical role in improving quality of team care. Evidence in this chapter suggests that communication accuracy, member resources, team resources and also human performance reliability were dependent upon interpersonal relationship management competence. Professional workers are required to control their work and to develop their knowledge, skills, attitudes and other characteristics for improving communication accuracy and performance reliability. In so doing, interpersonal relationship is enhanced in a recursive learning process with explicit and implicit knowledge, i.e. in the process of knowledge creation, and work organizational climate is constructed to be more transparent and responsible to the changing local needs by enhancing both types of communication and by developing their competence of interpersonal relationship management.

Team Reciprocity and Performance Reliability by the Degree of Appreciation

The degree of appreciation on the organizational context gave significant effect on team coherence, performance reliability and fairness perception. The higher degree of appreciation on organizational environment played a significant role in keeping higher perception of team reciprocity and performance reliability. Multiple causation between the higher and lower groups of appreciation differed in the intensity and direction of causation among three variables of work demand, organizational environment, and fairness perception. In the higher group of appreciation, work cooperation and understanding among staff led to the acceptance of equity of evaluation and maintaining pride in the work, while in the lower group of appreciation, working time, time required for patient care are strongly related to the overall or vague feeling of fairness. Evidence in this chapter suggests that having higher appreciation was required for approaching the substantiality of the cognitive world, while having lower appreciation means just following daily work without any development and autonomy.

FUTURE DIRECTION

Improvement of quality of care (QOC) has been a major goal in the healthcare system redesign. Care is a catalyst for changing organizational performance in terms of quality and security. Caring plays a critical role in innovating the healthcare organization. Work complexity due to the advancement of information technology (IT) requires healthcare workers to endeavor to enhance team reciprocity for improvement of QOC and performance reliability. Appropriate care to clients could hardly be maintained without strategic team reciprocity which is enhanced by means of communication style, communication accuracy and appropriate appreciation on team and organization goals. Adequate interpersonal relationship which is a key factor in knowledgeable or intelligent organizations play a crucial role in providing good care to meet the clients' need. Innovative organizational environments are aligned and enhanced by the enhancement of human relationship competence underpinned by advanced IT.

ACKNOWLEDGMENT

Author appreciates Murakami who is a Doctor course student in University of Kyoto after completed Master course in Saito Lab. in Dept. of Industrial and Management Systems Engineering, School of Science and Engineering, Waseda University, for collecting and analyzing data in the fields.

REFERENCES

Boyatzis, Goleman, & Rhee. (2000). Clustering competence in emotional intelligence: Insights from the emotional competence inventory (ECI). In R. Bar-On & J. D. A. Parker (Ed.), *The handbook of emotional intelligence: Theory, development, assessment, and application at home school and in the workplace.* Jossey-Bass.

Checkland, P. (1993). *Systems thinking, systems practice.* John Wiley and Sons, Inc.

Checkland, P., & Holwell, S. (1998). *Information, systems, and information systems: Making sense of the field.* John Wiley and Sons, Inc.

Checkland, P., & Scholes, J. (1999). *Soft systems methodology in action.* John Wiley and Sons, Inc.

Cherniss, C., & Goleman, D. (2001). *The emotionally intelligent workplace: How to selecmt for, measure, and improve emotional intelligence in individuals, groups, and organizations.* Jossey-Bass Wiley Company.

Deming, E. W. (1982). *Quality, productivity, and competitive position.* MIT Cambridge.

Hollnagel, E. (1998). *Cognitive reliability and error analysis method: CREAM.* Elsevier. Gomez, P. (1999). *Integrated value management.* International Thomson Press.

Holnagel, E. (1993). *Human reliability analysis: Context and control.* Academic Press.

Kaplan, R. S., & Norton, D. P. (2006). *Alignment: Using the balanced scorecard to create cooperate synergies.* Harvard Business School Press.

Maruyama, M. (1992). *Context and complexity: Cultivating contextual understanding.* Springer-Verlag.

Maruyama, M. (1994). *Mindscapes in management: Use of individual differences in multicultural management.* Dartmouth Publishing Co.

Minger, J., & Gill, A. (1996). *Multimethodology: The theory and practice of combining management science methodology.* John Wiley and Sons, Inc.

Murakami, G. (2005). *A study on care cognition and performance reliability in team nursing* (pp. 245-248). Dissertation abstracts for master's degree, Waseda University (in Japanese).

Nishida, K. (1911). *An inquiry into the good* (in Japanese). Iwanami.

Nishida, K. (1990). *An inquiry into the good* (in English). Translated by M. Abe & C. Ives. Yale University Press.

Nonaka, I., & Konno, N. (1998). The concept of 'ba': Building a foundation for knowledge creation. *California Management Review*, *40*(3), 1–15.

Nonaka, I., & Nishiguchi, T. (2001). *Knowledge emergence: Social, technical, and evolutionary dimensions of knowledge creation.* Oxford University Press.

Probust, G. J. B., & Gomez, P. (1992). Thinking in networks to avoid pitfalls of management thinking. In Maruyama (Ed.), *Context complexity: Cultivating contextual understanding* (pp. 910108). Springer-Verlag.

Rasmussen, J., Pejtersen, A. M., & Goodman, L. P. (1994). *Cognitive systems engineering.* John Wiley and Sons, Inc.

Reason, J. (1997). *Managing the risk of organizational accidents.* Ashgate Publishing Limited.

Saito, M., Ikeda, M., & Seki, H. (2000). A study on adaptive action development: Interference of mood states with perceived performance and perceived efficacy. In *Proceedings of the 14th International Congress of Ergonomics,* San Diego (Vol. 5, pp. 48-51).

Saito, M., Inoue, T., & Seki, H. (2004). Organizational control mode, cognitive activity, and performance reliability: The case of a national hospital in Japan. In Wickramasinghe, Gupta & Sharma (Eds.), *Creating knowledge-based healthcare organization* (pp. 179-192). Hershey, PA: Idea Group Publishing.

Saito, M., Murakami, G., & Karashima, M. (2007). Effect of communication and emotional types on team reciprocity in healthcare organization. *International Journal of Healthcare Technology and Management*, *8*(3/4), 196–208. doi:10.1504/ IJHTM.2007.013160

Saito, M., Murakami, G., Nishiguchi, H., & Seki, H. (2006, November 29-December 2). Job cognition-action causation I hospital nurses for evaluation of team care performance. In *Proceedings of the 9th ICBM,* Bangkok.

Saito, M., Watanabe, T., Murakami, G., & Karashima, M. (2005, August). Communication and emotional types and effectiveness of team care. In *Proceedings of the 4th International Conference on Management of Healthcare and Medical Technology*, Aalborg Univ. Denmark (pp. 336-345).

Schmitt, N., & Chan, D. (1998). *Personal selection: A theoretical approach.* Sage Publications.

Seers, A. (1989). Team member exchange quality: A new construct for role-making research. *Organizational Behavior and Human Decision Processes, 43,* 118–135. doi:10.1016/0749-5978(89)90060-5

Seers, A., Petty, M. M., & Cashman, J. F. (1995). Team-member-exchange under team and traditional management: A naturally occurring quasi-experiment. *Group & Organization Management, 20*(1), 18–38. doi:10.1177/1059601195201003

Vickers, G. (1965). *The art of judgment.* New York: Basic Books.

Vickers, G. (1983). *Human systems are different.* London: Harper & Row.

von Krogh, G. (2000). *Enabling knowledge creation: How to unlock the mystery of tacit knowledge and release the power of innovation.* Oxford University Press.

von Krogh, G., Ichijo, K., & Nonaka, I. (2001). Bringing care into knowledge development of business organization. In Nonaka & Nishiguchi (Eds.), *Knowledge emergence: Social, technical, and evolutionary dimensions of knowledge creation* (pp. 30-52). Oxford University Press.

Chapter 13

Interference of Mood States at Work with Perceived Performance, Perceived Efficacy, and Perceived Health

Murako Saito
Waseda University, Japan

ABSTRACT

The competencies of self-management and interpersonal relationship management play a crucial role in improving individual and organizational performance. Interference of mood states at work with perceived performance, perceived efficacy, and perceived health of individual workers needs to be clarified in redesigning an organizational environment which has an effect on enhancing the competence of individual self-management and interpersonal relationship management. This chapter provides some evidence on the relationship of mood states at work with perceived performance, perceived efficacy, and perceived health of the workers employed in beverage manufacturing plants and lapping chemicals manufacturing plants. The perceptions of performance, self-efficacy, and health status significantly differed among mood states at work. Vigorous mood at work gives positive effect on work perception which in turn leads to the enhancement of work ability and of interpersonal management competence. Vigorous mood at work gave effective power in changing organizational environment and in building in credibility among the participants, which promises a gain in intangible human assets in addition to tangible and extrinsic assets in redesigning innovative organization model.

DOI: 10.4018/978-1-60566-284-8.ch013

INTRODUCTION

Organizational management competencies are required for maintaining good in-interpersonal relationship in the advanced technological environment and for coping with the complexity in changing organizations and the diversity of social demands. The competencies of self-management and interpersonal relationship management play a crucial role in fostering human adaptability and in improving individual and organizational performance. Experiences of interpersonal relationship at work also play important roles in enhancing the values on work consciousness, mood states at work, members' work attitudes in addition to technical knowledge and skills in the course of the recursive organizational learning. Focus on organizational climate or culture has been the concern of many recent studies on organizational management. In a good atmosphere of work environment, especially organizational culture appreciated by all the participants, organizational performance is improved and a credibility is more smoothly built on among the participants, while erroneous actions, accidental occurrences, or withdrawal attitudes are more easily controlled than in the organizations without a good atmosphere to all the stakeholders (George and Jones, 1996, 1997, Schmitt and Chan, 1998). The participants in an organization are expected to take the initiative and act as a leader in developing both themselves and coworkers and in building the bond to collaborate with team members for providing a higher quality of service. Having shared goals among organizational participants harnesses their motivation as well as their volition, and generates their performances to assure a competitive advantage in coping with the turbulence in society (Schwalzer, 1996, Senge, 1990, Barrett, 2006, Gottschalg and Zollo, 2007)

This chapter is focused on the interference of mood states at work with perceived performance, perceived efficacy and workers' perceived health and also on causal relationship among structural variables in the case of workers engaging in manufacturing plants. Empirical evidence in this Chapter provides future directions on changing organizational climate or culture for workers to continue to work in a good mood, which leads to the assurance of competitive advantage.

METHODOLOGY FOR THE INVESTIGATIONS

Theoretical Backgrounds

As to emotional regulation competencies representing recognition of self and others' competences, the competences of self management and interpersonal relationship are important factors in controlling mood states at work and in improving the quality of care (QOC). Our studies in the healthcare sectors suggest that a collaboration

Figure 1. Hypothetical model of the relation between work environment and perceived health moderated or mediate by mood state work, self-efficacy and perceived health

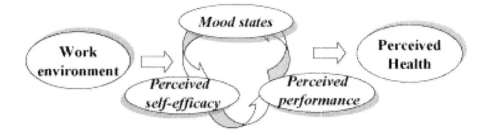

type of care categorized by two axes, i.e. the axis of group level and the axis of degree of care, plays an important role in improving the quality of team care and also organizational performances in comparison with three other types of care, egoistic, specialist, and bureaucratic types of care (Saito, Murakami, Karashima, 2007). In order to identify the important role of a dynamic collaboration type of care, mood states at work, perceived efficacy and perceived performance were placed as moderators or mediators, and perceived health as a criterion as one of the study hypothetical models in our studies. Our studies in the past suggested that job consciousness, emotional states at work, individual and organizational performances gave critical effects on occupational health status (Saito, Ikeda, Seki.2000, Saito, Konishi, Seki 2000). One of the theoretical images is illustrated in Figure1. This article describes classification of mood state at work, and the relation of mood state at work with perceived performance, perceived self-efficacy and perceived health status, and finally covariance structure model analyzed by using three variables, interpersonal communication, job demand and job control. The evidence provided in this chapter is very useful and gives some clues when preparing knowledge management process in the workplaces.

METHODS

The four kinds of questionnaires used in Study I and Study II include:

1.   The profile of mood states (POMS) developed by McNair, Lorr, and Droppleman (1971) which was applied in investigations as to the measurement of mood states at work. The questionnaire of the POMS has 65 question items with

5-point scale and is evaluated by six T-values, such as tension and anxiety (T-A), depression- dejection (D-D), anger-hostility (A-H), vigor (V), fatigue (F) and confusion(C).

2. Perceived health status was measured by applying the Todai Helath Index (THI) developed by Suzuki,S. Aoki,S. and Ynai,H.,1976, Suzuki,S. and Roberts,R.E.(1991). Perceived health status was depicted as a radar chart constituted of 12 scale values, vague complaints(SUSY), respiratory(RESP), eye and skin(EYSK), mouth and anal(MOUT), digestive(DIGE), irritabilities(IMPU), lie scale(LISC), mental instability (MENT), depressiveness(DEPR), aggressiveness(AGGR), nervousness(NERV) and life irregularity(LIFE). In addition to the pattern of health structure, health level was also diagnosed by using DF values (discriminant function values) for psychosomatics, for neurotics and for schizophrenics. The larger the DF value, the greater the probability of disease.

3. The questionnaire on self-efficacy was prepared for the survey by referring to a 20-item perceived self-efficacy developed by Schwalzer (1993, 1996).

4. Perceived performance was measured by actuality/potentiality (Beer, 1979, Flood, 1993, Espejo, Schumann, Schwaninger and Bilello,1996). Actuality is the current achievement with existing resources within existing constraints. Potentiality is what could be achieved by developing resources and removing constraints.

Subjects Surveyed in Study I and Study II

Survey subjects in Study I were 488 male workers engaging in beverage manufacturing plants located in four different areas in Japan. Average age of the workers surveyed and standard deviation are 44.7 ± 8.2 (Saito, Ikeda and Seki,2000). The subjects in Study II were 361 male workers engaging in a lapping chemical manufacturing plant located in Kanto district in Japan (Saito, Konishi and Seki, 2000, Saito, Inoue, Seki, 2002)

CLASSIFICATION OF MOOD STATES AT WORK

Subjects were classified into four groups, Group 1(n=158), Group 2(n=150), Group 3(n=47) and Group 4(n=133) in Study I) as shown in Figure 2, and into two groups in Study II, Group C (n=105) and Group D (n=101) as shown in Figure 3. Asymmetrical pattern of mood states at work measured by the POMS was observed between Group 3 and Group 4 in Study I. The T-values of vigor (V) were apparently lower in comparison with other five T-values, T-A, D-D, A-H, F and C in Group 3 in

Figure 2. Clustering of mood states at work, T-values variation of POMS among 4 groups clustered

Clustering of mood states at work in Study I

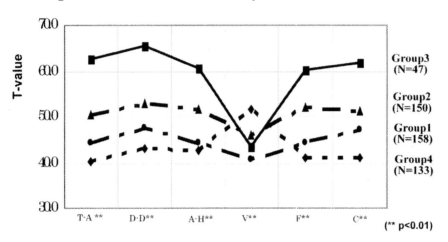

Figure 3. Clustering of mood states at work, T-values variation of POMS among 2 groups selected as the upper ¼ (Group C) and the lower ¼ (Group D)

Two groups in Study II

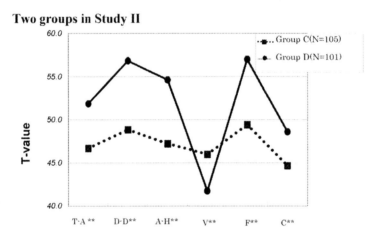

Study I and in Group D in Study II. Significant differences (P<0.01) were observed in six kinds of T-value among Groups in Study I and Study II.

PERCEIVED PERFORMANCE BY MOOD STATES AT WORK

Perceived performance was compared among four Groups in Study I. A significant difference (F (3, 484) = 21.54, P<0.01) was observed among four Groups as shown in Figure 4. Perceived performance (PP=actuality/potentiality) in Group3 appeared the lowest among four Groups, while perceived performance in Group 4 was the highest as shown in Figure 4. This study suggests that mood states at work have a significant effect on perceived performance. Perceived performance was significantly different (P<0.01) between some workers of Group 3 who engage in aseptic environment provided with the appliances of advanced technology and some others of Group3 engaging in traditional non-aseptic automated work environment. It was suggested that the work environment might give critical effect on workers' mood states at work. The relationship between physical environment changed by advanced technology and perceived performance was left for further study due to the limitation of subject number at that time of investigation. Few operators are in the most advanced technological environment because of full automation.

PERCEIVED EFFICACY BY MOOD STATES AT WORK

As shown in Figure 5, a significant difference (F (3, 484) = 11,61, P<0.01) of perceived self-efficacy extracted by PCA was observed among four groups. Factor scores were below 0, i.e. -0.15 in groups 1, -0.09 in group 2 and -0.34 in group 3,

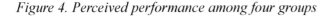

Figure 4. Perceived performance among four groups

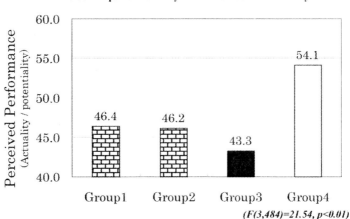

Figure 5. Perceived self-efficacy among four groups in Study I

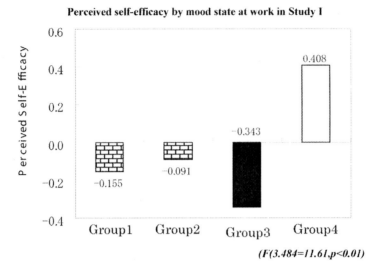

the lowest in group 3, while in group 4 the score was +0.41. A significant difference was also observed between aseptic and non-aseptic lines in group 3. The scores of perceived self-efficacy and perceived performance of the workers engaging in non-aseptic lines were significantly lower than those in aseptic lines in group 3. These results suggest that the conditions of work environment controlled by advanced technologies have an effect on the workers. The effects on workers have been neglected in large industries, but are required consideration for avoiding the decrement of performance, or withdrawal attitudes.

HEALTH STRUCTURE AND HEALTH LEVEL BY MOOD STATES AT WORK

Perceived health status was depicted as a radar chart constituted of 12 scales, such as vague complaints(SUSY), respiratory(RESP), eye and skin(EYSK), mouth and anal(MOUT), digestive(DIGE), irritabilities(IMPU), lie scale(LISC), mental instability (MENT), depressiveness(DEPR), aggressiveness(AGGR), nervousness(NERV) and life irregularity(LIFE) as shown in Figure 6 and Figure 7. In Group3 in Study Iand Group D in Study II, a deviated pattern of health structure, characteristically deviated in the scales of DEPR and MENT appeared in comparison with other Groups. The least deviation in the standard health pattern of Japanese workers was

Figure 6. Radar graph composed of 12 scales and discriminate diagnosis of perceived health among four groups in Study I

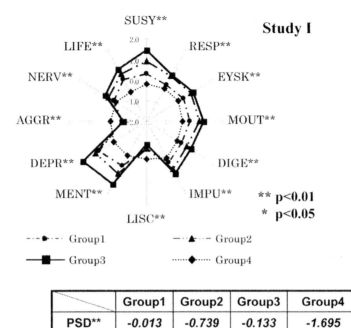

	Group1	Group2	Group3	Group4
PSD**	*-0.013*	*-0.739*	*-0.133*	*-1.695*
NEUR**	*-1.008*	*-0.751*	*0.399*	*-1.982*

seen in Group 4 of which T-value of Vigor was the highest among four groups, and DF values for diagnosing of psychosomatics, of neurotics and of schizophrenics were the lowest among four groups. Group 3 was the highest probability of psychosomatics, neurotics and schizophrenics. As also shown in the lower space of Figure 6, a significant difference in discriminant diagnosis of perceived health level was obtained among four groups ($F(3,484)=18.72$, $P<0.01$). The highest level of perceived health was in group 4 and the lowest was in the group 3. The larger the DF value, the greater the probability of disease. The largest deviation of perceived health structure and the highest probability of disease were observed in group 3. The deviation pattern on the radar chart obtained in this study was similar to those previously reported (Saito et al., 1991, Saito, 1991, Saito and Seki, 1998).

In Study II, the health structure of Group D was significantly deviated especially in the scales of DEPR and MENT, and DF values in Psychosomatics and neurotics were significantly higher than those of Group C. Mood states at work play a decisive role in improving perceived health.

Significant differences among four groups of mood states were observed in per-

Figure 7. Radar graph composed of 12 scales and discriminate diagnosis of perceived health among two groups in Study II

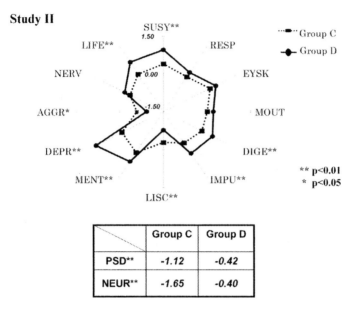

	Group C	Group D
PSD**	-1.12	-0.42
NEUR**	-1.65	-0.40

ceived performance, perceived efficacy and perceived health. Perceived performance, perceived efficacy and perceived health were interrelated and enhanced with higher vigorous mood and with lower mood states of T-A, D-D, A-H, F and C as observed in Group 4. In the group 3 in which the lower value of vigorous mood and the higher values of the other five mood states are observed, perceived performance, perceived self-efficacy were decreasing, and perceived health was deteriorated. These results suggested that an asymmetrical interference of mood states with perceptions of performance and efficacy and health was observed between group 3 and group 4, and that vigorous mood plays an important role in promoting an adaptive level of the job environment. Two types of workers engage in manufacturing plants, one type of worker accepts a controlled environment which is aseptic or coercive environment by advanced technology, the other type of worker feels isolated and tends to lose motivation. Appropriate allotment of work is needed for workers to keep a vigorous mood at work and a higher level of perceived health.

COVARIANCE STRUCTURE MODELS

Three variables, interpersonal communication, job demand and job control representing work environment of exogenous construct extracted by FA, and four endogenous variables obtained by PCA were hypothetically linked and analyzed. Four kinds of structural models were selected for explaining the causal relationship of the variables as shown in Figure 9.

Model 4 of moderated effect model in which the mood-state was dealt with as an exogenous variable was adopted as the most appropriate linkages to explain the reality of the work environment in terms of accountability (goodness of fit, GFI=0.93), stability (adjusted goodness of fit, AGFI=0.900) and residuals (RMR=0.044) among four hypothetical models obtained by Covariance Structure Analysis (CSA). This result suggested that these exogenous variables gave an effect on perceived performance or perceived self-efficacy and simultaneously perceived health. The mood states representing T-A, D-D, F and C gave direct and indirect effects on perceived health.

Figure 8. Cause-effect relation by CSA in Study I

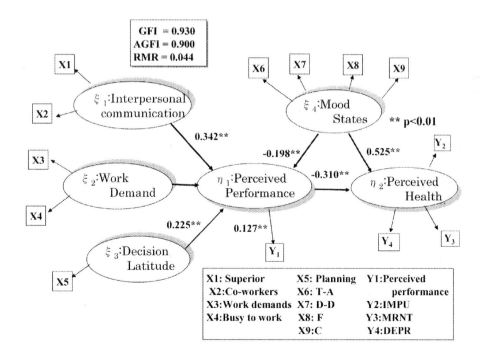

Figure 9. Comparison of covariance structure models

Model 1-4	GFI	AGFI	RMR	GFI-AGFI	variables
Model 1 Mediated effect model	0.906	0.846	0.091	0.060	3 ξ 4 η
Model 2 Moderated effect model	0.923	0.882	0.043	0.041	4 ξ 3 η
Model 3 Moderated effect model	0.941	0.906	0.046	0.035	4 ξ 2 η
Model 4 Moderated effect model	0.930	0.900	0.044	0.030	4 ξ 2 η

DISCUSSION AND LIMITATIONS

1. Significant differences in perceived performance, perceived self-efficacy and perceived health were observed between group 3 and 4 in which mood states at work are asymmetric. Higher perceived performance, higher perceived self-efficacy, higher perceived health level were observed in group 4 in which the T values of mood states at work were significantly higher in V. and significantly lower in T-A, D-D, A-H, F and C, while in group 3, a lower perceived performance, perceived self-efficacy and perceived health were observed, and the T values of mood states at work were lower in V. and higher in T-A, D-D, A-H, F and C. Mood status at work plays a crucial role in controlling perceived performance, perceived self-efficacy and perceived health. A vigorous mood state at work acts an important role in increasing perceived performance and promoting perceived health level.

2. A causation model with four exogenous variables (mood state, interpersonal relation, job demands and job discretion) and two endogenous variables (perceived performance and perceived health) was finally adopted as the most valid and stable model in comparing the four models selected by Covariance Structural Analysis. Perceived performance and perceived health were constrained by the states of the mood on the job. These results suggest that effective management needs to attain dual goals to control a work system and organizational environment supported by advanced technology, and also to enhance perceived health, perceived self-efficacy, perceived performance or adaptive competence of the participants by maintaining good and vigorous mood states at work.

3.   Empirical evidence on the effect of work in a physical environment could not adequately be provided to evaluate organizational performances. Subject collection in various working conditions was also limited in our studies. Further studies were left for the generalization of the results shown in this chapter. Environmental conditions inducing the difference of work environment, such as aseptic and non-aseptic conditions in manufacturing lines in plants need to be controlled for the participants to work in a good mood to maintain their motivation, to avoid the decrement of human performance or withdrawal attitudes. Management of a highly controlled environment by advanced technology was expected to improve for inducing the participants to work with vigorous mood.

CONCLUSION

Empirical evidence provided in this Chapter suggests that enhancement of a vigorous mood at work plays a great role in developing employees' work ability and management competence which leads to appropriately and promptly adapting to the changing technological and organizational environments, and leads to building in credibility among the participants. In redesigning organizational environment, alignment of organizational climate or culture is of importance to enhance mood states at work to be vigorous, which fosters the participants to improve perceived performance and perceived health level.

FUTURE TRENDS

It is very important to see reality in the workplace and to understand how workers' perceive self-efficacy, the work allotted, health status, and mood states at work which give significant effect on work performance. It is also very important to manage the participants to be able to sustain and act in positive moods, in vigorous moods and in good health. An innovative organization is redesigned by providing such an organizational climate for the participants to be able to act in a vigorous mood at work supported by advanced IT systems. The results suggest that alignment of organizational environment is required to create a meaningful atmosphere in providing vigorous moods at work which gives significant effects on perceived performance and perceived health of plant workers, and also suggest that development of more effective and innovative management methodology is made by complementary means of traditional human resources management and a new type of management for the future.

The results observed in the manufacturing plants may be seen in the other work-places, such as the ones in the healthcare sector. How to manage the participants by means of observing and analyzing workplace reality is absolutely effective in redesigning organizational environment to an innovative organization which leads to the achievement of the initial goals and to the enhancement of organizational competence with the advantage of overcoming complex society.

ACKNOWLEDGMENT

Author appreciates Seki, H. who is associate professor in Ryutsu Keizai University, Ibaragi, Japan after completed three-year duty as an assistant professor in Waseda University where he graduated, for collecting and analyzing data obtained in the fields.

REFERENCES

Barrett, R. (2006). *Building a value-driven organization: A whole system approach to cultural transformation.* Elsevier.

Beer, S. (1979). *The heart of enterprise.* Reprinted in 1995, John Wiley and Sons, Inc.

Espejo, R., Schumann, W., Schwaninger, M., & Bilello, U. (1996). *Organizational transformation and learning: A cybernetic approach to management.* John Wiley and Sons, Inc.

Flood, R. (1993). *Beyond TQM.* John Wiley and Sons, Inc.

George, J. M., & Jones, G. R. (1996). The experience of work and turnover inten-tions: Interactive effects of value attainment, job satisfaction, and positive mood. *The Journal of Applied Psychology, 81*(3), 318–325. doi:10.1037/0021-9010.81.3.318

George, J. M., & Jones, G. R. (1997). Experiening work: Values, attitudes, and moods. *Human Relations, 50*(4), 393–416. doi:10.1023/A:1016954827770

Gottschalg, O., & Zollo, M. (2007). Interest alignment and competitive advantage. *Academy of Management Review, 32*(2), 418–437.

Maddux, J. E. (1995). *Self-efficacy, adaptation, and adjustment: Theory, research, and application.* New York: Prenum Press.

McNair, D. M., Lorr, M., & Droppleman, L. F. (1971). *Manual for the profile of mood states(POMS)*. San Diego, CA: Educational and Industrial Testing Service.

Murakami, G., Inoue, T., & Saito, M. (2007). On cognitive reliability of hospital organizational environment and work performance. *International Journal of Healthcare Technology and Management, 8*(3/4), 388–398. doi:10.1504/IJHTM.2007.013170

Saito, M. (1991). Eyestrain in the context of total health from ergo-ophthalmological and psychosomatic ophthalmological viewpoints: A review. *Memoirs of the School of Science & Engineering, 55*, 221–240.

Saito, M., Ikeda, M., & Seki, H. (2000). A study on adaptive action development: Interference of mood states with perceived performance and perceived efficacy. In *Proceedings of the 14ᵗʰ IEA and HFES Congress,* San Diego (Vol. 5, pp. 48-51).

Saito, M., Inoue, T., & Seki, H. (2002). The effect of mood states on perceived performance and on perceived health. In *Proceedings of the 7ᵗʰ International Congress on Behavioral Medicine,* Helsinki, Finland.

Saito, M., Inoue, T., & Seki, H. (2003). Organizational control and performance reliability in hospital nurses. In *Proceedings of the IEA and HHEF Congress,* T-286.

Saito, M., Kishida, K., Aoki, S., & Suzuki, S. (1991). The relationship between eyestrain and health level in automated industrial work as evaluated by the Todai health index questionnaire. In Suzuki, Shosuke & R. E. Roberts (Eds.), *Methods and applications in mental health surveys: The Todai health index* (pp. 194-208).

Saito, M., Konishi, Y., & Seki, H. (2000). A study on information sharedness and active adaptability: Mood states at work as a mediator of the relation among occupational stressors and perceived health. In *Proceedings of the 6ᵗʰ ICBM,* Brisbane.

Saito, M., Murakami, G., & Karashima, M. (2007). Effect of communication and emotional types on team reciprocity in healthcare organization. *International Journal of Healthcare Technology and Management, 8*(3/4), 196–208. doi:10.1504/IJHTM.2007.013160

Schwalzer, R. (1993). *Measurement of perceived self-efficacy.* Berlin: Freie Universitat Press.

Schwalzer, R. (1996). Self-efficacy and health behaviors. In M. Conner & P. Norman (Eds.), *Predicting health behavior* (pp. 163-196). Open University Press.

Schwaninger, M. (2000). Managing complexity: The path toward intelligent organization. *Systemic Practice and Action Research, 13*(2), 207–241. doi:10.1023/A:1009546721353

Senge, P. (1990). *Fifth discipline: The art and practice of the learning organization.* New York: Doubleday.

Suzuki, S., Aoki, S., & Yanai, H. (1976). An introduction to a new health questionnaire, the Todai health index. *Progress in Medicine* (Igaku-no-ayumi, in, in Japanese), 99, 217-225.

Suzuki, S., & Roberts, R. E. (1991). *Methods and applications in mental health surveys: The Todai health index.* University of Tokyo Press.

Chapter 14

Causal Relationship among Perceived Organizational Environment, Leadership, and Organizational Learning in Industrial Workers

Murako Saito
Waseda University, Japan

ABSTRACT

It does not seem that recent social events occur simply due to the inappropriateness of a particular individual human action or a particular technological system. Most social events are caused largely by insufficient organizational management and inappropriate organizational climate in which the participants are scarcely motivated to develop them and to continue their work in a discretionary manner. Organizational performance is improved by designing the organizational environment where the participants are inspired to work in a recursive learning process underpinned by innovative operations management on the basis of systemic thinking. The purpose of this chapter is to present empirical evidence on organizational learning type shaped by strategic business unit (SBU) in industry and to compare organizational performance representing self-discretion, team reciprocity by learning type, and also to identify multiple causations among the structural variables of predictors,

DOI: 10.4018/978-1-60566-284-8.ch014

such as work environment, leadership and organizational learning, and criteria of organizational performance. Characteristic causation was identified among the predictors of work environment and the criteria of organizational performance with the mediators of leadership and organizational learning. The study results in this chapter suggest that organizational learning type is formed by depending on the goals and visions in the SBU or in the logical level of management, and that the recursive process of organizational learning and leadership play mediating roles of leverage in developing the participants' job capabilities and in improving organizational performances. Empirical evidence on the linkage of participants' perceptions and organizational performance described in this chapter may be meaningful in redesigning service delivery operation in healthcare sector as well as in the industrial area.

INTRODUCTION

It is most important to foster the participants of organization in which they are inspired to act and respond more effectively to the organizational visions and goals in a discretional manner than merely to work in accordance with the manual provided in a particular discipline. In an innovative organization underpinned by knowledge management, organizational learning and communication among leaders and followers or heterogeneous participants are a powerful means to enhance team coherence, team member reciprocity or dynamic stability of the organization (Saito, Inoue and Seki, 2002, Saito, Murakami, and Karashima, 2007) and to leverage the organization into being a more effective and intelligent organization which enables to cope with a changing society.

In this chapter, organizational learning, as one of the mediators between perceived work environment and perceived performance, is focused on as one of the effective means or catalysts in redesigning current workplace into an innovative organization. The following four points, namely, classification of organizational learning, organizational performances by cluster, causal relationship by learning type, and mediating roles of leadership and organizational learning, are discussed for improving organizational performance. Empirical evidence provided in this chapter suggests that organizational learning type depends upon organizational goals and business strategies, and that causal relationship among structural variables representing organizational environment, leadership and organizational learning differs depending upon organizational learning type, and also suggested that organizational learning and leadership play important mediating roles to determine the criteria of organizational performance

THEORETICAL BACKGROUNDS ON ORGANIZATIONAL LEARNING

In order to improve organizational performance, job ability of the participants has to be developed in the process of organizational learning. Organizational learning is developed in a recursive process constrained by the antecedents of the enterprise, such as organizational strategies, structure, and climate. In the recursive learning processes, the participants are able to acquire knowledge and skills, and interpret input information so as to transfer it and then implement it in the field. In the course of recursive learning in the organization, the participants consisted of heterogeneous disciplinary members, develop their skills through collaboration in order to enable them to overcome difficulties and disruptions which may happen in the course of doing daily work. Innovative ideas emerge through collaboration with a multi-disciplinary staff..

Improvement of organizational performance is leveraged by organizational learning which has been reported in the theories relevant to systemic thinking (Senge,1990, Flood,1998), and also by diversity management structured by three logical levels of management embraced with three types of organizational learning, such as single loop learning in operational management, double loop learning in strategic management and triple loop learning in legitimate management (Flood and Romm, 1996, Espejo, Schuhman, Schwaninger and Bilello, 1996, Schwaninger, 1997, 2000).

In the relation of information processing with organizational learning, knowledge acquisition and knowledge transfer are mainly dealt with predetermined or extrinsic knowledge information processing which represents single loop learning. Knowledge interpretation is dealt recursively together with intrinsic and extrinsic knowledge in addition with knowledge acquisition and transfer which represents double loop learning (Argyris,1992, 1994, 2004). All the processes of knowledge information processing, such as acquisition, transfer, interpretation and implementation are progressed in triple loop learning (Flood and Romm, 1996, 1998). In the relation of organization learning level with technology, single loop learning is supposed to be a tool of deficiency-supply technology, double loop learning is of new value or another action-inducing technology, and triple loop learning is of autonomy-emerging support technology, as described in Chapter 2. As far as we have observed in the workplace, the type of organizational learning is formed depending on organizational goals, or the goal of the strategic business unit (SBU). The recursive process with all types of learning plays a crucial role in changing organizational culture to develop into an innovative organization.

To identify the relationship among perceived organizational environment, leadership and organizational performance, three hypotheses are prepared as follows.

Survey methods and the results testified are in the following sections.

Hypothesis 1a: Organizational learning type is formed by organizational goals.
Hypothesis 1b: The participant's learning type differs by the role of the work allotted.
Hypothesis 2a: Self-discretion representing work environment differs by learning types of the participants.
Hypothesis 2b: Interpersonal relationship representing team reciprocity differs by learning types of the participants.
Hypothesis 3: Causal relationship among work environment, leadership and organizational learning exits by the type of organizational learning

SUBJECTS SURVEYED AND SURVEY METHODS

Subject numbers in this section were 252 employees engaging in industries, their average age and SD are 42.3 ± 9.2 in male worker and 31.7 ± 7.2 in female worker. All the subjects were asked to respond to the questionnaires on organizational work environment and organizational learning prepared for these surveys. In addition to the questionnaires we had made, Team Member Exchange (TMX) which has 34 question items developed by Seers, 989 (Seers, 1989, Seers, Petty, Cashman, 1995) was applied for extracting team reciprocity. Multifactor Leader Questionnaires (MLQ) which has 21 questionnaire items developed by Bass, 1999 (Bass, and Avolio, 1990, Graen and Uhl-Bien, 1995, Bass, 1999) was also applied for extracting leadership variables.

SURVEY RESULTS

Learning Type by the Work Allotted or the SBU in Enterprise

As shown in Figure 1, organizational learning was classified into three clusters, Cluster 1 with the higher factor loading in what and why types of learning, but the lower in how type of learning, Cluster 2 with the higher factor loading in how type of learning, but the lower in what and why type of learning, and Cluster 3 with the lowest factor loading all in how, what and why types of learning. Cluster 1 is constituted of knowledge workers belonging in the higher levels of organizational hierarchy and research workers in the Dept. of Research & Development, Cluster 2 is of the customer service area in the local level of the organization, in fact, most of them were female workers in charge of counter service work for customers and

Figure 1. Clustering employees by learning type, how, what, why

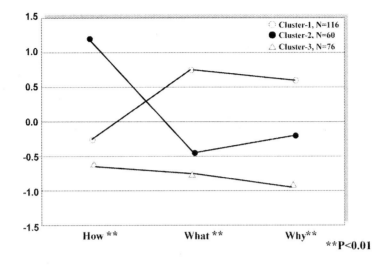

Cluster 3 is of part time workers, most of them were allotted the rule-based or manual work which is given, and they do not have any work autonomy. The results suggested that the formation of an organizational learning type was dependent upon the work allotted by the constraint of a strategic business unit (SBU) in the enterprise. Hence, Hypothesis 1a and 1b were supported as we predicted.

Perceived Work Environment and Team Reciprocity by Cluster

Self-discretion representing work environment, interpersonal relationship and team cooperation representing team reciprocity, were significantly different among Cluster 1, Cluster 2 and Cluster 3, as shown in Figure 2, 3 and 4. The workers in Cluster 1 who work through the process of critical and recursive organizational learning in the levels of what and why types of learning are able to act at a higher level of self-discretion, better interpersonal relation and better cooperation among team members than the workers in Cluster 2 and cluster 3. These results supported Hypotheses 2a and 2b as we predicted.

Causal Relationship by Learning Type

Causal relationships among structural variables on organizational environment and organizational learning were tested to find an independent causation by learning type. Each causation was mediated by characteristic leadership with higher values of good

Figure 2. Self-discretionary action by learning type

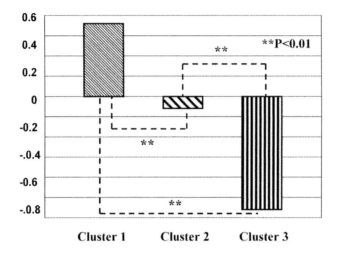

fitness index (GFI=0.940, AGFI=0.901, RMR=0.029 in how-learning, GFI=0.945, AGFI=0.915, RMR=0.028 in what-learning and GFI=0.925, AGFI=0.888, RMR=0.037 in why-learning) As shown in Figure 5, leadership was characterized by the learning type. How the type of learning is mediated by the leader who makes the effort to support subordinates' work by training, what type of learning is medi-

Figure 3. Interpersonal relationship by learning type

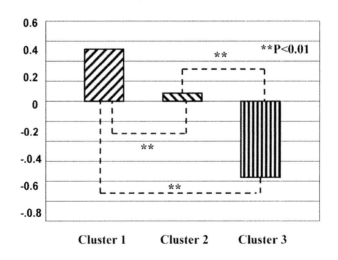

Figure 4. Cooperation amoung team members by learning type

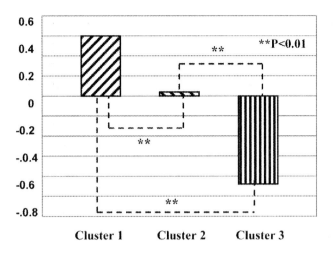

Figure 5. Causal relationship by how-learning, what-learning and why-learning

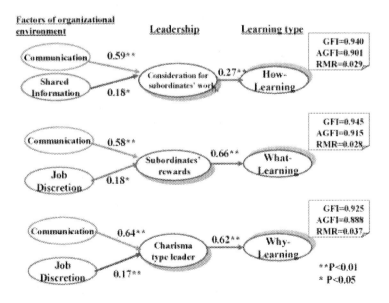

ated by the leader who watches if subordinates are appropriately rewarded, while why type of learning is mediated by a charismatic type of leader. The leadership appropriate to fit to the organizational context plays a role in affecting team performance in each level. The factors representing organizational environment extracted as exogenous factors were also characteristically dependant upon leadership and learning type, such as in the relationship between organizational environment and leadership, communication(γ=0.59, P<0.01) and shared information (γ=0.18, p<0.05) in how-learning, and communication(γ=0.58, P<0.01) and job discretion(γ=0.18, P<0.05) in what learning, communication(γ=0.64, P<0.01) and job discretion(γ=0.17, P<0.01) in why learning. Significant relationships between leadership and learning type were tested, such as significant levels are β=0.27, P<0.01 in how type of learning, β=0.66, P< 0.01 in what type, β=0.62, P<0.01 in why type respectively. These results supported Hypotheses 3 as we predicted.

Mediating Roles of Leadership and Organizational Learning in Improving Organizational Performance

Mediating roles of leadership and organizational learning were clarified by covariance structure analysis (Onozato,2004, Saito, Karashima, Nishiguchi, and Seki, 2007). Both mediators give significantly effective power on organizational performance, as shown in Figure 6. Significantly positive effect (γ= 0.79, P<0.01) of work environment representing shared information(X1), job discretion (X2) and communication (X3) was observed on leadership representing charisma(X4), considering subordinates' work(X5) and their rewards(X6). The mediating construct of leadership which gives

Figure 6. Causation among organizational environment, leadership, learning type and organizational performance

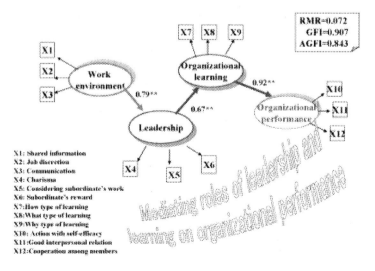

X1: Shared information
X2: Job discretion
X3: Communication
X4: Charisma
X5: Considering subordinate's work
X6: Subordinate's reward
X7: How type of learning
X8: What type of learning
X9: Why type of learning
X10: Action with self-efficacy
X11: Good interpersonal relation
X12: Cooperation among members

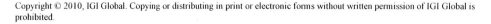

continuously positive effect on organizational learning (β= 0.67, P<0.01) and then makes powerful effect (β=0.92, P<0.01) on organizational performance representing action with self-efficacy(X10), good interpersonal relations (X11) and cooperation among members (X12). Multiple causal relationship constituted by two mediators, leadership and organizational learning, proved quite near to a real situation of workplace (GFI=0.907, AGFI=0.843, RMR=.072), as shown in Figure 5. The two mediators play crucial roles in improving organizational performance.

DISCUSSION AND IMPLICATIONS

In coping with complex and uncertain organizations, such as observed in the industrial domain, autonomy/or self-regulation and team reciprocity in the higher level are needed in transforming an organization into a more effective and innovative organization and in fostering individual proficiency. In assisting individual workers to work in a discretionary manner, recursive learning of what-learning and why-learning based on efficient operation of how-learning which is usually given from the top of organization by the unit of business strategy plays a crucial role as a leverage of organizational transformation. As observed in Cluster 1 with a higher level of what-learning and why-learning in comparison with those of Cluster 2 and Cluster 3, significantly higher performances are expected to transform into an innovative organization. Each local level constrained by the SBU has characteristic leadership type and organizational learning type as mediators to achieve organizational goals and to improve organizational performances. The recursive learning process in innovative organization is mediated by characteristic leadership to develop organizational performance. Organizational learning type is formed by depending upon strategic goals of the organization, such as the SBU in industrial organization. Flexibility or recursiveness in the learning process is needed in order to transform into an innovative organizational culture which leads the participants to achieve their desired reality in the future, and which develops further their individual job proficiency.

CONCLUSION

Organizational learning plays a decisive role in the leverage of developing organizational performance. Individual ability for achieving the work allotted and individual capability, for creating another action to induce an innovation and for developing job proficiency to acquire an insight from the present into the future is fostered in the processes of critical and recursive organizational learning. Empirical evidence provided in this Chapter suggests that an organizational learning type is formed in accordance with the logical level of strategic management, and that the recursive process of organizational learning that plays a role of leverage leads to inspire the participants' appreciation in the context of complex environment and converges into some purposeful actions for the individuals to act as an organizational citizenship.

FUTURE DIRECTIONS

Enhancing Organizational Competence in the Future

Job competence is the different between individual and collective levels. Individuals are expected to take action as an organizational citizenship, and are expected to make every endeavor to fit within individual and organizational future goals and perspectives through organizational learning process. To enhance organizational competence is to foster the participants to be a good organizational citizen or actor. Without organizational competence which enables the overcoming of turbulences and disruptions, redesigning an organization into an innovative organization is rarely achieved to the level planned in the initial stage and is equally rarely expected to sustain in the near future.

Management by Values as Well as by Instruction and by Objectives

Traditional management by instructions and by objectives which had been most popularly applied in the field and has been one of major tools in improving workplace conditions, is required to strengthen its management competence by complementary adoption of knowledge management which embraces another mean of management by values. Value congruence is very important in improving cognitive misfit between individuals and collectives, and also very important in predicting job satisfaction, or withdrawal behaviors. The results described in this chapter suggest that organizational learning and leadership leverage as the mediating roles in managing by values for all the stakeholders of the organization. Organizational learning and leadership are effective means and play mediating roles in improving organizational performance. Complementary approaches applying both traditional management and knowledge management may effect in redesigning work organizational environment not only in the industrial area, but also in the healthcare sector.

REFERENCES

Argyris, C. (1992). *On organizational learning.* Blackwell.

Argyris, C. (1994). *Theory in practice: Increasing professional effectiveness.* Jossey-Bass.

Argyris, C. (2004). *Reasons and rationalizations: The limits to organizational knowledge.* Oxford University Press.

Bass, B. M. (1999). Two decades of research and development in transformational leadership. *European Journal of Work and Organizational Psychology, 8*(1), 9–32. doi:10.1080/135943299398410

Bass, B. M., & Avolio, B. J. (1990). Training and development of transformational leadership: Looking to 1992 and beyond. *European Journal of Industrial Training, 14*, 21–27.

Espejo, R., Schuhman, W., Schwaninger, M., & Bilello, U. (1996). *Organizational transformation and learning: A cybernetic approach to management.* John Wiley and Sons, Inc.

Flood, R. (1998). Fifth discipline: Review and discussion. *Systemic Practice and Action Research, 11*(3), 259–273. doi:10.1023/A:1022948013380

Flood, R., & Romm, R. A. (1996). *Diversity management: Triple loop learning.* John Wiley and Sons, Inc.

Graen, G. B., & Uhl-Bien, M. (1995). Relationship-based approach to leadership: Development of leader-member exchange (LMX) theory of leadership over 25 years, applying a multilevel multidomain perspective. *The Leadership Quarterly, 6*(2), 219–247. doi:10.1016/1048-9843(95)90036-5

Onozato, T. (2004). *A study on realization of triple loop learning in enterprise organization* (pp. 49-52). Degree of master theses, Waseda University.

Saito, M., Inoue, T., & Seki, H. (2002, August 28-30). The effect of mood states on perceived performance and perceived health. In *Proceedings of the 7th International Congress on Behavioral Medicine,* Helsinki, Finland.

Saito, M., Karashima, M., Nishiguchi, H., & Seki, H. (2007, October). Organizational management developing individual job capabilities: Job cogniotion, organizational learning, and organizational performance. In *Proceedings of the 6th International Conference on Hospital of the Future,* Pisa, Italy.

Saito, M., Murakami, G., & Karashima, M. (2007). Effect of communication emotional types on team reciprocity in healthcare organization. *International Journal of Healthcare Technology and Management*, 8(3/4), 196–208. doi:10.1504/IJHTM.2007.013160

Schwaninger, M. (1997). Status and tendencies of management research: A systems oriented perspectives. In J. Minger & A. Gill (Eds.), *Multimethodology* (pp. 127-151). John Wiley and Sons, Inc.

Schwaninger, M. (2000). Managing complexity: The path toward intelligent organization. *Systemic Practice and Action Research*, *13*(2), 207–241. doi:10.1023/A:1009546721353

Seers, A. (1989). Team-member exchange quality: A new construct for role-making research. *Organizational Behavior and Human Decision Processes*, *43*, 118–135. doi:10.1016/0749-5978(89)90060-5

Seers, A., Petty, M. M., & Cashman, J. F. (1995). Team member exchange under team and traditional management: A naturally occurring quasi-experiment. *Group & Organization Management*, *20*, 18–38. doi:10.1177/1059601195201003

Senge, P. (1990). *Fifth discipline: The art and practice of the learning organization.* Century.

Section 4
Case Studies Illustrating Key Issues and Investigations at the Community Level

The final section presents four chapters as follows: Chapter 15, "Eye-Movement and Performance during Reading of Cerebral Palsy Patients," by Karashima, Chapter 16, "Roles of Home Care and Rehabilitation Equipment for the Aged who Need Care in Improving Performance," by Nishiguchi, Chapter 17, "The First Attempt of Intensive Approaches in Cognitive Rehabilitation in Clients with Severe Traumatic Brain Injury (TBI)," by Fujii, Chapter 18, "Further Directions in Cognitive Rehabilitation in Community- and Home-based Daily Trainings in Clients with Severe Traumatic Brain Injury (TBI)," by Fujii.

The objective of these chapters is to provide readers with empirical studies and investigations dealing with the CP patients, the aged, and the TBI clients in community life, which illustrate current problems in their lives without the benefits of the appropriate adoption of the tools and technologies of knowledge management. The idea of this book is to highlight all areas in innovative healthcare operations where the tools, techniques, and technologies of KM can be utilized. The empirical studies which make up Section 4 emphasizes an area within healthcare; namely, that of home-based and community-based care, one that is less well understood and more often than receives less attention, and shows that the need for KM is just as important and relevant in this context to facilitate the designing of innovative operations.

Supporting tools and technologies for the TBI patients, CP patients, or the aged peoples who have a social handicap have been developed in each disciplinary section. However, a particular disciplinary knowledge is not adequate for active people who want to develop their own future life styles. People require foresight in their future lives in society as well as deep insight into the current circumstances. Knowledge on sociotechnical systems in addition to the specific disciplinary knowledge is needed for the people who search future perspective/scenario of their lives. Redesigning appropriate mechanisms of sociotechnical systems makes socially handicapped people become empowered to see their desired reality. Appropriate application of knowledge management methodologies are hardly expected without the prudent inquiries to future scenario as well as to current problems for the socially handicapped people.

On the completion of this section, the reader will be equipped with some key points to understand how socially handicapped people perform their own cognition-behavioral coupling processes. Their reactions in cognition and behavior levels are so characteristic that you can not understand without adequate analytical data and study results, and also their future perspectives vary depending up their living environments whether or not they have family support and satisfactory living surroundings. Moreover, this section highlights that KM plays as an important role in the community, as well as other contexts of healthcare.

Section 4
Case Studies Illustrating Key Issues and Investigations at the Community Level

The final section presents four chapters as follows: Chapter 15, "Eye-Movement and Performance during Reading of Cerebral Palsy Patients," by Karashima, Chapter 16, "Roles of Home Care and Rehabilitation Equipment for the Aged who Need Care in Improving Performance," by Nishiguchi, Chapter 17, "The First Attempt of Intensive Approaches in Cognitive Rehabilitation in Clients with Severe Traumatic Brain Injury (TBI)," by Fujii, Chapter 18, "Further Directions in Cognitive Rehabilitation in Community- and Home-based Daily Trainings in Clients with Severe Traumatic Brain Injury (TBI)," by Fujii.

The objective of these chapters is to provide readers with empirical studies and investigations dealing with the CP patients, the aged, and the TBI clients in community life, which illustrate current problems in their lives without the benefits of the appropriate adoption of the tools and technologies of knowledge management. The idea of this book is to highlight all areas in innovative healthcare operations where the tools, techniques, and technologies of KM can be utilized. The empirical studies which make up Section 4 emphasizes an area within healthcare; namely, that of home-based and community-based care, one that is less well understood and more often than receives less attention, and shows that the need for KM is just as important and relevant in this context to facilitate the designing of innovative operations.

Supporting tools and technologies for the TBI patients, CP patients, or the aged peoples who have a social handicap have been developed in each disciplinary section. However, a particular disciplinary knowledge is not adequate for active people who want to develop their own future life styles. People require foresight in their future lives in society as well as deep insight into the current circumstances. Knowledge on sociotechnical systems in addition to the specific disciplinary knowledge is needed for the people who search future perspective/scenario of their lives. Redesigning appropriate mechanisms of sociotechnical systems makes socially handicapped people become empowered to see their desired reality. Appropriate application of knowledge management methodologies are hardly expected without the prudent inquiries to future scenario as well as to current problems for the socially handicapped people.

On the completion of this section, the reader will be equipped with some key points to understand how socially handicapped people perform their own cognition-behavioral coupling processes. Their reactions in cognition and behavior levels are so characteristic that you can not understand without adequate analytical data and study results, and also their future perspectives vary depending up their living environments whether or not they have family support and satisfactory living surroundings. Moreover, this section highlights that KM plays as an important role in the community, as well as other contexts of healthcare.

Chapter 15
Eye-Movement and Performance during Reading by Cerebral Palsy Patients

Mitsuhiko Karashima
Tokai University, Japan

ABSTRACT

This chapter introduced the characteristics of CP patients reading Japanese documents in comparison with fully abled students through two experiments. Experiment 1 was designed to study the characteristics in reading Japanese still documents and Experiment 2 was designed to study the characteristics in reading Japanese scrolling documents. The results of Experiment 1 revealed that the CP patients needed more time to read the documents than the students regardless of the difficulty of the documents. The eye fixation duration of the CP patients was generally the same as the students, although slightly longer with the most difficult documents. The frequency of eye fixation of the CP patients was greater than the students regardless of the difficulty. The distribution map of the intervals between the eye fixations revealed that the CP patients performed more eye movements. The results of Experiment 2 revealed that the most comfortable scrolling speed of CP patients was slower than that of the students regardless of the size of the scrolling window. The most comfortable scrolling speed of CP patients was stable regardless of the window size, while the most comfortable scrolling speed of the students increased as the window size increased from 3 to 5 characters and the scrolling speed was stable in 5 characters or more. Further discussions of the occurrence of the characteristics of CP patients reading both the still document and the scrolling document were done.

DOI: 10.4018/978-1-60566-284-8.ch015

INTRODUCTION

The characteristics of the fully abled people reading alphabetical text have been studied in many researches. The characteristics in reading alphabetical text were clarified by using the saccade length, the eye fixation duration, and the frequency of eye fixation. Taylor (1960) revealed the average collage student read 280 words per a minute. Rayner and Inhoff (1981) revealed that the distribution of the fixation duration had the range between 100 and 450 msec, and that the peak of the distribution was between 200 and 250 msec. They also revealed that the distribution of the saccade length has the range between 1 and 20 characters, and that the peak of the distribution was between 6 and 9 characters.

The characteristics of the fully abled people reading Japanese text have been also studied in many researches. Many researches clarified the characteristics in reading Japanese text by using the saccade length, the eye fixation duration, and the frequency of eye fixation; these were obtained by measuring eye movements during reading text. (Kanbe, 1986, Konosu, 1998) Osaka (1992) revealed that the averaged saccade length in reading Japanese text was 7.8 characters. Osaka (1989) also revealed that the averaged saccade length in reading vertical Japanese text was 5.8 characters. Kanbe revealed that the distribution of the fixation duration had the range between 100 and 400msec, and that the peak of the distribution was between 150 and 250 msec. Generally speaking, if the document is difficult to read or the text consists of only Japanese KANA characters, the saccade length is short, the eye fixation duration slightly long, and the frequency of eye fixation is greater in comparison with easy text or text that consists of Japanese KANA and KANJI characters(Osaka, 1987, 1992).

The characteristics in reading scrolling text have been also studied in many researches. Sekey and Tietz (1982) revealed that reading scrolling text took three times longer, 96 words per a minute, than reading still text, 278 words per a minute. Chujyo (1993) revealed that the scrolling speed, which the participants liked most, increased as the size of scrolling window increased, but that the scrolling speed was stable when the size of the window was 5 characters or more and the stable speed was 190 msec per character. Shina (2004) revealed the different results from Chujyo by using a different scrolling method. His method was that the text was moved pixel by pixel while Chujyo's method was that the text was moved character by character. Shina's results were that the scrolling speed quickly increased with the window size up to 5 characters and gradually increased from 5 up to 15 characters. The speed in 7 -15 characters was 150 msec per character.

However the characteristics of the disabled reading text have rarely been studied except in low vision disabilities (Ahn and Legge, 1995). The characteristics of cerebral palsy (CP) patients reading text have also rarely been studied. This study discusses the characteristic in reading the Japanese still text and scrolling text of CP patients by comparing CP patients with a group of university students through two experiments. This study especially focused on silent reading because it might be possible that there were the other constraints in the behavior of the CP patients in vocalized readings, e.g. difficulty with the smooth utterance of words.

EXPERIMENT 1

This experiment examined the characteristics of CP patients reading Japanese still text by comparing CP patients to the students.

Method

Participants

There were 15 participants, consisting of ten university students (mean age: 21.3 years, st.dev.: 0.7), who were not the CP patients, and five CP patients (mean age: 31.8 years, st.dev.: 7.1) were selected for this experiment. All participants had sufficient visual acuity to read the documents presented to them without any correctional optical equipment.

Apparatus

Eight Japanese documents were prepared for this experiment, from the Japanese language proficiency tests, and two documents were selected each for four levels of reading difficulty. Each document consisted of about 100 Japanese characters of KANA and KANJI. The classification by reading difficulty was based on the criteria of the Japanese language proficiency test itself (Association of International Education, Japan, 2000). Each document was presented on a white screen (150cm×80cm) using an overhead projector. The color of the characters presented was black and their size approximately 5cm×5cm. The viewing distance between the center of the screen and the eye position of the seated participant was approximately 3m. The viewing angle formed by the line of the viewing distance and the horizontal plane was approximately 0 degrees. An eye-marked recorder (EMR-8, nac corp.) was used for measuring the reading time and eye movements of the participants. The eye movements were recorded at a 60Hz sampling rate.

Procedure

The participants completed 8 sessions in this experiment. In each session one Japanese document was presented on the screen. The participants were required to sit in front of the screen with a 3 m viewing distance and 0 degree viewing angle, and to start reading the document silently and carefully as soon as the document was presented. They were also required to look at the dot, which marked the end of the document, as soon as they had finished reading. There was no constraint how to read the document, except for silence, nor any reading time limit. At the end of each session, the participants were required to answer four questions that were prepared to measure the degree of their comprehension of the document, and their retrospective self-reports were collected to assess how they read the document (e.g. their conscious re-reading). The sessions were ordered commencing from the easiest to the most difficult level document for all participants.

Measures

The reading times between the start and completion of reading were measured. The degree of comprehension of the document was measured by the correct ratio of the four questions. Some measurements of the eye movements were also measured as follows: the eye fixation duration, the frequency of eye fixation, and the interval between fixations. All these measurements depended on eye fixation. The eye fixation was based on the data from the eye-marked recorder. The eye fixation was defined by the gravity point method, and the criteria of the eye fixation was defined that the eye remained fixed for more than 150 msec within a circle whose diameter was 2 degrees of the visual angle. The manner of reading the document was measured by the participant's retrospective self-reports.

Results and Discussions

Calibration for the eye-marked recorder was successfully completed by the ten students and three CP patients, 1 male and 2 female. However the calibration could not be successfully completed for two of the CP patients because of their incapacity to control eye movements without noticeable head movements. The data used was that obtained from the ten students and three of the CP patients in this study.

In their retrospective self-reports all the CP patients declared that they did many conscious re-readings regardless of the reading difficulty, but the students declared that they did few conscious re-readings regardless of the reading difficulty. These results revealed that the CP patients needed more conscious re-readings of the docu-

Figure 1. Reading time in each reading difficulty level

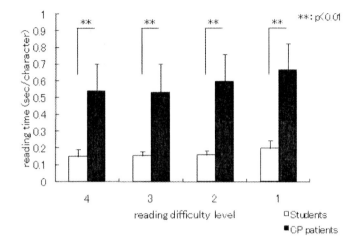

ments to achieve good comprehension than the students, regardless of the reading difficulty.

The reading time for one character of the students seemed to increase slightly as the level of reading difficulty increased, while the reading time of the CP patients increased obviously, as shown in Figure 1. ANOVA confirmed that the reading time for one character of the CP patients were longer than the students for all levels of reading difficulty (Level 4: $F(1,11)= 38.50$, Level 3: $F(1,11)=38.54$, Level 2: $F(1,11)= 55.63$, Level 1: $F(1,11)= 54.98$, $p<0.01$). These results revealed the reading time of the CP patients was influenced more by reading difficulty than it was for the students, moreover the CP patients spent more time reading the documents than the students, regardless of the reading difficulty.

All of the participants could perfectly answer each of the four prepared questions for all of the documents. It revealed that all of the participants, students and CP patients, could fully comprehend all of the documents.

The eye fixation duration for one gaze of the students was constant regardless of the reading difficulty, while the eye fixation duration of the CP patients seemed to increase slightly as the reading difficulty increased, as shown in Figure 2. ANOVA confirmed that the eye fixation duration of the CP patients was almost the same as the students except for Level 1 of the reading difficulty (Level 4: $F(1,11)= 0.02$, $p>0.05$, Level 3: $F(1,11)= 1.03$, $p>0.05$, Level 2: $F(1,11)= 2.87$, $p>0.05$, Level 1: $F(1,11)= 9.04$, $0.01<p<0.05$). These results revealed that the eye fixation duration for one gaze of the CP patients was slightly influenced by reading difficulty but the duration for the students was not, and that the CP patients spent almost the same time in gazing as the students.

Figure 2. Eye fixation duration in each reading difficulty level

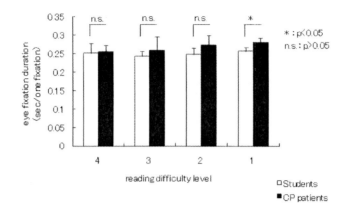

The frequency of eye fixation for one character of the students seemed to increase slightly as the level of reading difficulty increased, while the frequency of eye fixation of the CP patients increased markedly, as shown in Figure 3. ANOVA confirmed that the frequency of eye fixation of CP patients was larger than that of students at all levels of reading difficulty (Level 4: $F_{(1,11)} = 20.00$, Level 3: $F_{(1,11)} = 28.76$, Level 2: $F_{(1,11)} = 36.27$, Level 1: $F_{(1,11)} = 19.15$, $p < 0.01$). These results revealed that the frequency of eye fixation of the CP patients was influenced by reading difficulty more than that of the students, and that the CP patients gazed more frequently for reading the documents than the students, regardless of the reading difficulty.

Figure 3. The frequency of eye fixation in each reaading difficulty level

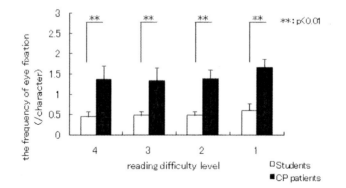

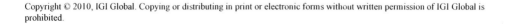

Figure 4. Distribution map of the intervals between eye fixations in each difficulty level

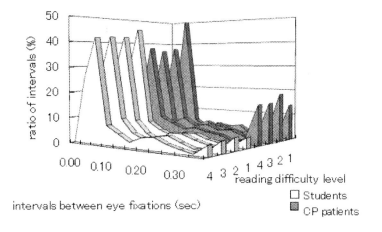

The distribution map of the intervals between the eye fixations of the CP patients was different from that of the students regardless of the reading difficulty, as shown in Figure 4. The characteristics of the CP patients in the distribution map were that the ratio of the long intervals, more than 0.3sec, was absolutely high compared with the students, regardless of the reading difficulty. This result suggested that the CP patients performed more eye movements, which were obviously different from the usual saccade and regression and it may be possible to be regarded as re-readings or return sweeps, to read the document than the students regardless of the reading difficulty.

The correlation coefficients between the reading time and the frequency of eye fixation revealed that the frequency of eye fixation correlated highly with the reading time, both for the CP patients and the students (CP: $r=0.91$ ($n=12$, $p<0.01$), Student: $r=0.99$ ($n=40$, $p<0.01$)). On the other hand, the results of the experiment revealed that the eye fixation duration of the CP patients was almost the same as the students, and the correlation coefficients between the reading time and the eye fixation duration revealed that the eye fixation duration correlated slight with the reading time with the CP patients but not with the students (CP: $r=0.59$ ($n=12$, $0.01<p<0.05$), Student: $r=0.24$ ($n=40$, $p>0.05$)). These results suggested that the difference of the reading time between the CP patients and the students were most influenced by the difference of the frequency of eye fixation.

EXPERIMENT 2

This experiment examined the characteristics of CP patients reading Japanese scrolling text by comparing CP patients to the students.

Methods

Participants

There were 15 participants, consisting of nine university students (mean age: 22.4 years, st.dev.: 0.5), who were not CP patients, and eight CP patients (mean age: 33.1 years, st.dev.: 9.2) were selected for this experiment. All participants had sufficient visual acuity to read the documents presented to them without any correctional optical equipment.

Apparatus

Nine Japanese documents were prepared for this experiment, from the Japanese language proficiency tests, and all the documents were selected from the most reading difficult level, Level 1. Each document consisted of about 350 Japanese characters of KANA and KANJI. Each document was moving character by character from right to left in the scrolling window on a 17 inch CRT display as Figure 5 shows. The window size was 3, 4, 5, 6, 7, 8, 9, 12, or 15 characters in width. The color of the characters presented was black, their size was approximately 0.7cm×0.7cm, and the between-character spacing was approximately 0.3cm. The viewing distance was approximately 0.5m. The viewing angle formed by the line of the viewing distance and the horizontal plane was approximately 10 degrees. An eye-marked recorder (EMR-8, nac corp.) was used for measuring the reading time and eye movements of the participants. The eye movements were recorded at a 60Hz sampling rate.

Procedure

The participants completed 9 sessions in this experiment. In each session one Japanese document was presented on the scrolling window whose size was 3, 4, 5, 6, 7, 8, 9, 12, or 15 characters in width. The order of the sessions was counterbalanced by Graeco-Latin square design for all participants. The participants were required to sit in front of the display with a 0.5 m viewing distance and 10 degree viewing angle, and to start reading the document silently and carefully as soon as the document was presented. They were simultaneously required to adjust the speed of scrolling characters to their own most comfortable scrolling speeds for reading

Figure 5. Text scrolling window

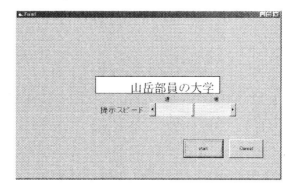

(MCS) by pressing two keys of the keyboard. A rightward- [leftward-] pointing arrow key increases [decreases] the scrolling speed. At the end of each session, the participants were required to answer four questions that were prepared to measure the degree of their comprehension of the document.

Measures

The MCSs were measured. The degree of comprehension of the document was measured by the correct ratio of four questions.

Results and Discussions

All of the participants could perfectly answer each of the four prepared questions for all of the documents. It was revealed that all of the participants, students and CP patients, could fully comprehend all of the documents.

The MCSs of the CP patients were significantly slower than that of the students in all the scrolling window sizes ($p<0.01$, $F_3(1,15)=18.28$, $F_4(1,15)=27.89$, $F_5(1,15)=18.65$, $F_6(1,15)=18.32$, $F_7(1,15)=26.78$, $F_8(1,15)=16.91$, $F_9(1,15)=13.84$, $F_{12}(1,15)=28.67$, $F_{15}(1,15)=21.21$) as shown in Figure 6. It revealed that the CP patients liked slower scrolling speed than did the students.

ANOVA confirmed that the MCSs of the students had some difference between the window sizes ($F(8,64)=10.95,p<0.01$). Multiple comparison (Turkey HCD) of the MCSs of the students between the window sizes revealed that the MCSs in 3 or 4 characters per window was significantly slower than that in more than 5 characters per window ($p<0.01$), while there was no difference in the MCSs between any two different window sizes which were more than 5 characters ($p>0.10$) and the averaged MCSs over 5 characters was 165 msec per character. These results confirmed

Figure 6. Most comfortable scrolling speed

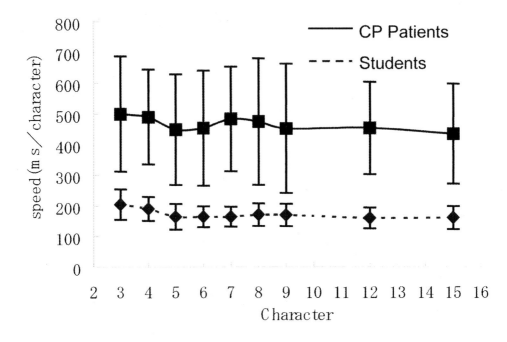

Chujyo's experimental results that the most comfortable scrolling speed increased as the window size increased from 3 to 5 characters, but that the scrolling speed was stable when the size of the window was 5 characters or more. Chujyo (1993) indicated that there were two different ways, serial processing and batch processing, one for reading the scrolling text of less than 5 characters and another for more than 5 characters. In reading the scrolling text of less than 5 characters that the fully abled persons added a new character to the pre-processed characters and judged whether they could recognize a group of characters as some word. He explained that was why the smaller the window size, which was regarded as the unit of the information processing, the slower the MCSs were. In reading the scrolling text of more than 5 characters, the fully abled persons could process the presented characters similarly to reading the still text by the batch processing. He also explained that was why the MCSs were stable. The research of Osaka and Oda (1991) supports Chujyo's explanation. The saccade length of the fully abled persons was 5~6 characters in reading the text in the moving window whose characteristics of reading documents was similar to the scrolling window.

On the other hand, the MCSs of the CP patients had no difference between the window sizes (F(8,56)=0.63,p>0.10) and the averaged MCS was 466 msec per character. These revealed that the CP patients had no characteristics, which the students revealed for the most comfortable scrolling speed, and the CP patients liked the same scrolling speed, which was slower than the students, regardless of the window size. This characteristic of the CP patients meant that regardless of the window size the CP patients might adopt the reading way the students read the scrolling text of less than 5 characters size of the scrolling window.

GENERAL DISCUSSION

In Experiment 1, the results suggested that the difference of the reading time between the CP patients and the students was mostly influenced by the difference of the frequency of eye fixation. We could assume two reasons why the frequency of eye fixation of the CP patients was more than that of the students. One reason might be that the frequency of the re-readings of the CP patients was more than that of the students. If the frequency of the re-readings increased, the frequency of eye fixation naturally increased in order to read the document completely. In this experiment only the CP patients reported that they performed many conscious re-readings regardless of the reading difficulty. The distribution map of the intervals between the eye fixations also revealed that the CP patients performed more eye movements, which were obviously different from the usual saccade and regression and might be able to be regarded as re-readings or return sweeps, than the students. The other reason might be that the saccade length of the CP patients was shorter than that of the students. If the saccade length decreased, the frequency of eye fixation naturally increased to read the document completely. Generally the saccade length decreased as the difficulty of the document increased, just as the saccade length decreased when Japanese read English documents, by comparison with Japanese reading Japanese documents (Kanbe, 1986) and the saccade length also decreased when Japanese read documents that consisted solely of KANA characters, by comparison with Japanese reading documents that consisted of KANA and KANJI characters (Osaka, 1987). On the other hand, the saccade length increased as they repeatedly read the same document (Kanbe, 1986). It would be possible that the saccade length of the CP patients was shorter than the students, because the documents were relatively more difficult for the CP patients if the reading ability of the CP patients, which consisted of their knowledge of grammar, words, and of their ability to process information, was lower than the students.

In Experiment 2, the results revealed that in reading the scrolling text the most comfortable scrolling speed of CP patients was stable regardless of the window size and slower than that of the students. As previously stated, by the results of Experiment 1 it was assumed as the characteristics of CP patients that the frequency of the re-readings of the CP patients was more and the saccade length of the CP patients was shorter in reading still text. The results of Experiment 2 could be explained by these two characteristics of CP patients.

The saccade length of the fully abled persons was 5~6 characters in reading the text through the moving window which was similar to the scrolling window (Osaka and Oda, 1991). The saccade length seemed to cause the most comfortable scrolling speed for a fully abled person to be stable in more than 5 characters of the scrolling window size. If the saccade length of CP patients was also shorter than that of a fully able person in reading the scrolling text, the saccade length of CP patients might be less than 5 characters in reading the scrolling text. That might be why the most comfortable scrolling speed of CP patients was stable in more than 3 characters of the scrolling window. Additionally, as CP patients want to do more conscious re-readings, CP patients might like the slower scrolling speed than fully abled persons in order to be able to do more re-readings in the scrolling window.

CONCLUSION

This chapter introduced the characteristics of CP patients reading Japanese documents in comparison with the fully abled students through two experiments. Experiment 1 was designed to study the characteristics in reading Japanese still documents and Experiment 2 was designed to study the characteristics in reading Japanese scrolling documents.

The results of Experiment 1 revealed that the CP patients needed more time to read the documents than the students, regardless of the difficulty of the documents. The eye fixation duration of the CP patients was generally the same as the students, although slightly longer with the most difficult documents. The frequency of eye fixation of the CP patients was greater than the students regardless of the difficulty. The time spent reading correlated highly with the frequency of eye fixation. The CP patients declared that they did many conscious re-readings, and the distribution map of the intervals between the eye fixations revealed that the CP patients performed more eye movements, which might be able to be regarded as re-readings or return sweeps. These results suggested the possibility that the longer time spent by the CP patients in reading was mostly influenced by the greater frequency of eye fixations, that might in turn depend on the frequent re-readings and the shorter saccade length.

The results of Experiment 2 revealed that the most comfortable scrolling speed of CP patients was slower than that of the students regardless of the size of the scrolling window. The most comfortable scrolling speed of CP patients was stable regardless of the window size, while the most comfortable scrolling speed of the students increased as the window size increased from 3 to 5 characters and the scrolling speed was stable with 5 characters or more. It was revealed that these characteristics of CP patients could be explained by the characteristics of the frequent re-readings and the shorter saccade length of CP patients which were suggested by the results of Experiment 1.

FUTURE RESEARCH

In Experiment 1, we could assume two reasons why the frequency of eye fixation of the CP patients was more than that of the students in reading Japanese still text. One was the more frequency of re-readings and the other was the shorter saccade length. In this chapter, however, it could not be clarified how much more the frequency of the re-readings of the CP patients was than that of the students, nor why the frequency of the re-readings of the CP patients was more than that of the students. Neither could it be confirmed that the saccade length of the CP patients was shorter than that of the students. Because any distance information of the eye movements could not be acquired by the experimental system of this study due to the constraints that the CP patient's head interlocked with their eye movements. Therefore, the assumptions about these reasons for the more frequent appearance of eye fixation with the CP patients, especially the latter reason, could not be verified in this study. In further studies more detailed analysis of the reading of CP patients will be investigated by adding the distance information of the eye movements in order to confirm that these reasons lead to the more frequent appearance of eye fixations of the CP patients.

In Experiment 2 we also could explain the slower and stable most comfortable scrolling speed of CP patients by the characteristics of the more re-readings and the shorter saccade length. In this chapter, however, as the eye movements of CP patients in reading the scrolling text could not be clarified, it could not be confirmed whether the frequency of re-readings of CP patients was more and the saccade length of CP patients was shorter. The reason why the information of the eye movements, especially the distance information, could not be acquired was because of the constraints of the uncontrollable head moving of CP patients. In further studies more detailed analysis of the reading of CP patients will be investigated by adding the distance information of the eye movements in order to confirm that the more re-readings and the shorter saccade occur in reading the scrolling text and that they lead to the slower and stable most comfortable scrolling speed of CP patients.

Moreover, the elderly and non CP disabled persons may have the different characteristics of reading the still and scrolling text. For example, the comfortable scrolling speed may be different. This difference will influence the social information accessibility for them. In further studies their characteristics of reading the still and scrolling text will be investigated and this research, including this chapter's research, effect to supply the tools of knowledge management by which the social information can become more accessible for the elderly and disabled persons.

Concretely the knowledge from this research will be able to supply the guidelines how to present the information not only in the public space, such as the flight information at the airport and headline news on street displays for example, but also in the private space, such as information in the portable information terminals, including mobile phone and breaking news on the TV to mention just two.

Finally the arrangement of the social information infrastructure and the proposal of the new information system according to the guidelines from the knowledge will support the independent activity of the elderly and disabled persons without the information barrier.

REFERENCES

Ahn, S. J., & Legge, G. E. (1995). Predictors of magnifieraided reading speed in low vision. *Vision Research, 35*(13), 1931–1938. doi:10.1016/0042-6989(94)00293-U

Chujyo, K., Notomi, K., & Ishida, T. (1993). The effect of the number of characters on the reading rate of character strings moving horizontally on a CRT. *Japanese Journal of Psychology, 64*(5), 360–368.

Kanbe, N. (1986). A review of the studies on the reading eye movements. *Report of the National Language Institute, 85*(7), 29–66.

Konosu, T., Jinbo, Y., Shigematsu, J., & Fukuda, T. (1998). An ergonomic study of Japanese graphical and phonological reading process. *The Japanese Journal of Ergonomics, 34*(5), 239–246.

Osaka, N. (1987). Effect peripheral visual field size upon eye movements during Japanese text processing. In J. K. O' Regan & A. Levy-Schoen (Eds.), *Eye movements: From physiology to cognition* (pp. 421-429). North Holland.

Osaka, N. (1989). Eye fixation and saccade during kana and kanji text reading: Comparison of English and Japanese text processing. *Bulletin of the Psychonomic Society, 27*(6), 548–550.

Osaka, N. (1992). Size saccade and fixation duration of eye movements during Japanese text reading: Psychophysics of Japanese text processing. *Journal of the Optical Society of America. A, Optics and Image Science, 9*(1), 5–13. doi:10.1364/JOSAA.9.000005

Osaka, N., & Oda, K. (1991). Effective visual field size necessary for vertical reading during Japanese text processing. *Bulletin of the Psychonomic Society, 29*(4), 345–347.

Rayner, K., & Inhoff, W. (1981). Control of eye movements during reading. In B. L. Zuber (Ed.), *Models of oculomotor behavior and control* (pp. 209-231). CRC Press.

Sekey, A., & Tietz, J. (1982). Text display by "saccadic scrolling". *Visual Language, 16*(1), 62–77.

Shina, K. (2004). Reading in scrolling and still presentations. *Kiso Shinrigaku Kenkyu, 23*(1), 70–75.

Taylor, S. E., Frackenpohl, H., & Pettee, J. L. (1960). Grade level norms for the components of the fundamental reading skill. *EDL Research and Information Bulletin, 3*, 22.

Chapter 16

Roles of Home Care and Rehabilitation Equipment for the Aged Who Need Care in Improving Performance

Hiromi Nishiguchi
Tokai University, Japan

ABSTRACT

In this chapter, some countermeasures are shown for the aged who need care to be able to live their own daily life not only at home, but also in the community, under the situation of worldwide aged society. At first we survey the present situation of the aging in the world. Next, it is explained what human functions are, and how they change by the aging with some research findings. Because of the fall of functions, the barrier often occurs that the aged cannot perform an objective daily life activity. Therefore, the methods to remove the barrier are examined. In the removal methods of the barrier, the commentaries are focused to the support technology, such as home care and rehabilitation tools which utilize survival functions effectively. Furthermore, the research is introduced on satisfaction and well-being of users of rehabilitation facility service of day care, and it is pointed out that kind of service as a social resource is important for the aged who need care to support the independence and well-being in daily life. Effective use of social resources is required to facilitate knowledge management in community life.

DOI: 10.4018/978-1-60566-284-8.ch016

Figure 1. The change of the aged population rate in the world. (Quoted from The United Nations. World Population Project (The 2000 Revision))

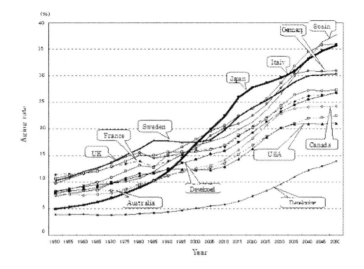

INTRODUCTION

We human manage our own daily life with physical and intellectual functions. It is said that human functions change by aging, and many of their functions tend to deteriorate (Charness, 1985). The aged society has being come in the many countries, as shown in Figure 1. Therefore many aged people whose physical or intellectual functions deteriorated need the help of others to live their own daily life.

ADL (Activities of Daily Living) are essential behavior to perform our daily life. ADL composes of the following activities; "Transfer from bed or chair", "Mobility", "Dressing", "Eating", "Toilet use", "Bathing", "Grooming", and "Communication". They are called "basic ADL", these are composed of fundamental and crucial self-care tasks. Furthermore, IADL (Instrumental Activities of Daily Living) are necessary functions to enable the individual to live independently within a community. They are as follows: "Using the telephone, "Community mobility", "Shopping for groceries", "preparing meals", "light housework", and "taking medications and managing money".

To support the aged who need care not only at home but also in community, many countermeasures have been carried out. "Social resources" as one of the countermeasures, are utilized very much to support to live independent at home and in a community for the aged who need care. The definition of "social resources" is as follows; It is a complex system composed of legal systems, welfare services, man power, support technology, and the aggregate of a fund / supplies, and it fills up needs of the aged who need care in the daily life at home and in community.

In this chapter, the author discusses about the relation between human functions and ADL, and countermeasures that make the aged who need care to be able to live an independent life at home and in community, from the viewpoints of support technology and home care.

HUMAN FUNCTIONS AND THEIR CHANGES BY AGING

Human Functions

A human being performs daily life by perception of various outside stimuli. The outside stimuli are obtained by "sense organs" such as sight or hearing at first. Next, this perception information is transmitted into "nervous system of the brain" via the centripetal tendency nervous system. And a perception / cognitive processing are performed there, and the order is decided by these processing. The order is sent to effectors such as hands or feet, and a reaction action is carried out at last.

The human functions are classified into three kinds. Those are sensory functions, perception / cognitive functions, and exercise (action) functions.

- Sensory functions; they are composed of five kinds as follows; sight by eyes, hearing by ears, sense of touch by skin, taste by tongue, and smell by nose.
- Perception / cognitive functions; perception function is to transform outside stimuli into significant information for human independent action. And cognitive function gives a behavior pattern that is decided by processing rules stored in long-term memories. There are three kind of process in cognition; skill base, rule base, and knowledge base (Rusmussen, 1986).
- Exercise (action) functions are mainly performed with a part of body site such as upper or lower limbs. And intention transmission to another person is also one of important behaviors of exercise functions.

A human information processing is usually explained by the S-R (Stimuli-Reaction) model shown in Figure 2.

Change of Human Functions by Aging

It is generally said that the human physical and intellectual functions change by aging. And many investigations clarified that most of these functions fall by aging. Especially the fall of the physical function causes various difficulties in daily life.

Figure 2. Human information processing (by S-R model)

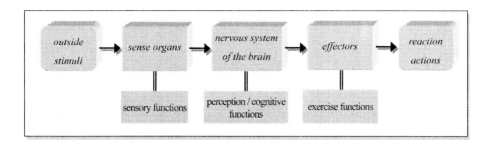

By such a background, many researchers have been trying to grasp the change of physical function by aging objectively, and also getting basic data for supporting the aged who need care in daily life.

There are two methods to grasp the change of the human being functions by the aging. One way is "longitudinal survey", and the other is "cross-sectional survey" (cf. Figure 3). Cross-sectional survey is the method that chases the change of the functions of a particular age group with time passage. By this way, the true characteristic of the change in functions can be got, but it costs much time and labor. On the other hand, longitudinal survey is to grasp functions of the different age group at the present time, and to examine the differences. However, we must add attention carefully to influential factors such as "the cohort effect" and "time effect" by this survey.

Studies about the Change of Physical Functions

Many of physical functions deteriorate by the aging. Physical Fitness Standards meeting for the study in Tokyo Metropolitan University (2000) reported the findings about various Japanese physical functions by cross-sectional survey, and some results are shown below.

Simple Reaction Time to the Light Stimulation (cf. Figure 4)

By this test, the reaction time from perceiving the light stimulation to pushing the button was measured. Its peak appears in late teens, and it is slowly deteriorating by the aging.

Figure 3. Cross-sectional survey and longitudinal survey

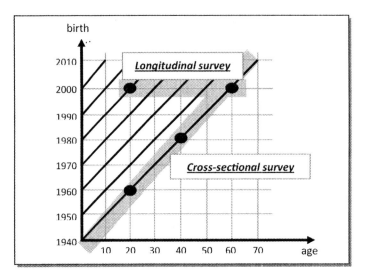

Grip Strength (cf. Figure 5)

The grip strength shows a static flexor power of the forearm. The grip shows the maximum in early twenties and falls from late thirties.

Figure 4. Simple reaction time

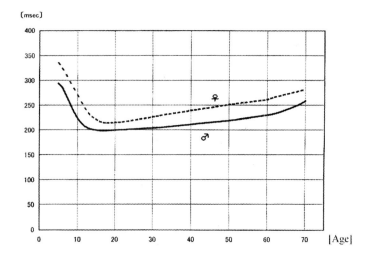

Figure 5. Grasp strength

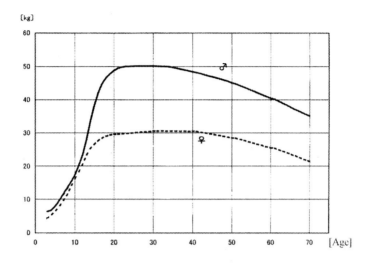

Vertical Jump (cf. Figure 6)

Vertical jump is a measuring method that had been devised as an index to evaluate leg power in U.S.A. The height of vertical jump reaches its peak in late teens and continues falling afterwards.

Figure 6. Vertical jump

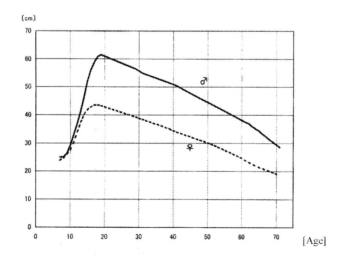

Studies about the Change of Intellectual Functions

It is known that some of intellectual function is maintained or raised (Dennis & Tapsfield, 1996). This Knowledge was reported by Horn, J. L. & Cattell, R.B. (1966), and they classified the intellectual ability into fluid intelligence and crystal-lized intelligence. Fluid intelligence is defined as follows; "on-the-spot reasoning ability, a skill not basically dependant on our experience." It is often explained from the biological standpoint, and this intelligence is activated when the central nervous system is at its physiological peak (Belsky, 1990). Crystallized intelligence is defined as follows; "the extent to which a person has absorbed the content of culture." And it is the store of knowledge or information that a given society has accumulated over time.

Furthermore, Thurstone, L. L. & Thurstone, T. G., (1941) proposed that intellec-tual ability of human being composed of seven ability factors. They are as follows; Memory (M), Number (N), Perception (P), Reasoning (R), Word fluency (W), Space (S), and, Verbal comprehension (V).

The authors made a description-style test to measure above seven ability factors (Nishiguchi & Saito, 2000). This test carried out to two subject groups; one is elder group (20 people and their average age is 63.1 years old) and the other is young group (20 people and their average age is 20.9 years old)). In this test, four phases of degrees of difficulty (a degree of difficulty rises by order from I to IV) are set for each question. Work performance was calculated by the following calculation type:

Work performance(%) = number of correct answers / number of problems * 100

Figure 7 showed the work performance ratio of the elders group for the young. In two ability factors (Memory (M) and Number (N)), the work performance ratio is high and a difference is not recognized between two groups when a degree of difficulty is low. But the difference between two groups grew bigger as the degrees of difficulty rise. These abilities are fluid intelligence and they decline by aging. Furthermore, the elders do not seem to be flexible for a change of the difficulty of the tasks comparison with the young. On the other hand, in Word fluency (W) and Verbal comprehension (V), which are crystallized intelligence, the elders were flexible in changing the difficulty although they performed lower in comparison with the young.

Figure 7.The work performance ratio of the elders group for the young

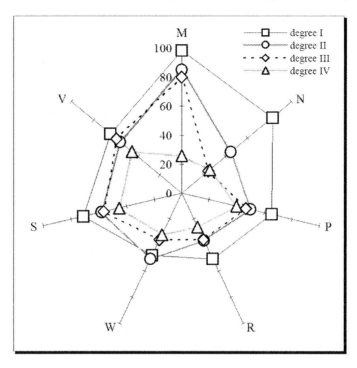

THE CAUSE OF BARRIER AND BARRIER-FREE DESIGN

The Cause of Barrier, and the Method to Remove It

In the situation that someone is going to accomplish some actions in everyday life, a barrier occurs when his/her ability does not satisfy the ability required shown in right side as (1) of Figure 8. When a survival or substituted function can be used, the barrier will be removed by using some jig or self-help device (Nishiguchi, Saito, & Ozeki, 1993), and then, the objective action becomes easy to perform for the elders who need care. In addition, it is effective to apply an architectural barrier-free design to house and public accommodation shown in left side as (2) of Figure 8.

By the way, a survival function is a function which has been left a little after disease and a substituted function has a supplementary roll for the function with disorder such as an auditory function in the blind.

In the next section, some example of the barrier-free design are shown, and these cases adopted the ways which assist deteriorated function or to substitute function.

Figure 8. The cause of barrier, and the method to remove it

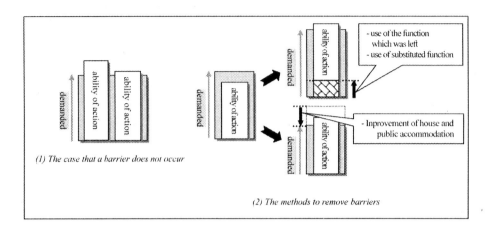

The Usage of Survival or Substituted Functions

In our daily life, various kinds of barrier-free designs have been carried out. Especially, barrier-free design for obtaining outside information is very useful for the people whose sensory function deteriorated as shown in Table 1.

The human being gets many of outside information by visual function and auditory function. However, when these sensory functions deteriorate we cannot take in outside information enough. In these cases, the barrier-free design is carried out to assist the deteriorated function shown as (1) and (5) of Table 1. Furthermore barrier-free design is utilized to obtain outside information using substituted sensory function in the case when visual function or auditory function does not work at all. These design is shown as (2), (4), and (7) of Table 1.

HOME CARE AND REHABILITATION EQUIPMENT AS SUPPORT TECHNOLOGY

"Home care and rehabilitation equipment" is used to support the aged who need care in daily life. These equipments are developed for the people who can not perform independent behavior in daily life because of functional deteriorating. However, it may invite the fall of the function in the future to depend on these equipments if they had an enough function to accomplish the behavior. Therefore, it is necessary to consider advice with the rehabilitation staffs and coordinators enough when the

Table 1. Barrier-free design for obtaining outside information

| | | Sensory function | |
		Fall of the visual function	Fall of the auditory function
Function to assist or substitute	**Sight function**	**(1) Assistance of visual function;** Eye grasses, Loupe The expansion reading machine for visually impaired persons	**(4) Presentation by sight information;** Conversation by sign language or writing Broadcast captioning Bulletin board such as Display of waiting number on service counter, and Refuge instruction display
	Auditory function	**(2) Presentations by auditory information;** Traffic signal with acoustic device The opening and closing message of the door, and the massage of the arrival floor	**(5) Assistance of auditory function;** Hearing aid Silver phone
	Touch function	**(3) Presentations by touch information;** Braille Walking stick, Tactile blocks A rising on the operation key The notch of the prepaid card	**(6) Presentations by touch information;** The call device with the vibration function
Other		**(7) Use of substituted function;** Taking a guide dog	

(Quoted from contribution of Nishiguchi, 2005)

aged who need care uses home care and rehabilitation equipments. Home care equipments also have an effect to reduce physical burden of the care-providers.

These home care and rehabilitation equipments are generally developed according to the classification of ADL (Activities of Daily Living). ADL are behavior to perform our daily life as follows; Transfer from bed or chair, Mobility, Dressing, Eating, Toilet use, Bathing, Grooming, and Communication. At first, the behavior in each ADL are explained, and next home care and rehabilitation equipments are commented that were developed to support for the aged who need care in this section.

About Home Care Equipment

Transfer from Bed or Chair

This behavior is composed of transfer to standing position and to wheelchair from bed, and it includes also the reverse movements. This kind of behavior occurs when getting up in the morning and going to bed. Various home care equipment to support transfer action have been developed for the aged who can not perform this behavior because their physical function had been deteriorated. For example, "adjustable bed" has functions such as changing the height of the bed and the angle of the back. It makes not only easy to transfer but also is effective in preventing a bedsore for the bedridden aged people. In addition, mattress, cushion, sidebar, and side table are prepared.

Mobility

Mobility is necessary when someone moves between places, such as from bed to toilet. Many kinds of wheelchair have been developed for the people who cannot walk because of their lower limbs function deterioration. "Wheelchairs" are classified into two kinds; they are "manual wheelchairs", and "electric powered wheelchairs". In addition, as equipments to assist mobility, there are walking stick and walker (walking frame), lifter, and home elevator.

Eating

Eating is an indispensable behavior so that a human being can maintain his own life. When we eat something, we use chopsticks or a spoon in a handedness or a practical use hand, and carry food into our mouth. The following equipments have been developed for persons having difficulty with eating because of upper limbs paralysis; chopsticks and a spoon that were designed for easy holding, and a bowl with the non-slip rubber at its bottom.

Toilet Use

Toilet use is required when we excrete the food which was digested in the body. To perform toilet use it is demanded to move to the restroom, to control of excreting, to keep cleanness after the excretion, and to dress. Many kinds of home care equipment are provided to support the excretion behavior. And also a portable toilet and diaper are developed for person who cannot move because of physical impairments.

Dressing and Grooming

Dressing is an act of wearing and taking off clothes or socks. Grooming is composed of following behavior; washing the face, brushing teeth, cutting nails, combing hair, and making up. When we perform these acts, it demands to use both hands. For the person who can use only one side for the paralysis, many equipments have been developed that enable one-handed operation.

Bathing

The bathing act is indispensable to maintain physical cleanliness and has the effect of fatigue recovery. In the bathing act, many kinds of equipments have been developed to remove dangers in case of stepping over the bathtub or walking on the wet floor.

Communication

The communication is an act of the understanding with person, and we use verbal function and auditory function. Talking aid was developed in particular as a communication tool for the person whose verbal function deteriorated.

Others

Various home care equipments have been developed for the aged who cannot live their independent daily life by the fall of the functions as mentioned above. "The emergency reporting system" for the aged of the single life, or "the search system" of the people who loiters in community with the dementia, has been introduced to secure their safety.

Recently, physical rehabilitation (or "power rehabilitation") with slight machine training has been introduced to improve physical functions and reduce care quantity. Many care providers and researchers began to perform scientific approach about its effect now.

The Database of Home Care Equipment

These home care and rehabilitation equipment can be searched by the database called "TAIS(Technical Aids Information System)" provided by "Association for Technical Aids in Japan". This database recorded 6,082 kinds of home care and rehabilitation equipments at a point of October 2007 (Association for Technical Aids in Japan, 2007). The breakdown of registered equipments is shown in Table 2.

CARE SERVICE IN COMMUNITY

The effectiveness of home care and rehabilitation equipments for the aged who need care to be independent in the daily life was mentioned above. Besides a support technology, the environment where the aged can spend positive daily life also must be provided by means of knowledge management technology.

Table 2. The breakdown of registered equipments with TAIS

Classification	Number
Treatment and rehabilitation equipments	523
Prosthesis and orthosis	12
Personal care equipments	1,082
Equipment for movement	2,478
Equipments for housework	42
Furniture / housing parts, building facilities	1,684
Communication-related equipments	189
Devices for operation	27
Improvement equipments for living environment	12
Recreational Equipments	13
Others	20
Total	6,082

The inventory survey was made to grasp the satisfaction and the feeling of well-being of the elders who use day care services, and to get some effective countermeasures for providing home care in community in order to facilitate social resources in our community to meet the needs of elders who need care. The subjects surveyed were fifty nine users of day care service provided by a certain geriatric health services facility (Nishiguchi, H. & Karashima, M., 2008).

The results are as follows: (1) The user held almost high feeling of satisfaction about offered service, and they were much satisfied to the care for bathing particularly. And there were differences of the satisfaction between the users of male and female in some service. Especially female users showed higher score of satisfaction in communication activity. (2) The feeling of well-being for the care service was influenced by sex differences, and human relation with the other users, and it showed higher score in female users and users who satisfied with human relations. According to the results, it is necessary that care service must be provided carefully by considering the sex differences in social and cultural viewpoint, i.e. gender as well as the age.

CONCLUSION

In this chapter, the characteristic of the change of the human being function by the aging was discussed considering the forthcoming aging society. And the methodology to remove the barriers which occur at home by functional decline was explained, and barrier-free design, home care tools and example of rehabilitation equipments to support the aged who need care were shown.

In these days, many manufacturing has been produced under "technology-oriented design", because of progress of the science technology. However, the human being function changes by the aging, and also the characteristics are different between persons. And it is necessary to design the equipment after considering the situation of the physical function and also having grasped what kind of equipment the client needs. Therefore, the making of "needs-oriented" home care and rehabilitation equipments is indispensable to support the independent life of the aged who need care in hyper aged society.

FUTURE TRENDS

I think that it is indispensable not only to perform independent daily life for the aged who need care, but also to take communication with friends or acquaintances in community. It is expected that social resources such as home care and rehabilitation equipments have been provided in a community, and the place such as "(Adult) day care" that provides "social support" must be increased for independent daily life of the aged who need care. Organizational environment in community is required to align social resources for providing an effective and equitable care services.

REFERENCES

Association for Technical Aids in Japan. (2007). TAIS (Technical Aids Information System). Retrieved from http://www.techno-aids.or.jp/system/index.shtml (in Japanese)

Belsky, J. K. (1990). *The psychology of aging theory, research, and interventions.* Pacific Grove.

Charness, N. (1985). *Aging and human performance.* John Willy & Sons, Inc.

Dennis, I., & Tapsfield, P. (1996). *Human abilities-their nature and measurement.* Lawrence Erlbaum Associates, Publishers.

Horn, J. L., & Cattell, R. B. (1966). Refinement and test of theory of fluid and crystallized intelligence. *Journal of Educational Psychology, 57,* 253–270. doi:10.1037/h0023816

Nishiguchi, H. (2005). Home care and rehabilitation equipment. In K. Itozawa, M. Sasaki & Y. Honna (Eds.), *Care technology* (new edition in Japanese) (pp. 105-124). Kenpakusha Press.

Nishiguchi, H., & Saito, M. (2000). *A study of the intellectual ability of the aged-the relationship between the degree of difficulty and performance.* In *Proceedings of the 14th Triennial Congress of the International Ergonomics Association* (Vol. 4, p. 99) (in Japanese).

Nishiguchi, H., Saito, M., & Ozeki, M. (1993). A study on the evaluation of functionality and effectiveness of self-help devices for the disabled. [in Japanese]. *Journal of Japan Industrial Management Association, 44*(3), 200–208.

Physical Fitness Standards Meeting for the Study, Tokyo Metropolitan University. (2000). *New physical fitness standards of Japanese people.* Fumaido Press (in Japanese).

Rusmussen, J. (1986). *Information processing and human-machine interaction: An approach to cognitive engineering.* Elsevier Science Co. Inc.

Thurstone, L. L., & Thurstone, T. G. (1941). *Factorial studies of intelligence.* University of Chicago Press. Nishiguchi, H., & Karashima, M. (2008). A study of the satisfaction and the situation of well-being of day care service users. [in Japanese]. *Journal of Japan Industrial Management Association, 59*(2), 137–144.

The United Nations. *World population project (the 2000 revision).* Retrieved from http://www.un.org/esa/population/unpop.htm

Chapter 17

The First Attempt of Intensive Approaches in Cognitive Rehabilitation in Clients with Severe Traumatic Brain Injury

Masako Fujii
Nonprofit Organization TBI Rehabilitation Center, Japan

ABSTRACT

Cognitive rehabilitation (CR) was undertaken by two clients, A and B, using pen and paper method by an exclusive and intensive approach. Client A with very severe TBI showed improved attention and memory deficits and after undergoing a step-by-step trial, he finally landed a satisfactory job and maintained it, with the support of a large organization. Client B underwent CR with considerable effort by himself and attained a normal cognitive level but was still half way to the satisfactory social integration owing to an insufficient support system. Through the long process undergone by the two clients, it was suggested that environmental factors (support system) are extremely important for a satisfactory social life in severe TBI clients, together with the recovery of cognitive functions by CR.

INTRODUCTION

Traumatic brain injury (TBI) shows unique problems as consequences of neuropsychological and cognitive sequelae. The most common causes of TBI are traffic

DOI: 10.4018/978-1-60566-284-8.ch017

accidents, falls, or sports/recreational accidents. The cognitive, behavioral and emotional changes in TBI include deficits of attention, speed of information processing, memory, planning and problem-solving, abstract thinking, initiative, flexibility, and control and regulation of behavioral and thought processes, egocentricity, changes in affect, and lack of self-awareness (Ponsford, 1995 p.27)

In a preliminary report of a recent official five-year model project for supporting persons with higher brain dysfunction including TBI by The Japanese Government(Ministry of Health, Labour and Walfare)the consequences with the specific symptoms of the dysfunction were defined. These consequences were reported to be deficits of attention, memory, executive functions, and/or social behavioral disturbances in the post-acute phase. It is considered that the deficits are typically expressed after TBI. Of the four dysfunctions the former three deficits of attention, memory, and executive functions are the most common deficits in TBI and they were determined as the most important targets of our CR. The social behavioral disturbances are considered to arise sometimes from certain dysfunction of the executive functions and more related to emotional disturbances than to cognitive deficit. With the aim to restore the three cognitive functions, our CR was started and continued using workbooks and dictation tasks in a daily intensive training for creating brain reorganization, as demonstrated with the stroke model (Taub et al., 2002).

The most challenging and complex issues regarding TBI clients together with the restoration of cognitive functions are how to return to work or how to find and maintain a new suitable work for TBI clients with an altered personality and/or with decreased cognitive abilities. Recently, factors that allow TBI clients to return to work have been argued more than before, indicating many problems in post-acute phase of TBI. Such arguments were carried out in the broad domain, for example, in relation to early neuropsychological functioning and severity (Machamer et al., 2005), behavioral aspects (McCrimmon and Oddy, 2006), differences in Neurobehavioral Rating Scale (Franulic et al., 2004), interventions in behavior and disability (Winkler et al., 2006) or injury severity and self-awareness on TBI deficits (Shames et al. 2007). Problems on returning to work are being recently discussed in Japan, but CR as the basic remediation of brain function as a background factor for returning to work has been disregarded because CR requires several years, sometimes as a life-long CR. During CR client's considerable efforts is essential for cognitive recovery and CR often requires great support from the environment in the broad sense, such as significant relations including the family or teachers. We have developed CR original programs simply on the basis of the concept that the more the brain is trained, the better it is activated, thus reorganizing previous and present cognitive functions in the prefrontal and lateral cortices, which are mainly affected by brunt head trauma caused by the traffic accidents or falls. Furthermore, it was also developed, taking into consideration that during CR, the contralateral unaffected side of the injured brain region plays important roles in the functional recovery and reorganization of the ipsilateral affected brain region. In the implementation of CR, four principles; namely; (1) daily, (2) at home, (3) with family, (4) outcome measures, were proposed from the first time in our program.

BACKGROUND OF COGNITIVE REHABILITATION

The main purposes of our intensive CR are to restore lost brain functions through daily training of cognitive functions, using a restorative (rather than comprehensive) approach. It was considered that our CR is the most appropriate approach based on the new paradigm for brain reorganization (Nadeau, 2002; Taub et al., 2002), according to brain plasticity recently demonstrated even in a mature brain (e.g., my previous research, Fujii and Hayakashi, 1992). The actual goal of CR is to repair the three cognitive deficits of attention, memory, and cognitive functions, caused by TBI. Attention is a basic function of human cognition involving accepting and manipulating information in the brain. Under a clear arousal state and a certain degree of concentration attention is essential to manipulating information related to writing, reading, and hearing. The visual catching (partly auditory) of many small targets such as letters in words and sentences is the usual conventional method for visual attention rehabilitation. Reading and writing trainings usually carried out in early educational processes can be used also in attention CR. The tools already available for CR in English such as Attention Process Training (Sohlberg and Mateer, 2001) were not easy to use in Japan; therefore, workbooks and audiotapes for dictation tasks were originally made in our center (see Appendix 1).

Although the workbooks used for the remediation of attention deficits are often relatively simple, more elaborate workbooks for the remediation of memory deficits using sentences and stories are more favorable for TBI clients and such workbooks have been prepared including those for verbal rehearsal, elaboration, and executive training, along with other verbal techniques. The reason why we used these materials for CR was that it is very useful for long-term CR and cost-effective. Intensive and repeated use of various types of such materials gradually improved neuropsychological test scores, suggesting the recovery of brain functions in clients with TBI, even if their deficits were very severe. We consider that an intensive CR accelerates brain reorganization with the intensive training stimulation, as shown in a stroke model (Taub et al., 2002; Nadeau 2002).

In the case of severe TBI clients whose memory deficits are difficult to improve (Rees et al. 2007) an external compensatory approach for memory rehabilitation may be recommended. In contrast to the compensatory approach, the other concept is that by using external aids patients do not have to worry about their memory but the aids are ultimately compensatory technique and are not rehabilitation technique, and that the compensatory technique is not recommended if it might interfere with neuropsychological rehabilitation (Leon-Carrion, 1997). The restorative approach, aiming for the intrinsic recovery of memory function, is the main approach used in our center, although compensatory techniques are also used as a supplementary approach. The purpose of many memory workbooks made in our center is not only for memory training in the long-term but also for the general purpose of language training and attention remediation. They also played a rehabilitative role anytime in attention improvement. CR devices for executive function remained as our future problem to be solved. The recoveries of attention and memory then became the realized goals in our CR.

The Japanese versions of neuropsychological tests (RBMT, BADS, and JART, see in Appendix 2) were recently published in Japan, which made follow-up studies of clients more practical than before. Clients A and B in cases of the subject in this chapter already attained the time of their readiness for training, as three years have already passed since their serious vehicular accidents, and at this time, CR was necessary in both clients to improve their cognitive deficits to a higher level.

CLIENT A

Client A was a 25-year-old man who lived with his parents, sister and grandmother when he suffered a very severe TBI from a vehicular accident (Fujii et al., 1998). At the time, he was delivering newspaper in the early morning and he collided with a light truck running at a high speed. He was in coma for one month. He was discharged after 3 months, and he began to participate in the day-service center for persons with mental illness, near hospital in the same organization. He received short-term speech therapy, without any other rehabilitation. The bus of the day-service center was door to door; thus, he went there everyday. Magnetic resonance imaging (MRI) showed focal lesions in the posterior part of his right lateral lobe with hemorrhage and with cranial bone fracture (direct injury). Furthermore, the left lateral lobe was considerably injured with damage to the posterior part of the frontal lobe (contre-coup injury). Although he showed no physical symptoms, his cognitive deficits were extremely severe with severe deficits of attention, memory, and executive functions. He was not able to talk well perhaps because of his word-finding disorder. His mother worked as a hairdresser in her beauty salon in her own house and his father was a retired school official. Both parents were very supportive of him. Three years after the injury, the patient was referred to us and he participated in our home-based daily training program.

Table 1. Changes in scores of five neuropsychological tests of client A. Regarding the tests, see Appendix 2

	Baseline	1 year	2 yrs.	3 yrs.	4 yrs.	5 yrs.	6 yrs.	7 yrs.	8 yrs.	9 yrs.
WAIS-R (IQ)	47	46			43					
TEA total score (attention)			17	31			30	41	52	39
RBMT standard profile score (memory)				9	8		9	5	11	6
BADS (executive function)							33	33	33	27
JART (adult reading ability)					30		30		28	25
Social reentry							waiter, kitchen assistant			

CR of Client A and Results

In Table 1, the changes in test scores of client A over 9 years are summarized. Numbers and years (yrs) are the times from the start of the cognitive rehabilitation. After 3 years of TBI, client A began to undergo CR, trying at first various activities such as those in workbooks for primary schools, dictation tasks, and explanations of four-item comics. Client A mostly preferred dictation tasks, and from the following year, the dictation tasks became his main home-based training from Monday to Friday. The trainings of the dictation task showed positive result, demonstrated by his scores of tests that we originally developed (Matsuoka et al., 2000). One year after the start of CR, his mother said that he always concentrated well on the tasks, and that he was able to listen to family talks for about half an hour, which seemed to be signs of attention improvement. His mother also said that his personality before TBI was characterized by calmness and honesty, whereas after the accident he became rather talkative and bright without any antisocial behavior.

After two years of dictation and other tasks he began to use our workbooks; the first set of workbooks was listening attention and the second was for visual attention. He used the next set of memory workbooks in addition to the dictation tasks everyday from Monday to Friday. Generally, he used the same workbooks four times; the first workbook was carried out together with his mother, and he did the second, third and fourth workbooks by himself. After returning home from the day-service center at about 4 p.m., he accomplished the tasks of the workbook and dictation for about 2 hours everyday. The success of this continuous rehabilitation was perhaps enhanced by his preservative tendency of behavior as a TBI aftereffect. The practical availability of this preservative tendency was the strong backup for the daily cognitive training. His first TEA scores were all lower than 5 (5 is the cutoff score) in nine subtests. After his one year long training using workbooks and dictation tasks, his score of the fourth TEA subtest of visual elevator became 11 (10 is the average score), although the time score of the fifth subtest was still lower than 5. These findings showed that his works were accurate but it took much time for him to accomplish them. The total score of TEA then increased to 31 from 17 (Table 1).

In addition, the mean scores in a scale of 5 (0, no; 1, slight; 2, some improvement; 3, improvement; 4, large improvement) in a questionnaire on the improvement of his behavior answered by his mother were as follows: 1. attention 2.7; 2. memory 2.4; 3. communication 2.8; and 4. behavior 3. This questionnaire consisted of 18 questions that need to be answered on the basis of her subjective impression after three years of training (Fujii et al. 2002). The most improved item was "starting trouble" in behavior with the mother's additional comment that he could start doing things promptly. She also said that he relied on his mother at home, but outside, he could do things on his own will without depending on others. This scores in attention, communication, and behavior were higher than those in memory. His mother also noticed that his memory deficit improved in tasks on prompt memory and writing sentences recollection. Staff members in the day-service center also noticed his improved cognitive function and behavior and he was able to help the staff in putting in order and cleaning the room after their activities in the day-service center were finished. As his work at the center gradually increased and he returned home using two bus routes at around 6 p. m., which was later than before and trainings in his weekday using workbooks was moved to the weekend. He stopped practicing the tasks on the workbooks when he started as a café waiter.

Toward Effective Social Reentry of Client A

In the first workplace at a café as a waiter, client A gradually showed a decline in memory function: forgetting orders or errors in calculation and recollection of changes. Neuropsychological tests showed a decreased RBMT score from 9 to 5 (Table 1) without any change in BADS score. However, in the questionnaire (DEX) attached to BADS, he indicated clear confusion, as shown in Table 2.

Change of one point such as a change from Never to Occasionally are omitted. The total score was 4 in the first answers and 18 at the second using Dex questionnaire with 20 items with unchanged BADS scores (both 33, see Table 1). The Dex score changes showed his subjective confused experiences in the daily life. Difficulties in controlling himself are well expressed in the change in the response to item 14 as from Never to Very often. Lack of continued attention, irritability, and restlessness are shown in the changes in the responses to the other four items from

Table 2. Answer to part of Dex questionnaire (self-rating) attached to BADS in the first (at the time of working as a café waiter) and the second (one-year after), indicating changes in his behavior. The numbers 0, 1, 2, 3 and 4, denote Never, Occasionally, Sometimes, Fairly often, and Very often, respectively. Clear changes from 0 to 2 or 4 are shown in five items out of 20.

10. I really want to do something one minute, but couldn't care less about it the next. Change from 0 to 2 indicates change from Never to Sometimes
12. I lose my temper at the slightest thing. Change from 0 to 2 indicates change from Never to Sometimes.
14. I find it hard to stop repeating saying or doing things once I've started. Change from 0 to 4 indicates change from Never to Very often.
15. I tend to be very restless, and can't sit still for any length of time. Change from 0 to 2 indicates change from Never to Sometimes.
17. I will say one thing, but will do something different. Change from 0 to 2 indicates change from Never to Sometimes.

Never to Sometimes. These data revealed his difficulties in doing his work as in one-year before. Perhaps it might be the main cause of the decrease in the score of his memory functions from 9 to 5 in RBMT.

His caregiver from the community support division of the same organization looked for a suitable job for him, using the network of the organization. After three months of apprenticeship, he was employed as a kitchen staff (washing used tableware, putting tableware in order, carrying meats in pans, or cleaning the cooking room), in a company that has a contract with a home for mentally retarded children. The work as a kitchen staff suited him well and his confusion at the time when he worked as a cafe waiter disappeared: he is now working as a kitchen staff with satisfaction. TEA and RBMT scores increased (Table 1) with unchanged BADS and JART scores. In addition, in comparison with TEA total score of the past five tests; the scores at 8 yrs. in Table 1 were the highest, showing improvement to the borderline or near borderline level. Furthermore, the eighth subtest that reveals a possibility of doing two tasks at the same time showed a borderline score of 5. This is the best subtest score among the five TEA tests examined. It must be noted that the scaled score is changed at 35 years of age and without a marked difference in raw score scaled score change was shown as positive data between data, for 6 and 7 yrs. in Table 1(see also TEA Manuals, Robertson et al., 1994). At least, the attention scores, at 7 and 8 yrs. on the same scale of the scaled score showed increased scores from 41 to 52 (see Table 1), suggesting real improvement of attention.

Next is his letter to us:

I am working at --- center, washing dishes, pushing the trolley pan, and cleaning the entrance of the drainage. During my work I happily talk to many working ladies. Yesterday, I pushed the trolley pan and cleaned the entrance of the drainage as well. I am working happily and enjoy talking with other kitchen staff. At first, I cut my second and fifth fingers during the cutting of vegetables. I felt satisfied pushing the trolley pan, and I intend to work hard from Monday to Friday. I can also enjoy in today's personal computer class. I work hard from Monday to Friday. I am enjoying my work.

Half a year after working at his suitable workplace, he had epileptic seizures every Friday. Various examinations as an inpatient of the hospital in the organization showed that his seizures could be controlled, and again he returned to work. His scores for cognitive functions shown in Table 1 in the last year examined outcome measure decreased in all the test scores. Decreased test scores owing to the epileptic seizure were often encountered in our center. Epileptic seizure was considered to affect cognitive function more than results of his previous maladjusted work, which resulted only in memory score decline from 9 to 5.

It took 10 years from the time of the client suffered from TBI caused by a vehicular accident at 25 years of age to time of finding a suitable and satisfying employment at 35 years of age. Still he was able to maintain his work happily. It can be said that his CR and gradual work reentry of client A is an ideal model of CR and social reentry. During this course, his tendency of preservation (after effect of TBI) must be added as an important factor that could not be found in the literature. After his discharge from hospital, he attended the day-service center everyday with almost perfect attendance and this tendency to continue with his daily activities was maintained until now. Although the preservative tendency was not found among the multifactor recommended in social reentry (Wilson, 1998; Kowalske et. al., 2000; Levack et al., 2004), it was a potent factor for CR maintenance and may be a more important factor for his job maintenance. Poor self-awareness and severity of TBI-induced deficits (Shames et al., 2007) seemed not to interfere with his social integration and job maintenance. The support system worked well for him, advancing step by step towards social integration. The preservative tendency as an after effect of TBI may play an important role in TBI clients with very severe cognitive deficits such as client A.

CLIENT B

Client B was a 27-year-old man who suffered from severe TBI caused by a motor vehicle accident. Coma lasted for 45 days. He was diagnosed as having diffuse axonal injury, right hemiplegia, articulation disorder, hearing loss in the right ear, and memory disorder. He received hypothermia treatment without surgery. MRI showed focal lesions in the left-hemisphere deep white matter including the internal capsule. The anterior and dorsal portions of his lateral cortex were also injured. He was referred to a hospital rehabilitation facility for gait training and he was discharged after gaining the ability to walk with the aid of a cane. He returned home without specific cognitive rehabilitation. Before the accident, client B was a fulltime worker at a printing company and a sport instructor in a high school. He could not return to work owing to his physical and cognitive impairments. After his discharge, client B continued gait training with his own plan for gait rehabilitation (walking around his home daily for four hours). This lasted for two years. He lived with his parents. The patient was referred to us three years after the accident through a family support group and participated in our daily home-based cognitive training program.

CR Outcome and Social Reentry of Client B

In Table 3, changes in test scores of client B over 5 years are summarized. Numbers and years (yrs) are from the start of CR. Memory rehabilitation was the main focus from the first time in his CR because the results of his initial interview and cognitive assessment showed an impaired memory, with relatively normal attention and concentration. Using tapes for dictation tasks, memory workbooks, and newspapers, he carried out his daily cognitive training tasks for 4 hours on his own effort with the following schedule: approximately 30 minutes for the dictation task (10 minutes for writing, 20 minutes for spelling or kanji character checking), approximately 90 minutes used for the workbook (75 minutes for answering, 15 minutes for error checking) every morning; approximately 90 minutes for transcription of newspaper articles at the library every afternoon; and approximately 30 minutes for writing in a diary, remembering activities in the daytime, every evening. In a monthly meeting held every third Saturday with other TBI members he was able to report smoothly his progress or daily activities by referring his diary.

Client B earnestly kept to his cognitive training schedule for two years and repeated the workbook series four times in consecutive weeks. These workbooks included memory workbooks 1-8 for 32 weeks, reading, writing, remembering workbooks 1-12 for 48 weeks, and remembering by cues workbooks 1-4 for 16 weeks. Client B spent approximately 700 hours in cognitive training during the first eight months and continued his cognitive training for more than two years until his start of to one-year training course for the disabled. During the course, he continued the dictation tasks as his evening cognitive training. His preparation for entrance examination for the training course was also a part of his CR. Through 8 months of cognitive trainings, the RBMT standardized profile scores of client B

Table 3. Changes in scores of four neuropsychological tests of client B. Regarding the tests, see Appendix 2

	Baseline	1 year	2 yrs.	3 yrs.*	5 yrs.
TEA total score (attention)	71	89	86	95	102
RBMT standard profile score (memory)	12	19	20	23	21
BADS(executive function)			97	97	118
JART(adult reading ability)	35			46	52
Social reentry				Workshop	

* Job training course for disabled for a year

improved from 12 to 19 (Fujita et al., 2003), which was the borderline (cutoff) for a full score of 24. After that, he attained a normal cognitive level with RBMT scores of 20 and 23 (Table 3). His TEA total scores also increased to 89 and 95 (normal score ranges) 1 and 3 years after the start of the training, respectively, from the baseline score of 71 (Table 3). It was considered that an early improvement of his memory function was due to his daily intensive CR (4 hours every day) and rather unaffected attention ability.

The subjective impression of TBI recovery from the response to 70 items of European Brain Injury Questionnaire (EBIQ Martin et al., 2001) and 7 additional items showed a general recovery of his cognitive function. Client B showed "very improved" for 8 item, "improved" for 20 items, and "better" for 15 items as compared with the start of CR. One of his parents reported "improved" for 14 items and "better" for 35 items (Table 4). Client B showed all items "improved" among the 5 items in Table. 5 with one exception of "no symptom" for one item, in contrast with the parent's response of "better" for all 5 items. These results suggest that client B feels more improvement through CR than his parent. It may result from some overestimation in his self-assessment. His assessment of his memory improvement also agreed with that of his parent, although the assessment of the degree of improvement was somewhat different, as shown in Table 5. His memory improvement extended to his social integration. First, it was attendance in a training course for a year, and next was a welfare workshop for three days a week, and then a place of community service one day a week. He may still have a long way, to go, as full time work is his final target.

Table 4. Parent and client scores for 70 items of questionnaires improvement (63 from EBIQ and additional 7 items on memory improvement)

	Client B	Parent
Very much improved	8	0
Improved	20	14
Better	15	35
No change	1	1
No symptoms	24	18
N/A	2	2
Total	70	70

0: No symptoms. 1: No change. 2: Better. 3: Improved. 4: Very improved

DISCUSSION

These analyses of CR of two clients provided us much knowledge on the process of improving cognitive functions, particularly in attention and memory, although 1000 or more training hours were required in both clients A and B. The improvement of attention and memory deficits by CR using drill methods has not been positively reported in severe TBI (Rees et al., 2007). It was considered that our success in CR came from long-term intensive and exclusive daily training. Furthermore, it was suggested that CR as a daily activity was more effective than experimental and clinical training of comprehensive rehabilitation (Sarajuuri et al., 2005). It was also said that rehabilitation of hobby-like fashion only gained one-third effect of intensive training (Taub et al., 2006). Preservative tendency as a TBI aftereffect was played a crucial role in the continuation of CR by daily home-based trainings for a long term in client A. Although his physical problems such as epileptic seizures caused damage to his overall cognitive function and maladjustment as a café waiter, which

Table 5. Scores for 5 out of 70 items of questionnaire concerning memory. Grading of items is the same as that in Table 4

	Client B	Parent
Forgetting the day of the week	0	2
Forgetting appointments	3	2
Forgetting anything	3	2
Recall immediately and not delayed	3	2
Taking time to recall	3	2

reduced his memory ability, he successfully continued with his job as a kitchen staff everyday from Monday to Friday. Earnest daily training of client B for 4 hours caused increased RBMT score from 12 to 19 (cutoff score) and finally attained an almost normal cognitive level in all neuropsychological tests conducted although he still in a way to final target.

It was also considered that intensive CR produces brain (perhaps association cortices) reorganization (Taub et al., 2002; Nadeau, 2002) and good effects for work reentry. CR played an important preparatory role in social integration. One of the two clients successfully landed a job, even if with relatively poor cognitive functions, as shown by his low RBMT, BADS, and JART scores (lower than the minimum required neuropsychological test scores for reentry to work mentioned in chapter 18) and he lack of self-awareness of his own deficits. Perhaps improvement of attention plays a role in his success. In addition, a support system in a large organization made his work continuation possible. In contrast, client B who showed good cognitive recoveries that reached almost normal levels (within normal ranges in all the four tests and over than minimum required test scores for social reentry) could only gain a part time work without a potent support system such as that for client A.

CONCLUSION

On the basis of the results of CR of the two clients and the follow up after the CR, following conclusions are:

(1) Intensive CR is effective for attention and memory recoveries, and the cognitive improvement is a preparation for a satisfactory social life.
(2) Preservative tendency as a TBI aftereffect is often useful for CR continuation.
(3) The negative factors are unsuitable work and epileptic seizures, both of which cause a certain deterioration of cognitive functions, perhaps in clients with severe TBI.

These results of the first attempt of our CR provided us practical knowledge on real improvement of TBI cognitive deficits through intensive CR, suggesting brain reorganization in associational cortices (perhaps prefrontal and lateral cortices). This reorganization is considered to cause a permanent improvement of the cognitive function. In addition to the positive results, a support system for severe TBI clients was considered to be essential for a social reentry.

FUTURE TRENDS

Our CR program is based on a practical idea in Japan where there is no CR course. This report demonstrated that the home-based practices formed an effective model for CR. From our first attempt of CR, it was suggested that the exclusive and intense cognitive training was essential factor for improving cognitive deficits caused by TBI. The follow-up study of these clients up to now showed us various additional new findings for future CR advances and taught us that life long activities including CR with clients, family and care givers, as a cooperative system, are ideal for their satisfactory lives. Activities for expanding the CR model in every city must be planned as a community resource.

ACKNOWLEDGMENT

The author thanks Dr. Kumiko Imahashi, for her earnest participation in this work, particularly her work with client B, and also thank the two clients who participated in the yearly meeting of the follow-up study and permitted us to use their personal data.

REFERENCES

Franulic, A., Gloria, J., Carbonell, C., Patricia, P., & Sepulveda, I. (2004). Psychosocial adjustment and employment out come 2, 5, and 10 years after TB. *Brain Injury : [BI], 18*(2), 119–129.

Fujii, M., Fujita, K., Hiramatsu, H., & Miyamoto, T. (1998). Cases of two patients whose food aversions disappeared following severe traumatic brain injury. *Brain Injury, 12*(8), 709–713. doi:10.1080/026990598122278

Fujii, M., & Hayakashi, T. (1992). Axons from the olfactory bulb transplanted into the cerebellum form synapses with dendrites in the granular layer, as demonstrated by mouse allelic form of Thy-1 and electron microscopy. *Neuroscience Research, 14*(1), 73–78.doi:10.1016/S0168-0102(05)80007-0

Fujii, M., Inutsuka, K., Matsuoka, Y., Fujita, K., & Shikimori, H. (2002). Report on home-based three-year-cognitive training for a man who had received severe bilateral brain injuries with traffic accident. *Cognitive Rehabilitation 2002.* Tokyo: Sinkoh Igaku Shuppan (in Japanese).

Fujita, K., Fujii, M., & Shikimori, H. (2003). A home-based memory training for severe traumatic brain injury through the use of training books and dictation tasks. *Brain Injury, 17*(Suppl. 1), 120.

Kashima, H. (Ed.). (2003). *Behavioural assessment of the dysexecutive syndrome* (Japanese version). Tokyo: Sinkoh Igaku Shuppan (in Japanese).

Kowalske, K., Plenger, P. M., Lusby, B., & Hayden, M. E. (2000). Vocational reentry following TBI: An enablement model. *The Journal of Head Trauma Rehabilitation, 15*(4), 989–999. doi:10.1097/00001199-200008000-00003

Leon-Carrion, J. (1997). Rehabilitation of memory. In J. Leon-Carrion (Ed.), *Neuropsychological rehabilitation: Fundamentals, innovations, and directions* (pp. 371-398). Delray Beach, FL: GR/Saint Lucie Press.

Levack, W., McPherson, M., & McNaughton, H. (2004). Success in the workplace following traumatic brain injury: Are we evaluating what is most important? *Disability and Rehabilitation, 26*(5), 290–298. doi:10.1080/09638280310001647615

Machamer, J., Temkin, N., Fraser, R., Doctor, J. N., & Dikmen, S. (2005). Stability of employment after traumatic brain injury. *Journal of the International Neuropsychological Society, 11*(7), 807–816. doi:10.1017/S135561770505099X

Martin, C., Viguier, G., Deloche, G., & Dellatolas, G. (2001). Subjective experience after traumatic brain injury. *Brain Injury : [BI], 15*(11), 947–959. doi:10.1080/02699050110065655

Matsuoka, K., & Kim, Y. (2006). *Japanese adult reading test (JART)*. Tokyo: Shinko-Igaku Syuppansya.

Matsuoka, K., Uno, M., Kasai, K., Koyama, K., & Kim, Y. (2006). Estimation of premorbid IQ in individuals with Alzheimer's disease using Japanese ideographic script (Kanji) compound words: A Japanese version of NART. *Psychiatry and Clinical Neurosciences, 60*(3), 332–339. doi:10.1111/j.1440-1819.2006.01510.x

Matsuoka, Y., Fujii, M., Fujita, K., Kanae, K., & Shikimori, H. (2000). Efficacy of the dictation test to evaluate the social reentry ability in young persons with traumatic brain injury. [in Japanese]. *Hokenno-Kagaku, 42*(9), 759–764.

McCrimmon, S., & Oddy, M. (2006). Return to work following moderate-to-severe traumatic brain injury. *Brain Injury : [BI], 20*(10), 1037–1046. doi:10.1080/02699050600909656

Nadeau, S. E. (2002). A paradigm shift in neurorehabilitation. *The Lancet Neurology, 1*(2), 126–130. doi:10.1016/S1474-4422(02)00044-3

Ponsford, J. (1995). *Traumatic brain injury: Rehabilitation for everyday adaptive living.* Taylor & Francis. In M. Fujii, Nisimurasyoten & Niigata (Japanese translation 2000).

Rees, L., Marshall, S., Hartridge, C., Mackie, D., & Wiser, M. (2007). Cognitive interventions post acquired brain injury. *Brain Injury : [BI], 21*(2), 161–200.

Robertson, I. H., Ward, T., Ridgeway, V., & Nimmo-Smith, I. (1994). *The test of everyday attention.* Suffolk: Thames Valley Test Company.

Sarajuuri, J. M., Kaipio, M. L., Koskinen, S. K., Niemela, M. R., Servo, A. R., & Vilkki, J. S. (2005). Outcome of a comprehensive neurorehabilitation program for patients with traumatic brain injury. *Archives of Physical Medicine and Rehabilitation, 86*, 2296–2302. doi:10.1016/j.apmr.2005.06.018

Shames, J., Treger, I., Ring, H., & Giaquinto, S. (2007). Return to work following traumatic brain injury: Trends and challenges. *Disability and Rehabilitation, 29*(17), 1387–1395. doi:10.1080/09638280701315011

Shinagawa, F., Kobayashi, S., Fujita, K., & Maekawa, H. (1990). *Japanese wechsler adult intelligence scale-revised.* Tokyo: Nihon-Bunkakagakusya.

Sohlberg, M. M., & Mateer, K. (2001). *Cognitive rehabilitation: An integrative neuropsychological approach.* New York: Guilford Press.

Taub, E., Uswatte, G., & Elbert, T. (2002). New treatments in neurorehabilitation founded on basic research. *Nature Reviews. Neuroscience, 3*, 228–236. doi:10.1038/nrn754

Taub, E., Uswatte, G., Mark, V. W., & Morris, D. M. (2006). The learned non-use phenomenon: Implications for rehabilitation. *Europa Medicophysica, 42*(3), 241–255.

Watamori, Y., Hara, H., Miyamori, T., & Eto, F. (2002). *The rivermead behavioural memory test, Japanese version.* Tokyo: Chiba Test Center.

Wilson, B. A. (1998). Recovery of cognitive functions following nonprogressive brain injury. *Current Opinion in Neurobiology, 8*(2), 281–287. doi:10.1016/S0959-4388(98)80152-9

Winkler, D., Unsworth, C., & Sloan, S. (2006). Factors that lead to successful community integration following severe traumatic brain injury. *The Journal of Head Trauma Rehabilitation, 21*(1), 8–21. doi:10.1097/00001199-200601000-00002

APPENDIX 1

List of workbooks originally issued by the NPO-TBI Rehabilitation Center. One book is usually used for a week's practice from Monday to Friday.

1. Workbooks for words 1-8 (a book for two weeks, total of 16 weeks)
2. Workbooks for elderly persons, 1-4 (a book for two weeks, total of 8 weeks)
3. Workbooks for word exercise, 1-6 (a book for two weeks, total of 12 weeks)
4. Workbooks for listening attention, 1-4 (a pair of books one for the examiner and the other for the client; a book for a week, total of 4 weeks)
5. Workbooks for visual attention, 1-4 (a book for a week, total of 4 weeks)
6. Memory workbooks for first attempt, 1-4 (a book for a week, total of 4 weeks)
7. Easier memory workbooks, 1-6 (a book for a week, total of 6 weeks)
8. Easy memory workbooks, 1-4 (a book for a week, total of 4 weeks)
9. Memory workbooks, 1-8 (a book for a week, total of 8 weeks)
10. Listening, writing, remembering workbooks, 1-5 (a pair of books one for the examiner and the other for the client; a book for a week, total of 5 weeks)
11. Reading, writing, remembering workbooks, 1-12 (a book for a week, total of 12 weeks)
12. Remembering by cue workbooks, 1-4 (a book for a week, total of 4 weeks)
13. Listening memory workbooks, 1-8 (a pair of books one for the examiner and the other for the client; a book for a week, total of 8 weeks)
14. Reading memory workbooks, 1-8 (a book for a week, total of 8 weeks)
15. Workbooks for head training, 1-4 (a book for a week, total of 4 weeks)
16. Executive workbooks, 1-6 (a book for a week, total of 6 weeks)
17. Thinking workbooks, 1 (a book for 6 weeks)

Workbooks 1-3 are for language practice; 4-5, for attention practice; 6-14, for memory practice; 15-17, for executive function exercise.

About 25 types of audiotape of stories composed of 200, 300, and 500 words per day practice including 5 days per week are also available.

APPENDIX 2

Assessments used by our NPO-TBI Rehabilitation Center

Out of six tests and questionnaires of cognitive function, we usually employ four tests (from 1 to 4), while the other tests and questionnaires are used as needed.

1. Test of Everyday Attention (TEA). This test can assess attention and speed of information processing using everyday materials (Robertson et al., 1994).
2. Japanese version of the Rivermead Behavioural Memory Test (RBMT) and the questionnaire by Watamori et al. (2002). This test can assess various memory functions, using everyday materials.
3. Japanese version of the Executive Function Disorder Syndrome (BADS) and questionnaire (Dex) edited by Kashima (2003). This test can assess six types of executive items.
4. Japanese version of National Adult Reading Test (Japanese Adult Reading Test, JART). This test can assess language function by determining the ability to read 100 Kanji characters (Matsuoka et al., 2006; Matsuoka et al., 2006).
5. Japanese version of Wechsler Adult Intelligence Scale-Revised by Shinagawa et al. (1990).
6. Questionnaire on recovery impression based on the European Brain Injury Questionnaire (Martin et al., 2001). This questionnaire can assess subjective recovery changes in daily life. There were originally 63 questionnaire' items and we added 7 more. Answers were collected separately from TBI persons and their families.
7. The other test is a dictation test for hearing and writing originally made for our research on language ability (Matsuoka et al., 2000).

Chapter 18

Further Directions in Cognitive Rehabilitation in Community– and Home–based Daily Trainings in Clients with Severe Traumatic Brain Injury

Masako Fujii
Nonprofit Organization TBI Rehabilitation Center, Japan

ABSTRACT

Community- and home-based daily intense cognitive rehabilitation (CR) of traumatic brain injury (TBI) clients was initiated on the basis on knowledge mentioned in Chapter 17. In the CR, statistically significant changes were demonstrated in attention and reading abilities in sixteen severe TBI clients by one-year daily CR. Improvement of memory and executive functions required more training periods as shown later. The temporary minimum scores of four neuropsychological tests required for social reentry, namely, 50 in TEA, 15 in RBMT, 80 in BADS and 40 in JART, were determined as a goal of our CR. In addition to the drill (pen and paper) method mainly using workbooks, a more advanced program for CR, particularly in clients who reached the required level, was developed together with the clients.

DOI: 10.4018/978-1-60566-284-8.ch018

INTRODUCTION

The remediation of cognitive deficits caused by TBI is particularly important because TBI clients are often young people (men are approximately 3 times more than women), who have just reached their productive stage or their last educational level (high school or university). Therefore, it is indispensable for the clients to improve their impaired cognitive functions such as attention, memory, and executive functions for their work reentry. TBI clients desire a convenient center for a daily training CR program near the place of their residential area, which is particularly necessary because they are widely distributed in a community and TBI remediation takes much time, even if they practiced without missing their daily trainings. A center for CR will be therefore indispensable in every city or prefecture, but community-based intensive CR centers are currently lacking in Japan. Under such a condition, the need for an effective community-based CR model increases. With progress in motorization, more developmental approaches in community-based and cost-effective CR become indispensable for TBI clients (Rehabilitation of persons with TBI, 1999), generating positive effects that can supersede residential-, hospital- or comprehensive day-treatment-based rehabilitation.

Home-based daily CR is a practical idea in the local areas where a convenient CR center is not available as is the case in Japan. In general, the rehabilitation of clients with TBI has been discussed mainly in terms of behavioral aspects or family dynamics, and also cost effectiveness as compared with residential- and hospital-based rehabilitation (Wood et al., 1999). Although there is some effort in hospital-based comprehensive rehabilitation in Japan (Hashimoto et al., 2006), it does not relate to long-term CR, which results in brain reorganization. Generally, CR as a part of daily activities may be ideal. The future establishment of local- and community-based CR center will make it easy to provide permanent services to local population cost-effectively (Oddy and McMillan, 2001). This process in our center may be supported by continuation of self-transcending process of knowledge creation (Nonaka and Takeuchi, 1995) for a better quality of life (QOL) in TBI clients. In addition to the psychosocial aspect, the concept of our daily intensive CR also agrees closely with the recent paradigm shift in neurorehabilitation to form reorganized cortical system for a permanent remediation of cortical functions, as mentioned in chapter 17. According to the concept, our CR is aimed to create the reorganization in the prefrontal and lateral cortical association areas although the anatomical demonstration of the cortical reorganization may remain difficult.

The CR of TBI clients has already started in Europe and USA but its outcomes are not always consistent (Pace et al., 1999; Boman et al., 2004) due to different rehabilitation methodologies and concerns related to TBI remediation. We considered that the CR of TBI clients was most effective in the case of exclusive cognitive daily practices at home in an area where there is no CR center nearby. The pen-and-paper trainings using workbooks or dictation tasks are familiar for daily practice and are cost-effective. The effects of training in an educational system (as a place of training and development of human cognitive function) seemed in a sense to be similar final goal of brain reorganization.

From 1997 to 2001, our research on CR of TBI clients was started at the Human Science Laboratory, in a university (a part of the CR mentioned in chapter 17). From the results of a study of CR over five years and the follow-up studies after that, fundamental information concerning CR of TBI clients has been accumulated. Further knowledge could be obtained from a practical book for TBI (e. g., Ponsford, 1995) and the World Congress of Brain Injury started from 1995. From 2002 up to now, the Nonprofit Organization (NPO) TBI Rehabilitation Center was initiated in Tokyo for the implementation of the knowledge on CR, previously gained. The basic administration principle is community- and home-based rehabilitation service for daily practices at home. In addition to productions of CR tools, various workbooks and audiotapes for dictation tasks, CR classes (the name of our group session) once a week was also started to promote daily home-based CR in the community setting. These activities proved the efficacy of CR tools we made. This is the first attempt of applying the CR approach as a community- and home-based daily practice in Japan.

The intended services to be provided by our center are as follows:(1) Daily home-based CR, in which a practical guide of weekly training is checked at the rehabilitation class once a week; (2) Production of CR tools such as rehabilitation workbooks and audiotapes for dictation tasks mentioned in Appendix 1 of chapter 17; and (3) Dissemination of a dispersed network of cognitive rehabilitation practice in Japan through lectures, consultations, or delivery of rehabilitation tools.

PRINCIPLES OF THE CR ADMINISTRATION

It is well known that the brain regions affected by TBI are the prefrontal and lateral cortices (Figure 1), which are phylogenetically new cortical areas in human beings and also the main regions in which information is manipulated in a broad sense using language (including numbers). As mentioned above injuries to these regions cause deficits of attention, memory, executive function, and behavioral disturbances. The first three deficits are the main concern in this chapter and these deficits are demonstrated in association with information- related activities. Deficit of attention causes poor input of language, and memory deficit affects language encoding, consolidation, and retrieval in the brain. The executive function involves the most elaborate language manipulation and is also damaged by TBI. CR or neuropsychological

Figure 1. Schematic drawing of brain regions mostly affected by TBI based on our findings and Courville's pictures cited in a book by Sohlberg et al., 2001

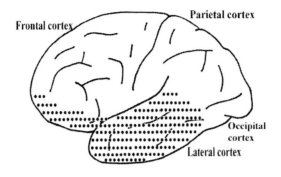

rehabilitation usually encompasses many types of deficits that must be improved (Johnstone and Stonington, 2001). However, we used the term, CR, with a limited definition, that is, for the improvement of affected language manipulation and related functions that are commonly revealed by deficits of information processing. Our CR is then limited to a training at first mainly using language drills similar to those used in school. For an effective CR the following principles were considered; (1) daily, (2) at home, (3) with family, (4) outcome measures. An effective home-based daily CR training program was then planned involving an increase in the total amount of training hours. Generally, outpatients who return home from the hospital have much time during the day, and the training at home with family member are considered to be able to reconstruct a new family organization in addition to obtaining training efficacy. The training program is usually carried out by the pen and paper method, using workbooks and/or audiotapes for dictation tasks, and it is a cost effective and familiar work to do. One workbook is usually made for one week of training and it is made to be handy and light for daily practice, compared with 4-week workbooks and paired books (one book for the client and the other book for the trainer) (Malia et al., 1997). Workbooks and audiotapes for dictation tasks as rehabilitation tools were prepared using letters, words (kanji, kana), or/ and sentences (and also pictures as cues to induce words and sentences) (for details on workbooks, see Appendix 1 in chapter 17). An additional effect of CR was considered to be an increase in self-awareness of TBI clients (Matsuba et al., 2003).

Results of daily trainings are checked by members of our center in a CR class held once a week for two hours, and a family support meeting is held once a month, every third Friday from 18:30. Furthermore, a 64-page-booklet entitled "Brain and Recovery" is distributed to family member to inform them on cognitive deficits and

Table 1. Changes in neuropsychological test score before and after one-year CR of 16 TBI clients in our center. Regarding the neuropsychological tests, see Appendix 2 in previous chapter. Repeated measurement of analysis of variance (ANOVA) was used to examine the one-year changes.

Mean (SD)	Baseline	after one year	statisticalvalueF(df=15)
TEA total score	61.50(20.85)	71.69(23.73)	16.404**
RBMT standard profile score	14.44(5.62)	14.56(5.39)	0.013
BADS age-adjusted scaled score	83.75(21.65)	89.56(17.38)	1.273
JART-100 total score	60.06(17.38)	63.94(16.07)	7.512*

†$p < 0.10$ *$p < 0.05$ **$p < 0.01$.

CR, which is issued four times a year. Neuropsychological tests (see Appendix 2 in chapter 17) before (baseline scores) and after the training are carried out yearly to assess the recovery of attention and memory abilities and executive function. Data on the clients are collected as follows: (1) The submitted workbooks and other materials after checking weekly are collected in our center; (2) Individual files of test records and questionnaires are collected as background data; (3) The training program is recorded and delivered with individual scores of four tests and results of questionnaire survey to clients and their families; (4) In a semiformal interview, data on the clients and their families are collected; (5) In a monthly meeting, a client's actual activities are discussed with family.

OUTCOME MEASURES

The neuropsychological tests (see Appendix 2 in chapter 17) are carried out first to examine the participant's baseline (before the practice) abilities, and after which, yearly outcome measures of attention, memory, executive function, and reading ability is collected. Table 1 shows the one-year mean scores of 16 TBI clients who are recent participants in our center and who usually performed CR at home 5 days a week, from Monday to Friday.

As shown in Table 1, attention improvement was statistically significant and the most prominent in changes in TEA total scores. Furthermore, the TEA subtest scores (data are not shown) suggested that the duration of visual selective attention (duration of information processing) improve ($p < 0.05$) and switching of visual and auditory attention also tended to improve ($p < 0.1$). Increase in the TEA attention scores realized using our workbooks have already been reported as preliminary results

(Yamamoto-Mitani et al., 2007). The second significant improvement was in the score of JART (Japanese Adult Reading Test. See Appendix 2 in chapter 17). The significant changes in the score of JART suggest that the reading ability decreased by TBI was recovered during practices using workbooks or writing sentences in dictation tasks, which had offered many chances of using Japanese language. The demographic data of all the 16 clients are as follows:(1) age (mostly 23 to 40 years, 11 persons 41 to 49 years, 5 persons, mean 42 years), (2) gender (2 women and 14 men), (3) years from TBI onset to start of CR (2 to 39 years; mean, 10 years; with spontaneous recovery already ceased), and (4) cause of TBI (14 persons, traffic accidents; 2 persons, a fall or recreation accident). These clients required workbook-practices of 511 weeks, an average of 34 weeks. The workbooks were those for language practice (32%), attention practice (10%), memory practice (43%), and executive function practice (15%).

These results suggest that attention and reading abilities improved, particularly through the first-year of trainings and that the reason for this improvement was the large amount of training time, approximately 170 hours (34 mean weeks x 5 days x daily 1 hour), which is more than the effective cognitive training times of over 100 hours (a report by Prigatano cited in the literature by Johnstone et al. 2001, p.114). A longer time may be required to maintain improvements of attention and reading abilities. The daily practice may be a reasonable method because it can be carried out in daily efforts outside the conventional training procedure (Boman, 2004).

The success in the first year of CR using our training materials needs the second step of maintaining the improvement perhaps for more than a year. Several kinds of workbooks (approximately more than 100 workbooks) make it possible. After that, more complex and comprehensive steps are performed considering client's interest and preference. This community- and home-based daily practice by pen and paper method were demonstrated to be a good first step towards cognitive recovery, forming a basis of social reentry or return to work, because attention ability plays an important role in social life. The other outcome measures such as those for memory and executive function were not statistically significant, suggesting no clear difference between the start of CR and one-year after in 16 clients. The executive functions of these clients was often retained from the first time with minimum required scores of 80 for reentry to work even if the other scores of cognitive abilities seemed to be decreased by TBI. Memory ability that is commonly affected by TBI was sometimes recovered through long-term CR, as demonstrated by increased RBMT or/and WMS-R scores. As examples, data of two individuals showed improvement of memory function after long-term CR. These are shown in Tables 2 and 3. The tables also showed increases in three other scores in both clients. Perhaps the recovery of memory function was accompanied by the overall improvement of cognitive function. A part of the results was already reported in a

Table 2. Cognitive improvements in client C through our CR.

	Baseline	2 yrs.	3 yrs.	4 yrs.*	5 yrs.
TEA total score (Attention)	65	82	90	90	92
RBMT standard profile (Memory)		12	15	14	17
BADS (Executive function)		86	86	91	108
JART (Adult reading ability)	55		71	70	71

poster in the 7th World Congress of Brain Injury 2008.

Information on client C: His CR was involved intensive practices for 2 and 1/4 yrs. with followed by precedent infrequent practices for 2 yrs. After interruption of CR owing to his landing a job (*), his memory and executive function scores increased, suggesting the positive effects of his new job, with negligible change in attention scores.. Abbreviations: yrs. showed years after. As to the neuropsychological tests, see Appendix 2 in chapter 17.

Information on client D: Gradual increases in TEA and JART scores were noted over four yrs. of daily workbook trainings, with additional practices using e-mail in the past three yrs. Increases in RBMT and WMS-R scores were clearly observed at

Table 3. Cognitive improvements in client D through our CR.

	Baseline	1 year	2 yrs.	3 yrs.	4 yrs.*	5 yrs.
TEA total score (Attention)	30	36	47	46	59	57
RBMT standard profile (Memory)	13	13	16	14	19	23
BADS (Executive function)	81	91	91	102	91	102
JART (Adult reading ability)	66	69	73	74	83	76
WMS-R(Wechsler memory)						
Verbal memory				79	103	86
Visual memory				87	94	104
General memory				78	101	89
Attention/concentration				50	81	84
Delayed retrieval				71	73	84

4 years. After landing a job increased scores at 5 years were also noted in RBMT and WMS-R at 5 yrs.

These results of the two TBI clients showed a possibility to recover memory function through CR and a good gain for employment after CR. For both clients the time of their landing a job was four years after CR and it was of interest that memory improvement as indicated by RBMT scores was also observed after landing a job. The positive effect of employment may be expressed in memory improvement although it is not sure whether this effect always occurred after landing a job. Both clients showed in four tests higher than our minimum scores required for reentry to work (TEA, 50; RBMT, 15; BADS, 80; JART, 40 as discussed below).

TEMPORARY MINIMUM REQUIRED SCORES IN FOUR NEUROPSYCHOLOGICAL TESTS FOR REENTRY TO WORK

Through the advancement of community services of CR in our center, a goal decision required for reentry to work based on the following purposes: (1) comparison of results among scores of four tests TEA, RBMT, BADS and JART, to know of which test score in these four test still remain under the required level (2) formation of a guideline for TBI clients, their families and TBI professionals to know a possibility of returning to work, and (3) decision of a training target that should be checked with our cognitive program that has an unlimited rehabilitation term. The determination of the clients' readiness to return to work or school reentry in TBI clients has been discussed from various aspects using different measures (for example, Petrella et al., 2005; Cantagallo et al., 2006; Shames et al., 2007) but there has been a lack of an exact scale for cognitive goal or the minimum cognitive function required scores for social reentry. Through data of cutoff or borderline scores in test manual or using empirical assessment of daily life we decided to determine temporarily minimum required test scores for return to work. TBI clients in our center who already returned to work and still participate in CR class inform us various useful information on actual work, in addition to their test scores. Scores of the neuropsychological tests differ from each other. However, four tests, TEA for attention, RBMT for memory, BADS for executive function, and JART for reading ability can be used to determine the clients' readiness for work reentry on the basis of their total scores.

In TEA, 5 is the cutoff score in each nine subtest. If a TBI client scores 5 in all the nine subtests, the client has a total score of 45. A TBI client with a TEA total score of 51 can maintained her work after securing a job. It was considered that approximately 51, is the minimum score for social reentry, which is slightly higher than 45. The minimum required total score was then determined to be 50 for TEA.

The RBMT cutoff score is determined within the test manual. The cutoff score for a person younger than 40 years of age is 19/20. Two above-mentioned clients C and D showed RBMT, scores of 17 and 19, respectively, which are relatively good scores for social reentry. Because of a general difficulty in memory recovery, the minimum score had to set to be relatively lower than the cutoff score. The minimum required memory test score (RBMT) is therefore determined as 15 for RBMT, which is the cutoff score for persons over 60 years of age. The borderline BADS score is 70 in this test manual and clients C and D scored over 80 in all their tests and mean of BADS in Table 1 was over 80 from the first time. As mentioned above, the executive function tends to be retained after TBI when an accident occurs in adulthood. Thus, it was decided that the minimum score should be 80. It was considered that the BADS score shows roughly a part of executive function because more than one measure is recommended to use in a comprehensive assessment of executive function (Bamdad et al. 2003). From these findings, the minimum BADS score was determined to be 80. The JART cutof score is 40 therefore out of 100 words (personal communication with Matsuoka, see Appendix 2 in chapter 17). Therefore, the minimum score of JART for social reentry of TBI clients is determined to be 40. As a result, 50 for TEA, 15 for RBMT, 80 for BADS, and 40 for JART were determined as our temporary minimum scores of cognitive function required for work reentry.

EFFICACY OF COGNITIVE CR SERVICES AND SOCIAL REENTRY

Home-based CR by the pen-and-paper methods is not always reported to be effective (Willer et al., 1999; Rees, 2007). However, as expected in the literature (Cicerone et al., 2005) our long-time intensive home-based CR demonstrated that the pen-and-paper method effectively improved attention and reading abilities in a district where there are no residential- and hospital-based rehabilitation resources, and effective home-based CR activities may be promising for TBI clients. The success of home-based activities could be obtained owing the support of the families of young clients, who were just at the starting point of their productive lives. With a strong family support, home-based practice became possible for a client who has a somewhat poor self-recognition of his/her cognitive deficits (see chapter 17, Client A). Our practices differ from other conventional comprehensive program (Malec and Basford, 1996; Sarajuuri et al., 2005) in four points: (1) Long-term in CR (life-long practices as a part of TBI client's life are desirable). (2) The use of the various workbooks that are made for daily use or new books made considering client's needs and preference, (3) everyday practices at home and feedback once a week in group sessions., and

(4) Cost-effective during the CR. A restricted environment has been suggested to offer more comprehensive services, but it may cost much (perhaps several times more, Kirn, 1987), than the services provided by our center.

Our previous report on 13 clients and their families (Matsuba et al., 2003), studied using the same questionnaire and by asking them individually in both subjects. The scores in a client was paired with a family member and the pair was instructed to evaluate the subjective experiences of TBI symptoms with the lowest score indicating mild symptoms and the highest scores indicating severe symptoms. Differences between the client and family scores increased from middle family scores but for the last two clients the scores were almost similar between the clients and families. It was suggested that these unexpected findings were attributable to the fact that the last two clients completed CR more than one year using our workbooks, suggesting that the daily trainings played a role in developing self-awareness of their deficits. If the reduced differences between the client and family scores among two clients, that may be another results of CR in contrast with findings that impaired awareness is a major factor for the severity of TBI symptoms (Sherer et al, 1998). It may be also considered that the self-awareness induced better productive activities (Petrella et al 2005) in the client's daily life and also indicated the readiness to return to work (Shames et al., 2007). However, it was demonstrated in one client described in chapter 17 that the supported system played a greater role than self-awareness. Perhaps multi-factors may affect the social reentry in TBI clients.

At the time when our center started, all the clients did not hold a job. Three years after (at least after one year training), four clients landed and maintained their jobs. Another client worked in a nursing home as a volunteer and later became a staff of the same home. They still continue CR, and this may play some role in the maintenance of their jobs. The weekly rehabilitation class for clients with daytime work is after 5 p. m. on a weekday or Saturday afternoon. Two clients still continued their fulltime jobs (one client, for four years and the other client, for one year), whereas another client decreased her working time and felt happier than before because fulltime work was too much for her.

Two or three years after the CR in TBI clients in our center, using workbooks, a more advanced CR for social integration was tried, for example, two clients enjoyed a daily E-mail program in which daily announcements with some sentences taken from his favorite novel and its summary, or summaries of columns of newspaper of the day were sent. The purpose of the E-mail program is to promote the understanding of sentences. The other client made training books for other participants, in which there are various questions to answer (so-called Q and A), for 6 weeks. Another client translated a English book written by a TBI client in USA to English. These works were selected in accordance with the client preferences and experiences.

Seventeen young TBI clients of our center were asked about the role of rehabilitation class in social reentry and their responses were as follows: Out of the ten questions asked, the most frequent answer were "good to be able to meet other persons, 53%," and "good to talk well with each other, 47%". Interestingly, this rehabilitation class partly played a role in social reentry, as a transition place between a conventional rehabilitation setting and reentry to the society, such as in the case of landing a job. It was suggested from these responses that severe TBI persons was generally lack a place for their socialization, such as transitional living center (Ponsford, 1995), aside from the rehabilitation hospital and day-services for mentally ill or elderly persons.

DISCUSSION

Our community- and home-based intensive CR, yielded positive results as follows: (1) Daily CR using the pen and paper (workbooks and dictation tasks) method for one year led to statistically significant improved attention and reading abilities (in terms of mean TEA and JART scores). (2) More than one year of CR plays a role in the development of self-awareness of cognitive deficit. (3) Varied CR tools prepared, weekly feed back system, and cost effectiveness of CR made daily CR continuation easy. The effective, inexpensive and an elaborated method of CR was a daily home-based cognitive training, using workbooks and dictation tasks originally prepared. The drill method is not widely used in severe TBI but the cognitive improvement may be obtained using home-based CR program with unlimited and continuous daily training, sometimes as a part of the daily TBI client's life. These community-based CR program was not always accepted (Cullen et al. 2007), but it was considered to be reasonable center in the area where a convenient center is not available.

Our results also showed that attention improvement was appropriate as the first-year goal in CR, which was accompanied by the improvement of reading ability. Some clients attained the required score for social reentry from the first time in the executive function (BADS, score, 80) similarly to clients C and D whose BADS scores increased with further CR as shown in Tables 2 and 3. The most difficult goal in CR therefore was memory improvement. However some clients showed memory recovery although much time was needed as case of client D, in contrast to unbelievable goals of time-limited programs of adult post-acute brain injury rehabilitation (Kern, 1987). Then the second most difficult goal following the first goal of improving attention in our center was memory recovery for obtaining required score for work reentry, that is, RBMT score of 15 for young TBI clients. Some of the positive results were already reported (see in Chapter 17). The primary aim of CR is cognitive recovery that is brain reorganization through daily intensive practices. Positive productive activities were demonstrated by comprehensive day treatment of TBI client (Sarajuuri 2005) but there is no effort to prove directly the recovery of cognitive functions.

The reason why our CR program results in cognitive recovery, which has not been demonstrated in severe TBI (Rees et al. 2007), is that brain function is improved slowly and gradually through daily (sometimes taking several years) training and is manifested by high test scores, as in clients C and D, particularly concerning memory recovery. One more positive change as determined by RBMT in client C manifested after landing a job may be attributable to long CR before that time obtaining the job. Long daily efforts of TBI clients may realize the positive results in our center. Community- and home-based CR makes it easy because CR as a community service near residential place lasts long and restarts easily if it is sometimes interrupted.

Now we are working with a large organization, developing support systems for the work reentry of TBI clients. The main part of the support system will be research on how to maintain their work, namely, adaptation to their new social life. The success of a large organization in helping the social reentry of very severe TBI clients mentioned in chapter 17 pushes forward this planning. It will be a new model of TBI clients in the post-acute period on how to lead happy healthy social life.

CONCLUSION

The positive results of home-based daily CR of TBI clients are as follows:

1. There are statistically significant improvements in attention and reading abilities after a one-year cognitive training. These improvements provided important knowledge for further CR and could be the basis for the next process of CR,
2. Recoveries of memory were demonstrated in some clients who underwent a considerably long time, (over 2 years) of intensive CR, and executive function often retained cutoff level from the first time if TBI had occurred in adulthood.
3. Workbook trainings for over one year seemed to play a role in developing client self-recognition or self-awareness of TBI deficits.
4. Group training once a week plays a role as a first step towards social reentry.

The above mentioned processes led to the development of creating self-awareness in addition to recovery of the cognitive functions and provide knowledge to each TBI client through daily cognitive exercises at home with the family and rehabilitation classes with rehabilitation specialists. Furthermore, the most important trial of this kind of process is the creation of life space of a durable CR throughout a TBI client's life. This kind of project must move forward to support everyday life (as a model system in every city or prefecture) as a community-based health service because the number of TBI clients increase every year in a contemporary motorized society, and the clients are widely distributed throughout the country.

FUTURE TRENDS

Fine and delicate deficits in communication were often observed after TBI, e.g., word-finding disturbance or worse understanding on written and spoken information, as a part of deficit of executive functions. Computer software for pragmatics and the effective way of using appropriate words may be expected for good social integration and suitable human relationship of TBI clients. Furthermore, a community-based CR system including CR of communication, operating within a social health care program for TBI as a social resource is another essential factor for their work reentry. Although various elaborated efforts were indispensable in TBI clients, their families and CR specialists, through success of this system, their employment ratio increases and the quality of life of TBI clients and their families increases.

ACKNOWLEDGMENT

As a provider of our services from 2003 to 2005 the author thanks Dr. Keiko Matsuoka for her earnest effort in developing effective rehabilitation services and also for her help in data analysis. The author also thanks TBI clients for their cooperation in this study. A part of this study was financially supported by the Mitsubishi Zaidan in Japan.

REFERENCES

Bamdad, M. J., Ryan, L. M., & Warden, D. M. (2003). Functional assessment of executive abilities following traumatic brain injury. *Brain Injury : [BI]*, *17*(12), 1011–1020. doi:10.1080/0269905031000110553

Boman, I.-L., Lindstedt, M., Hemmingsson, H., & Bartfai, A. (2004). Cognitive training in home environment. *Brain Injury : [BI]*, *18*(10), 985–995. doi:10.1080/02699050410001672396

Cantagallo, A., Carli, S., Simone, A., & Tesio, L. (2006). INDFIN: A measure of disability in high-functioning traumatic brain injury outpatients. *Brain Injury : [BI]*, *20*(9), 913–925. doi:10.1080/02699050600832742

Cicerone, K. D., Dahlberg, C., Malec, J. F., Langenbahn, D. M., Felicetti, T., & Kneipp, S. (2005). Evidence-based cognitive rehabilitation: Updated review of the literature from 1998 through 2002. *Archives of Physical Medicine and Rehabilitation*, *86*, 1681–1692. doi:10.1016/j.apmr.2005.03.024

Cullen, N., Dhundamala, J., Bayley, M., & Jutai, J. (2007). The efficacy of acquired brain injury rehabilitation. *Brain Injury : [BI]*, *21*(2), 113–132.

Hashimoto, K., Takatsugi, O., Watanabe, S., & Ohashi, M. (2006). Effectiveness of a comprehensive day treatment program for rehabilitation of patients with acquired brain injury in Japan. *Journal of Rehabilitation Medicine*, *38*, 20–25. doi:10.1080/16501970510038473

Johnstone, B., & Stonington, H. H. (2001). *Rehabilitation of neuropsychological disorders. A practical guide for rehabilitation professionals*. Psychological Press. Psychology Press Philadelphia. Japanese translation by K. Matsuoka, K. Fujita, M. Fujii (2004). Tokyo: Sinkoh-igaku Shuppansha.

Kirn, T. F. (1987). Cognitive rehabilitation aims to improve memory functions in survivors of head injury. *Journal of the American Medical Association*, *257*(18), 2400–2402. doi:10.1001/jama.257.18.2400

Malec, J. F., & Basford, J. S. (1996). Postacute brain injury rehabilitation. *Archives of Physical Medicine and Rehabilitation*, *77*(2), 198–207. doi:10.1016/S0003-9993(96)90168-9

Malia, K., Berwick, K. C., Raumond, M., & Bennet, T. (1997). *Brainwave-R, cognitive strategies, and techniques for brain injury rehabilitation*. Texas: PRO-ED.

Martin, C., Viguier, D., Deloche, G., & Dellatola, G. (2001). Subjective experience after traumatic brain injury. *Brain Injury : [BI]*, *15*(11), 947–959. doi:10.1080/02699050110065655

Matsuba, M., Sikimori, H., Fujii, M., & Iitsuka, T. (2003). Subjective awareness on the disability after traumatic brain injury. Preliminary study. *Cognitive Rehabilitaion 2003*. Tokyo: Sinkoh-Igaku Schuppansha (in Japanese).

Nonaka, I., & Takeuchi, H. (1995). *The knowledge-creating company*. New York: Oxford University Press.

Oddy, M., & McMillan, T. (2001). Future directions: Brain injury service in 2010. In R. L. I. Woods & T. M. McMillan (Eds.), *Neurobehavioural disability and social handicap following traumatic brain injury* (pp. 287-296). Philadelphia, PA: Psychological Press.

Pace, G., Schlund, M., Hazard-Haupt, T., Christensen, A. L., Lashno, M., & McIver, J. (1999). Characteristics and outcomes of a home and community-based neurorehabilitation programme. *Brain Injury : [BI]*, *13*(7), 535–546. doi:10.1080/026990599121430

Petrella, L., Mccoll, M. A., Krupa, T., & Johnston, J. (2005). Returning to productive activities: Perspectives of individuals with long-standing acquired brain injuries. *Brain Injury : [BI]*, *19*(9), 643–655. doi:10.1080/02699050410001671874

Ponsford, J. (1995). *Traumatic brain injury. Rehabilitation for everyday adaptive living.* Hillsdale: Lawrence Erlbaum Associates.

Rees, L., Marshall, S., Hartridge, C., Mackie, D., & Wiser, M. (2007). Cognitive interventions post acquired brain injury. *Brain Injury : [BI]*, *21*(2), 161–200.

Rehabilitation of Persons with Traumatic Brain Injury. (1999). NIH consensus development panel on rehabilitation of persons with traumatic brain injury. *Journal of the American Medical Association*, *282*(10), 974–983. doi:10.1001/jama.282.10.974

Sarajuuit, J. M., Kaipio, M. L., Loskinen, S. K., Niemela, M. R., Serbo, A. R., & Bilkki, J. S. (2005). Outcome of a comprehensive neurorehabilitation program for patients with traumatic brain injury. *Archives of Physical Medicine and Rehabilitation*, *86*, 2296–2302.

Shames, J., Treger, I., Ring, H., & Giaquinto, S. (2007). Return to work following traumatic brain injury: Trends and challenges. *Disability and Rehabilitation*, *29*(17), 1387–1395. doi:10.1080/09638280701315011

Sherer, M., Boake, C., Levin, E., Silver, B. V., Ringholz, G., & High, W. Jr. (1998). Characteristics of impaired awareness after traumatic brain injury. *Journal of the International Neuropsychological Society*, *4*(4), 380–387.

Sohlberg, M. M., & Mateer, C. (2001*). Cognitive rehabilitation.* London: Guilford Press.

Willer, B., Button, J., & Rempel, R. (1999). Residential and home-based postacute rehabilitation of individuals with traumatic brain injury: A case control study. *Archives of Physical Medicine and Rehabilitation*, *80*(4), 399–406. doi:10.1016/S0003-9993(99)90276-9

Wood, R., Mc, L. I., Crea, J. D., Wood, L. M., & Merriman, R. N. (1999). Clinical and cost effectiveness of post-acute neurobehavioural rehabilitation. *Brain Injury : [BI], 13*(2), 69–68. doi:10.1080/026990599121746

Yamamoto-Mitani, N., Matsuoka, K., & Fujii, M. (2007). Home-based rehabilitation program for older adults with cognitive impairment: Preliminary results. *Psychogeriatrics, 7*(1), 14–20. doi:10.1111/j.1479-8301.2007.00193.x

Epilogue

We set out to present in one concise volume a discussion of the fundamental issues of knowledge management (KM) as they relate to innovative organizations. The preceding chapters present critical issues that cover important concepts and methodologies as well as providing evidence from industry, healthcare, and the community. We do not claim to cover the whole gamut of issues, indeed this would not be possible if we are to present a concise volume on the subject matter, however we have attempted to provide the reader with the most important aspects and trust that spurred by this introduction further research and reading into this vital area will occur. We are also confident that the material presented will enable all our readers to develop a greater appreciation of core aspects of KM and innovative organizations and this in turn will serve to develop a sustained extant knowledge base which will be beneficial to both practitioner and academician.

In closing, we would like to highlight one important aspect about knowledge management in general. KM is indeed a new, nascent field and as such is still developing and evolving. To facilitate such an understanding and appreciation it is useful to recall Everett M. Rogers' theory of innovation and diffusion to first understand diffusion in organizations and then apply it to see how knowledge management could be used differently according to different organizational contexts.

When trying to define knowledge management, as we have discussed in several chapters, it seems as though everyone's opinion is different. One of the primary reasons for this is due to the many fields where KM is utilized. In practice, knowledge management often encompasses identifying and mapping intellectual assets within an organization, generating new knowledge for competitive advantage within an organization, making vast amounts of corporate information accessible, sharing of best practices, and technology that enables all of the above.

Specifically, KM draws from a wide range of disciplines and technologies including:

- **Cognitive science.** Insights from how we learn and know will certainly improve tools and techniques for gathering and transferring knowledge.
- **Expert systems, artificial intelligence, and knowledge base management systems (KBMS).** AI and related technologies have acquired an undeserved reputation of having failed to meet their own and the marketplaces high expectations. In fact, these technologies continue to be applied widely, and the lessons practitioners have learned are directly applicable to knowledge management.
- **Computer-supported collaborative work (groupware).** In Europe, knowledge management is almost synonymous with groupware and therefore with Lotus Notes. Sharing and collaboration are clearly vital to organizational knowledge management with or without supporting technology.
- **Library and information science.** We take it for granted that card catalogs in libraries will help us find the right book when we need it. The body of research and practice in classification and knowledge organization that makes libraries work will be even more vital as we are inundated by information in business. Tools for thesaurus construction and controlled vocabularies are already helping us manage knowledge.
- **Technical writing.** Also under-appreciated as a professional activity, technical writing (often referred to by its practitioners as technical communication) forms a body of theory and practice that is directly relevant to effective representation and transfer of knowledge.
- **Document management.** Originally concerned primarily with managing the accessibility of images, document management has moved on to making content accessible and reusable at the component level.
- **Decision support systems.** Researchers working on decision support systems bring together insights from the fields of cognitive sciences, management sciences, computer sciences, operations research, and systems engineering in order to produce computerized artifacts for helping knowledge workers in their performance of cognitive tasks and to integrate such artifacts within the decision-making processes of modern organizations; i.e. various aspects of KM however, in practice the emphasis has been on quantitative analysis rather than qualitative analysis, and on tools for managers rather than everyone in the organization.
- **Semantic networks.** Semantic networks are formed from ideas and typed relationships among them (i.e., hypertext without the content), but with far more systematic structure according to meaning. Often applied in such arcane

tasks as textual analysis, semantic nets are now in use in mainstream professional applications, including medicine, to represent domain knowledge in an explicit way that can be shared.

- **Relational and object databases.** Although relational databases are currently used primarily as tools for managing "structured" data and object-oriented databases are considered more appropriate for "unstructured" content, we have only begun to apply the models on which they are founded to representing and managing knowledge resources.
- **Simulation.** This covers computer simulations, manual simulations, as well as role plays and micro arenas for testing out skills.
- **Organizational science.** The science of managing organizations increasingly deals with the need to manage knowledge often explicitly.

This is at best only a partial list. Other technologies include: object-oriented information modeling; electronic publishing technology, hypertext, and the World Wide Web; help-desk technology; full-text search and retrieval; and performance support systems.

"Knowledge management" has been a buzzword in the corporate world for several years and many are even cynical that it is essentially "old wine in new bottles." KM efforts have met with varying degrees of success as organizations hire knowledge managers with different skills and expect them to make order out of chaos. The knowledge management movement has made obvious what librarians have known for a long time: Collecting information is a good first step, but if you do not have pertinent information, relevant data, and germane knowledge, the collected information is useless. Knowledge management is the process of identifying, capturing, disseminating, and using the knowledge created by an organization. KM involves both technology and non-technology elements.

As can be seen, KM has its roots in many different fields. This has both advantages as well as disadvantages. The advantages are that there are endless resources to draw from when trying to find one that will fit with a specific application. The disadvantage is that it may be challenging to narrow down a specific plan to work for a specific context, be it within healthcare or for a particular innovative organization.

According to one of the most well known and early social science researchers in the area of diffusion, Everett Rogers (1995), innovation is an idea perceived as new by the individual and diffusion is the process by which an innovation spreads. Rogers used well established theories in sociology, psychology, and communications to develop a concise and easily understood approach to the diffusion of innovations. Originally, Roger's model was used by rural sociologists to study the diffusion of agricultural technologies in social systems. It has also been successfully applied to specific information technology products.

Change agents actively work to promote an innovation. The innovation spreads slowly at first and then picks up speed as more and more people adopt it. Eventually it reaches a saturation level, where virtually everyone who was going to adopt the innovation has done so.

A key point, early in the process, is called take-off. After the forward-thinking change agents have adopted the innovation, they work to communicate it to others in the society by whatever means they believe appropriate. When the number of early adopters reaches a critical mass-between 5 and 15%-the process is probably irreversible. The innovation has a life of its own, as more and more people talk about or demonstrate the innovation to each other. What makes an innovation successful? Innovation diffusion theorists have identified five critical characteristics that may be helpful in explaining this. Note that these are not requirements for a successful innovation, but their presence or absence could greatly affect the rate at which it gets adopted.

Succinctly stated, key aspects of Rogers' Theory include:

- **Relative Advantage:** Is the innovation better than the status quo? Will people perceive it as better? If not, the innovation will not spread quickly, if at all.
- **Compatibility:** How does the innovation fit with people's past experiences and present needs? If it doesn't fit both well, it won't spread well. Does it require a change in existing values? If members of the culture feel as though they have to become very different people to adopt the innovation, they will be more resistant to it.
- **Complexity:** How difficult is the innovation to understand and apply? The more difficult, the slower the adoption process.
- **Trialability:** Can people "try out" the innovation first? Or must they commit to it all at once? If the latter, people will be far more cautious about adopting it.
- **Observability:** How visible are the results of using it? If people adopt it, can the difference be discerned by others? If not, the innovation will spread more slowly.

According to Rogers, the individuals within a social system do not adopt an innovation at the same time. Rather, they adopt in an over-time sequence, so that individuals can be classified into adopter categories on the basis on when they first begin using an idea. We know more about innovativeness (the degree to which an individual or other unit of adoption is relatively earlier in adopting new ideas than other members of the system), than about any other concept in diffusion research. Because increased innovativeness is the main objective of change agencies, it became the main dependent variable in diffusion research. Innovativeness indicates overt behavioral change, the ultimate goal of most diffusion programs, rather than just cognitive or attitudinal change.

For innovation diffusion theorists, innovativeness is related to such independent variables as: (1) individual (leader) characteristics, (2) internal organizational characteristics, and (3) external characteristics of the organization.

The internal organizational characteristics include:

- **Centralization:** The degree to which power and control in a system are concentrated in the hands of relatively few individuals. Centrality has usually been found to be negatively associated with innovativeness; that is, the more power is concentrated in an organization, the less innovative the organization tends to be. The range of new ideas in an organization is restricted when a few strong leaders dominate the system. In a centralized organization, to leaders are poorly positioned to identify operational-level problems, or to suggest relevant innovations to meet these needs.
- **Complexity:** The degree to which an organization's members possess a relatively high level of knowledge and expertise, usually measured by the members' range of occupational specialties and their degree of professionalism expressed by formal training. Complexity encourages organizational members to conceive and propose innovations, but it may be difficult to achieve consensus about implementing them.
- **Formalization:** The degree to which an organization emphasizes following rules and procedures in the role of performance of its members. Such formalization acts to inhibit the consideration of innovations by organization members, but encourages the implementation of innovations.
- **Interconnectedness:** The degree to which the units in a social system are linked by the interpersonal networks. New ideas can flow more easily among an organization's members if the organization has a higher network of interconnectedness. This variable is positively related to organizational innovativeness.
- **Organizational slack:** The degree to which uncommitted resources are available to an organization. This variable is positively related to organizational innovativeness, especially for costly innovations. Socioeconomic and personality individual characteristics will define the individual's role in the diffusion process, which can be one of the following: (1) innovators, (2) early adopters, (3) early majority, (4) late majority, and (5) laggards.

Returning to what we have presented in the preceding material then, we must also remember, irrespective of industry and /or context, that as the field of KM evolves, so too will the manifestation of KM in a particular context. Innovating organizations are continually adapting and changing and thus, at all times if they are to maximize the full potential benefit of the specific KM initiative they have embraced it is vital for them to be aware of the fundamental dynamics captured by Rogers' model of innovation and diffusion and realize that incorporating KM is a dynamic and on going process. We close by quoting a famous ancient saying, "even the thousand mile journey has a first step" and wish all our readers success as they traverse the KM path.

Nilmini Wickramasinghe and Murako Saito

REFERENCE

Rogers, E. (1995, May). *Diffusion of Innovation, 4th ed.* Free Press.

About the Authors

Masako Fujii is a director of the non-profit organization of TBI (Traumatic Brain Injury) Rehabilitation Center located in Tokyo. Dr.Fujii had been an associate professor in Medical School, Hamamatsu University and a professor in Nursing School of Hamamatsu University after making carrier of psychological clinician and also brain researcher as being an assistant and instructor at Bain Research Institute of University of Tokyo. Dr.Fujii has a wide experience of consulting with many clients with TBI and their families by giving them progress programs on the abilities of attention, memory and executive functions she prepared for each client and his/her families, and she has also conducting lectures on cognitive rehabilitation for the practitioners and for the classes in nursing schools in Japan.

Eliezer (Elie) Geisler is a distinguished professor at the Stuart School of Business, Illinois Institute of Technology and director of the IIT Center for the Management of Medical Technology. He holds a doctorate from the Kellogg School at Northwestern University. Dr. Geisler is the author of nearly 100 papers in the areas of technology and innovation management, the evaluation of R&D, science and technology, and the management of healthcare and medical technology. He is the author of several books, including: *Managing the Aftermath of Radical Corporate Change* (1997), *The Metrics of Science and Technology* (2000) also translated into Chinese, *Creating Value with Science and Technology* (2001), and *Installing and Managing Workable Knowledge Management Systems* (With Rubenstein, 2003). His forthcoming books are: *Knowledge and Knowledge Systems: Learning from the Wonders of the Mind*, and a textbook: *Knowledge Management Systems: Theory and Cases* (with Wickramasinghe). He consulted for major corporations and for many U.S. federal departments, such as Defense, Agriculture, Commerce,

EPA, Energy, and NASA. Dr. Geisler is the co-founder of the annual conferences on the Hospital of the Future, and the Health Care Technology and Management Association, a joint venture of several universities in 10 countries. He serves on various editorial boards of major journals. His current research interests include the nature of knowledge management in general and in complex systems, such as healthcare organizations.

Mitsuhiko Karashima is an associate professor in Dept. of Management Systems Engineering, School of Information Technology and Electronics, Tokai University. He received PhD in Engineering from Dept. of Industrial and Systems Management Engineering, School of Science and Engineering, Waseda University where he graduated. Dr. Karashima's major research fields are Cognitive Ergonomics and Usability Engineering. His primary research interests of these fields are characteristics on human information processing and information systems development process from a view point of usability He is currently one of directors of Health Care Technology Management Research Center and a councilor of Human Centered Design Organization which are nonprofit organization.

Hiromi Nishiguchi is an associate professor in Dept. of Management Systems Engineering, School of Information Technology and Electronics, Tokai University. He had been an associate professor in School of Nursing and Social Welfare, Kyushu University of Nursing and Social Welfare located in Kumamoto prefecture, and also an associate professor in Yamanashi Gakuin University after three years of assistant professor in Dept of Industrial Management system Engineering, Waseda University immediately after he graduated from Waseda University. His main interests in his research work are physical ergonomics in term of Welfare Engineering for support of the handicapped and aged people. He is currently associated with the developer of new types of wheel-chair and the tools for supporting the handicapped people.

Murako Saito is Representative of Health Care Technology Management Research Center in Tokyo, and Research Adviser in Institute of Future Healthcare Policy in Waseda University. She had been a Professor of Cognitive Ergonomics, Organizational Ergonomics in Graduate and Undergraduate Courses in Industrial and Management Systems Engineering, School of Science and Engineering, Waseda University, and as the position that preceded Waseda University, she had been a professor of Industrial Health, Healthcare Management in Dept. of Health Sciences, School of Medicine, University of Ryukyu. She received PhD of Health Sciences from Faculty of Medicine, University of Tokyo where she graduated. She had been a Fulbright Scholarship Grantee authorized by US Department for continuing to study in Graduate School of Public Health and Teachers College, Columbia University,

New York, USA . Dr. Saito has been involved in several associations and served as editorial boards of national and international journals. She serves currently for NPO Joint Lecture-Consultation Plans. Her major research interests are on organizational redesign and transformation into innovative organizations by strategic knowledge management in the processes of cognition-action coupling or the recursive processes of organizational learning, and by fostering the participants to be a healthy actor and harnessing potentiality of the participants in individual and collective levels.

Nilmini Wickramasinghe (PhD) researches and teaches within information systems domain with particular focus on the applications of these areas to healthcare and thereby effecting superior healthcare delivery. She is well published in all these areas with more than 90 referred scholarly articles, several books and an encyclopaedia. In addition, she regularly presents her work throughout North America, as well as in Europe and Australasia. Nilmini Wickramasinghe is a professor at the Business Information Technology School at RMIT University Australia. In addition she is the U.S. representative of the Health Care Technology Management Association, the associate director of the IIT Center for the Management of Medical Technology in Chicago, USA and the editor-in-chief of two scholarly journals published by InderScience.

Index

G

genetic algorithms 131
goal alignment (GA) 113
Gross Domestic Product (GDP) 126, 143

H

Healthcare Information Portability and Accountability Act (HIPAA) 145
Health Insurance Portability and Accountability Act (HIPAA, Public Law 104-191) 127
home-based daily CR 269, 277
Home care and rehabilitation equipment 234, 242, 248
human action development 81, 82
human cognition-action coupling 57, 58, 62, 63, 65

I

IADL (Instrumental Activities of Daily Living) 235
ICT 25, 60
ICT (information communication technologies) 2
indirect experience 64
Informal socialization 38
information and communication technologies (ICTs) 106
information interpretation 75, 76
information processing levels 75
information systems (IS) 118
information technology (IT) 186
infrastructure 31, 32, 33, 34, 35, 39, 40 , 41, 42, 43, 44
initiative, flexibility 250
innovating organizations 1, 2, 6, 7, 11, 12, 13
innovative organization model 190
intelligence continuum 91, 92, 93, 101, 105
intelligent organization 58, 61, 74
interface 131, 132
interpersonal relationship management 190, 191

Interpersonal relationship management competence 185
intranet 133
ipsilateral 251
irritabilities(IMPU) 193, 196

K

KDD 8, 9
KM 31, 32, 34, 35, 36, 42, 43
KMI 31, 32, 42
knowledge assets 1
knowledge-based economy 1
knowledge construct 1, 2, 5, 10, 11, 12
knowledge creation 4, 6, 7, 8, 9, 10, 11, 14
knowledge discovery in databases (KDD) 8, 94
knowledge economy 1, 2, 3, 4, 12, 13, 92, 106, 107, 120
Knowledge Generation 51
knowledge management 2, 4, 5, 6, 9, 10, 11, 12, 13, 14, 15, 17, 18, 19, 22, 24, 26, 27, 31, 32, 33, 35, 36, 37, 39, 42, 43, 44, 45, 106, 125, 126, 129, 130, 131, 132, 133, 137, 138, 139, 140, 141, 144, 145, 147, 151, 152, 153, 154, 234, 245
Knowledge management 18, 22, 28, 34, 71, 96
knowledge management infrastructure (KMI) 31
knowledge management (KM) 4, 31, 91, 125, 126
Knowledge Management Systems(KMS) 145
knowledge spiral 7, 8, 11, 144, 146, 147, 148, 149, 150, 153
Knowledge Transfer Network 34
knowledge worker 111, 112, 115, 116, 117, 118, 119, 123
KPMG 37

L

labor 1, 3
lack of self-awareness 250, 260

V

W